IMAGES
of Modern America

SANTA FE

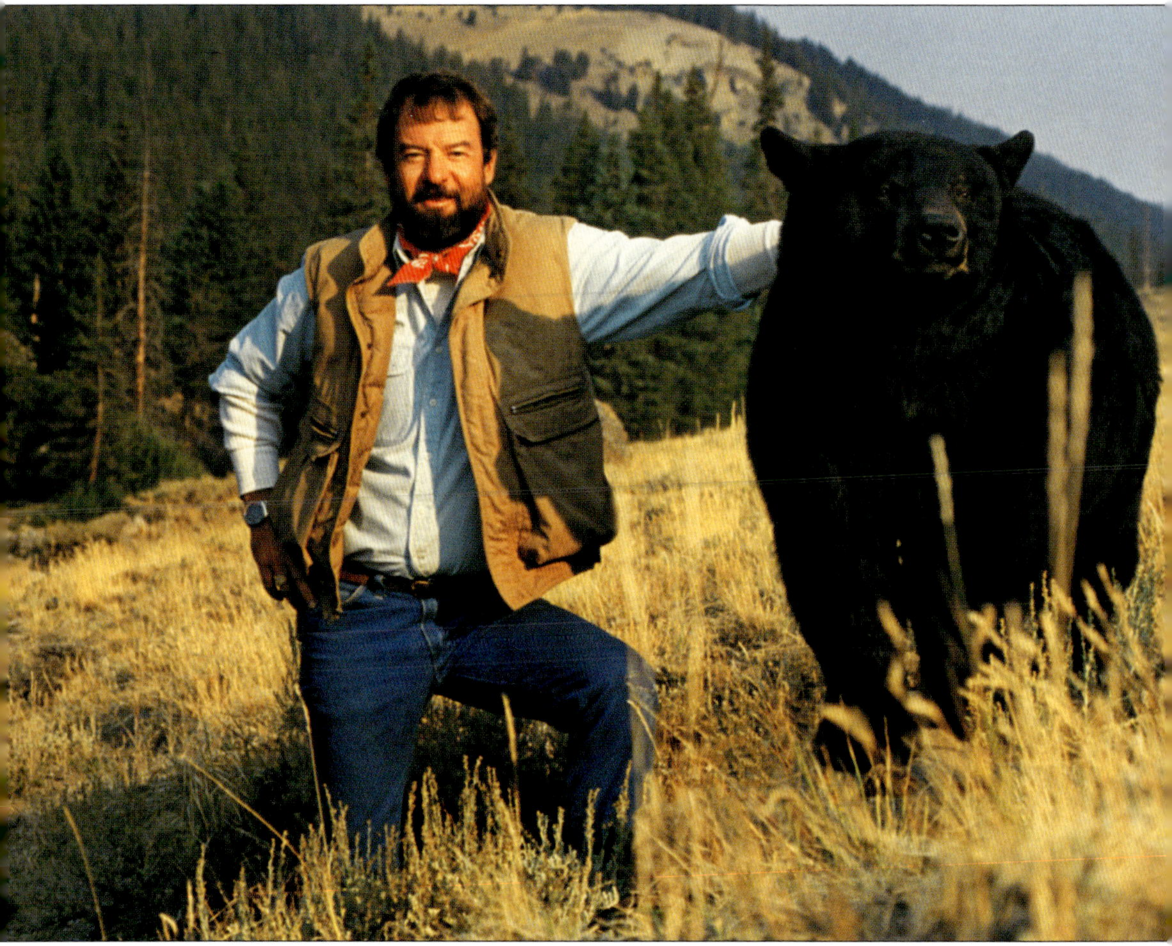

Santa Fe native Buddy Mays is a freelance lifestyle photographer and writer whose images of, and articles about, northern New Mexico's people and places have appeared in hundreds of national and international publications. He is the author of 12 previous books, including 2012's *Hard to Have Heroes*, a prize-winning novel about the American Southwest, and *People of the Sun: Some Out-of-Fashion Southwesterners*, which he coauthored with historian Marc Simmons in 1979. Mays attended New Mexico State University and is a vertebrate zoologist by education. He is also an avid hiker, skier, hunter, and fisherman, having spent much of his life enjoying the wildlife and wildland of the American Southwest.

On the Front Cover: Clockwise from top left:
Inn at Loretto on Christmas Eve (see page 20), a bleached cow skull and chile *ristras* on a downtown adobe wall (see page 12), mystery writer Donald Hamilton (see page 45), the famous *Homage to the Burro* sculpture by artist Charles Southard in Burro Alley (see page 33), a goatherd at the Las Golindrinas Historical Museum (see page 76)

On the Back Cover: From left to right:
Happy Ley at the Terrero Store (see page 48), San Miguel Chapel (see page 34), sunbathing at a Santa Fe spa (see page 92)

IMAGES
of Modern America

SANTA FE

Buddy Mays

ARCADIA
PUBLISHING

ISBN 978-1-4671-3312-8

Published by Arcadia Publishing
Charleston, South Carolina

Printed in the United States of America

Library of Congress Control Number: 2014954332

For all general information, please contact Arcadia Publishing:
Telephone 843-853-2070
Fax 843-853-0044
E-mail sales@arcadiapublishing.com
For customer service and orders:
Toll-Free 1-888-313-2665

Visit us on the Internet at www.arcadiapublishing.com

Contents

Acknowledgments 6

Introduction 7

1. A Historical Primer on Santa Fe Style 9
2. The Plaza, Santa Fe's Historic Hub 27
3. Some Memorable Santa Feans 43
4. Native Faces, Special Places 59
5. The Great Santa Fe Outdoors 81

ACKNOWLEDGMENTS

I owe a hefty debt of gratitude to my wife, Stephanie, for her skillful proofreading and editing assistance and to the dozens of Santa Feans who helped me research locations, check facts, and find mistakes. Special thanks as well to all of the memorable New Mexicans, living and deceased, who allowed me to take their photographs during the late 20th century. I'll be forever grateful. Unless otherwise noted, all photographs are by Buddy Mays.

Hallelujah, comes the Gypsy, bring he glory to your soul
But his essence begs sustaining, lay a coin inside his bowl
Then he'll snare your secret parable with his sword of sober truth
The gnomic gleam unbearable of fleeting, tender youth

—El D Odell, from *Ode to Santa Fe*, 1979

INTRODUCTION

Nestled in the piñon-covered western foothills of the Sangre de Cristo Mountains, the settlement of Santa Fe was established in 1608 by Spanish soldier Juan Martinez de Montoya. The city is one of the oldest, continuously inhabited communities built by Europeans in the United States—surpassed in age by only St. Augustine, Florida, and Jamestown, Virginia. It is the site of the oldest public building in America, the Palace of the Governors, and the oldest church, the San Miguel Mission, both constructed about 1610. It is also home to the nation's longest-running communal celebration, the Fiesta de Santa Fe, first held in 1712. The city is a world-class art and music center, providing visitors and residents with an all-season menu of activities. It is little wonder that historic Santa Fe is also New Mexico's most popular tourist destination, attracting more than one million visitors each year.

In the early 1600s, Santa Fe was a small, isolated community of soldiers, farmers, and Franciscan missionaries—the latter dedicated to converting thousands of Pueblo Indians to Christianity. Surrounding a main square or plaza, the central part of the settlement was walled and fortified against potential attack from any of two dozen nearby Indian pueblos. The colonists made two fundamental errors during Santa Fe's formative years, both concerning their Indian neighbors. First, they introduced the *encomienda*, a system of taxation that gave government and church officials the right to extract an annual tribute—mostly in the form of food, human labor, or personal service—from each Indian household. Second, the Franciscan friars prohibited Pueblo residents from practicing their centuries-old religious ceremonies and, using forced Indian labor, erected large mission churches in almost every native community.

Most Puebloans hated both the encomienda and the Franciscan missionaries. Pueblo men and boys were forced to labor long hours in their fields to pay the tribute, while Indian women and girls working in Spanish households were often sexually abused by their masters. By 1680, the Pueblo people had endured enough. Late that summer, 2,000 angry warriors pillaged and burned much of Santa Fe, slaughtering settlers and missionaries as they went. Other war parties attacked churches, farms, and outlying communities throughout New Mexico. A combined 400 colonists and 21 Franciscan friars were slain during the first few hours of this Pueblo Revolt, and at least 2,000 others were sent scurrying south toward Mexico. The success of the uprising was short-lived, however. In 1693, just 13 years later, Spanish conquistador Don Diego de Vargas led an army of 800 soldiers, settlers, and friendly Indians back to Santa Fe and ordered the occupying Indians to surrender. They refused, and in the bloody battle that followed, the heavily armed Spaniards killed 79 warriors and sentenced every family member of the slain Indians to 10 years in slavery.

Once again under Spanish control, Santa Fe grew slowly but steadily over the next century as more colonists arrived each year from Mexico City. In 1821, Mexico won its independence from Spain, and Santa Fe's ownership and political jurisdiction reverted to the Mexicans. That same year, American William Becknell led a string of pack mules loaded with trade goods into the Santa Fe Plaza, having journeyed all the way from Missouri on a new trade route he called the Santa Fe Trail. Becknnell's arrival nudged Santa Fe out of the dark ages. Within a few years, a steady stream of wagons bearing American and European merchandise was pouring into the city, where amenity-starved residents eagerly purchased it for exorbitant prices. In 1845, the United States declared war on Mexico after 16 Americans were slain by a Mexican cavalry unit on the US side of the border. Pres. James Polk immediately ordered a large force of American soldiers to occupy Santa Fe and lay claim to the New Mexico Territory. The campaign was swift and bloodless; commanding general Stephen Kearney took the city without firing a shot and established a joint civil and military government to run the territory. The Treaty of Guadalupe Hidalgo was signed two years later, ending the war and officially surrendering Santa Fe and New Mexico to the United States.

In 1880, the Atchison, Topeka & Santa Fe Railway (AT&SF) reached the village of Lamy, 18 miles south of Santa Fe. Surveyors deemed the terrain too difficult for a main line track, so a small spur line was built that would carry passengers and freight from Lamy into the city. In the years that followed, Santa Fe's population increased slightly, but the economic prosperity that residents had hoped for with the railroad's arrival did not materialize. In the 1930s, however, a group of farsighted business leaders and city officials began to advocate a novel idea: tourism, not industry, was the key to an affluent future. The idea took root, and shortly thereafter, city fathers and business leaders initiated a five-decade-long cultural and architectural face-lift that aimed to transform Santa Fe into a major tourist destination.

By the late 1970s, the city was riding high, both aesthetically and economically. Santa Fe Style—a visually appealing meld of traditional Pueblo and Spanish mission architecture—had become a common catchphrase throughout the western hemisphere. Community get-togethers like the Indian Market, Spanish Market, and Fiesta de Santa Fe had been expanded into internationally acclaimed events, and Canyon Road, Santa Fe's 80-year-old artist colony, had become an American mecca for art lovers and one of the world's top art markets. The icing on the cake was the opening of the Santa Fe Opera, a world-class outdoor facility that not only attracted wealthy music aficionados but also the country's preeminent operatic talent.

In the early 1980s, however, Santa Fe's popularity suddenly became its albatross. From 1981 to 2000, an incessant cloudburst of publicity in the national media trumpeted everything from the city's tri-cultural heritage and mañana lifestyle to its bicycle paths and public art exhibits. Scores of magazines suddenly decided that Santa Fe was the new "in" spot, a delightful place to live, the nicest place to retire, and the best place to bike, ski, hike, shop, drink, eat, or even start a family. As publicity increased, tourism escalated as well, and so did Santa Fe's population. By 1990, suburban sprawl had run amok as new homes sprouted by the thousands from the fragile high-desert earth like dandelions. Even as city water supplies dwindled and traffic congestion on Santa Fe's narrow streets reached the point of gridlock, the deluge of national exposure continued. Crime shot up, residents complained, developers got rich, businesspeople desperately tried to catch up, and the city fathers pulled out their hair.

Today, the population of Santa Fe County has increased from 75,000 in 1980 to more than 146,000 in 2014. In the summer, traffic congestion continues to be unmanageable in some areas, but the construction of new homes has slowed, and with heavy usage restrictions in place, water supplies seem to be handling the load. Many longtime inhabitants feel that much of Santa Fe's old-world charm and southwestern ambience disappeared in the 1980s, but newcomers who never experienced the "Old Santa Fe" seem to love the city just as it is. Only time will tell what lies in Santa Fe's future. Few would argue, however, that the present-day version of this historic, 400-year-old northern New Mexico community is one of America's most fascinating and alluring places—irresistible to visitors and residents alike.

One

A Historical Primer on Santa Fe Style

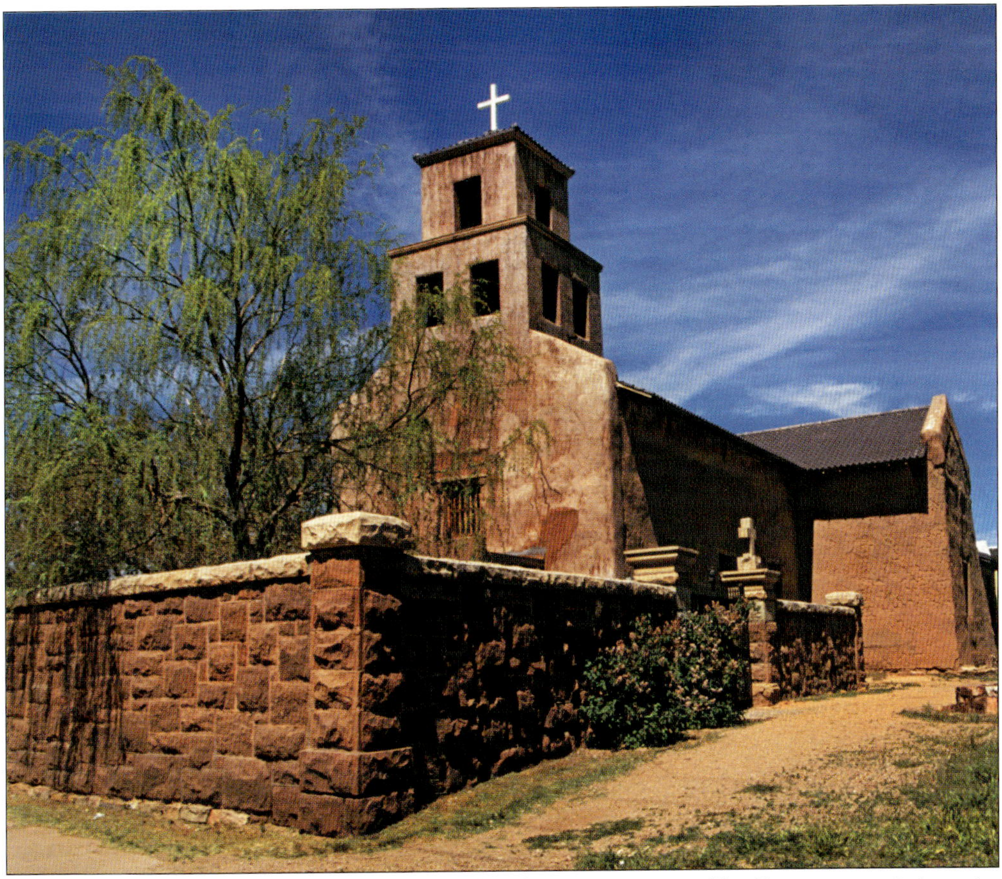

The venerable El Santuario de Guadalupe Church was constructed by Franciscan missionaries around 1777 and is the oldest shrine to Our Lady of Guadalupe in the United States. Located just west of the Santa Fe Plaza, it was an active parish for more than 180 years but was retired from the Santa Fe Archdiocese in 1961. It is now a museum that houses a large collection of santos—hand-carved wooden depictions of saints.

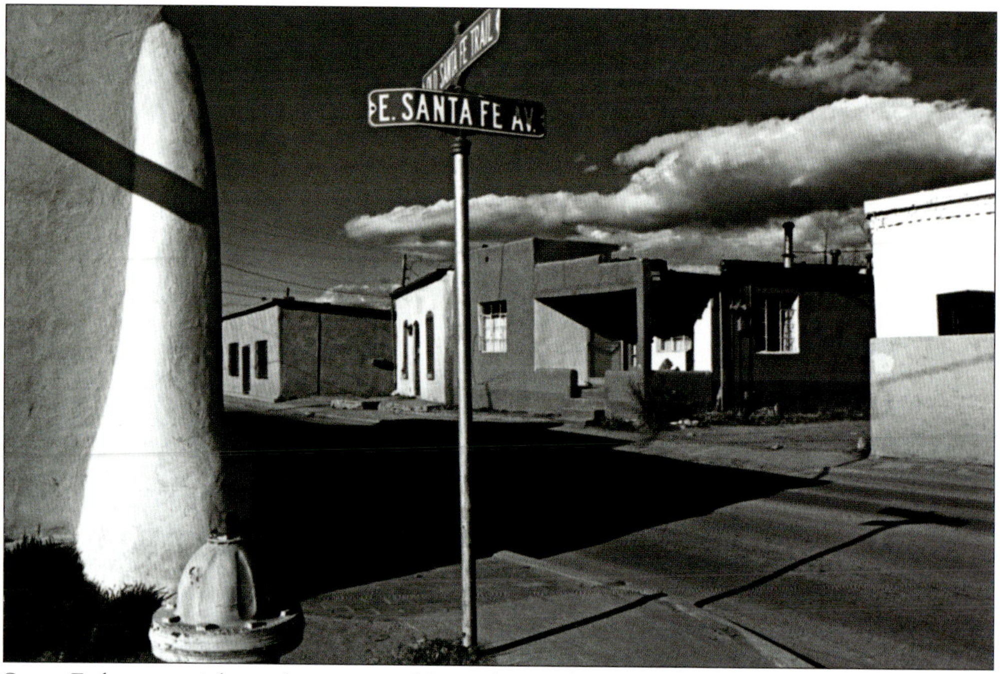

Santa Fe boasts a rich amalgamation of Spanish, Anglo, and American Indian building styles, which have helped create one of the most recognizable communities in the United States. Except for a few layers of pavement and considerably more traffic, the city's main streets have changed very little since this photograph was taken in the 1960s. (Courtesy of Eduardo Fuss Photography Collection, Center for Southwest Research, University Libraries, University of New Mexico.)

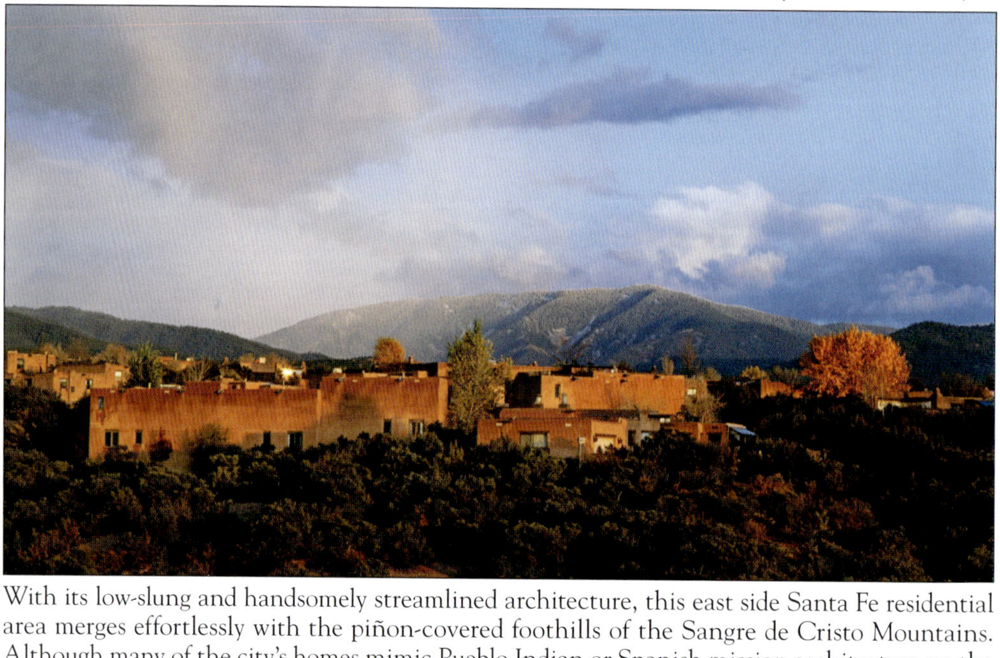

With its low-slung and handsomely streamlined architecture, this east side Santa Fe residential area merges effortlessly with the piñon-covered foothills of the Sangre de Cristo Mountains. Although many of the city's homes mimic Pueblo Indian or Spanish mission architecture on the outside, houses built after 1975 were usually fashioned from concrete blocks and stucco instead of the traditional sandstone blocks or adobe bricks.

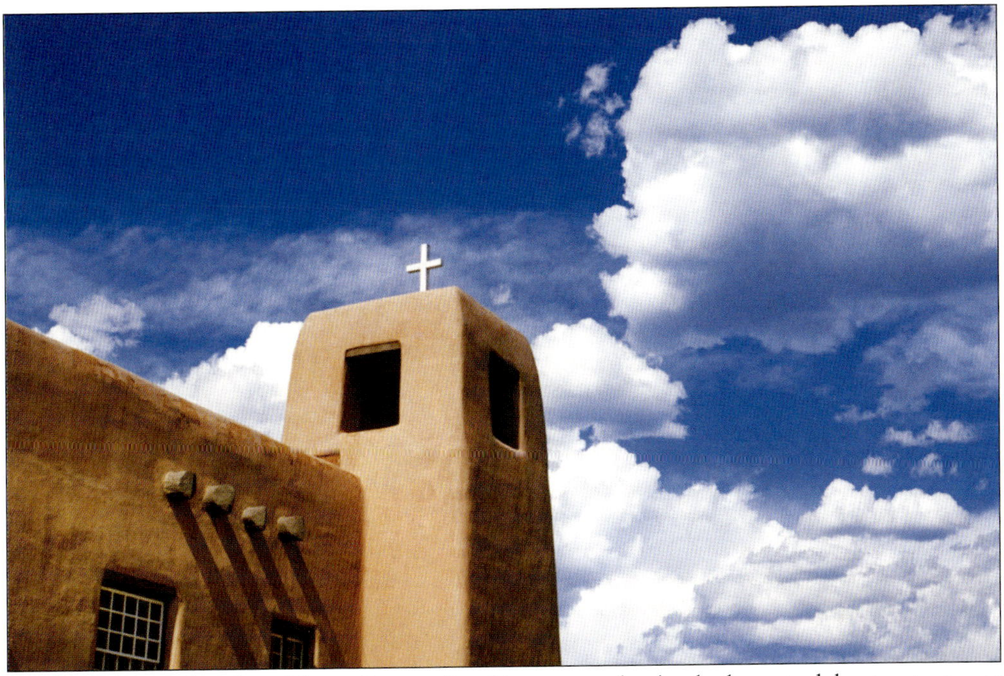

The Cristo Rey Church on Upper Canyon Road is purported to be the largest adobe structure ever built at one time in the United States. Designed by John Gaw Meem (the father of Santa Fe Style architecture), the church is 350 feet long and has walls that are as much as nine feet thick. Approximately 100,000 handmade adobe bricks were used to construct the church in the late 1930s.

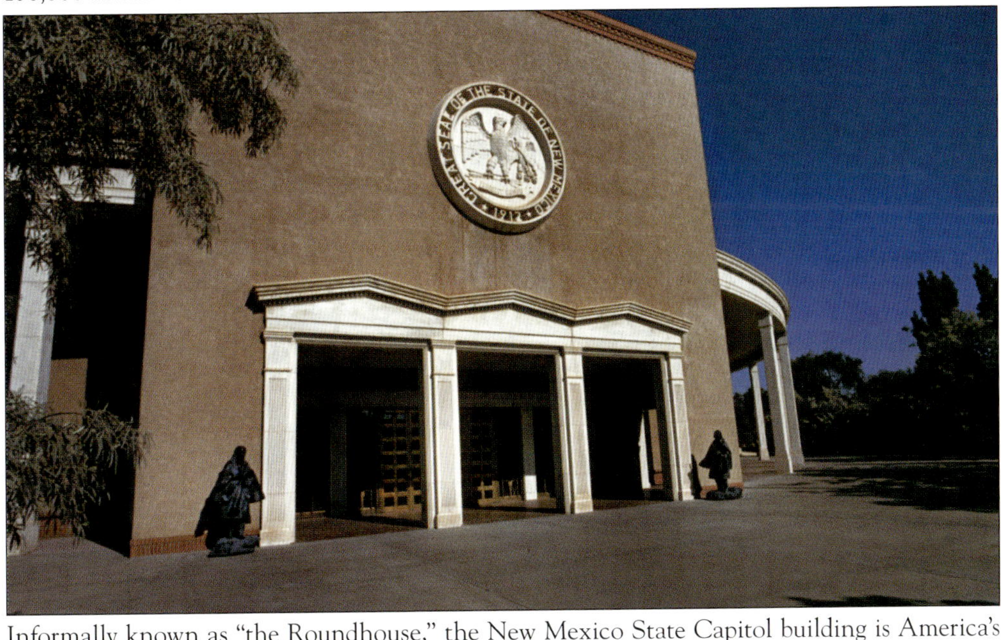

Informally known as "the Roundhouse," the New Mexico State Capitol building is America's only circular statehouse. Constructed in 1966 and designed to resemble a Zia Indian sun symbol when viewed from above, this 232,346-square-foot structure is a blend of Neoclassical and New Mexico Territorial Revival architectural styles. The Roundhouse is home to both the executive and legislative branches of New Mexico's government.

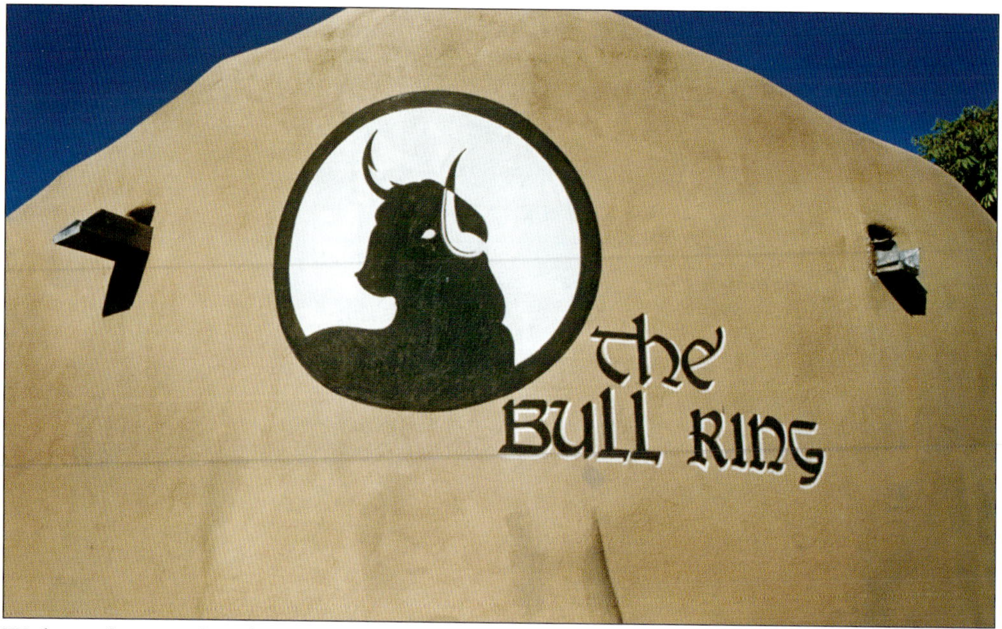

Within a few months of its grand opening in 1971, the Bull Ring restaurant became Santa Fe's most popular watering hole for politicians and political reporters. Ideally situated just a short walk from the Roundhouse, it was where three-martini-lunch legislators could wheel and deal informally and where journalists on the prowl for partisan gossip usually could find something to write about.

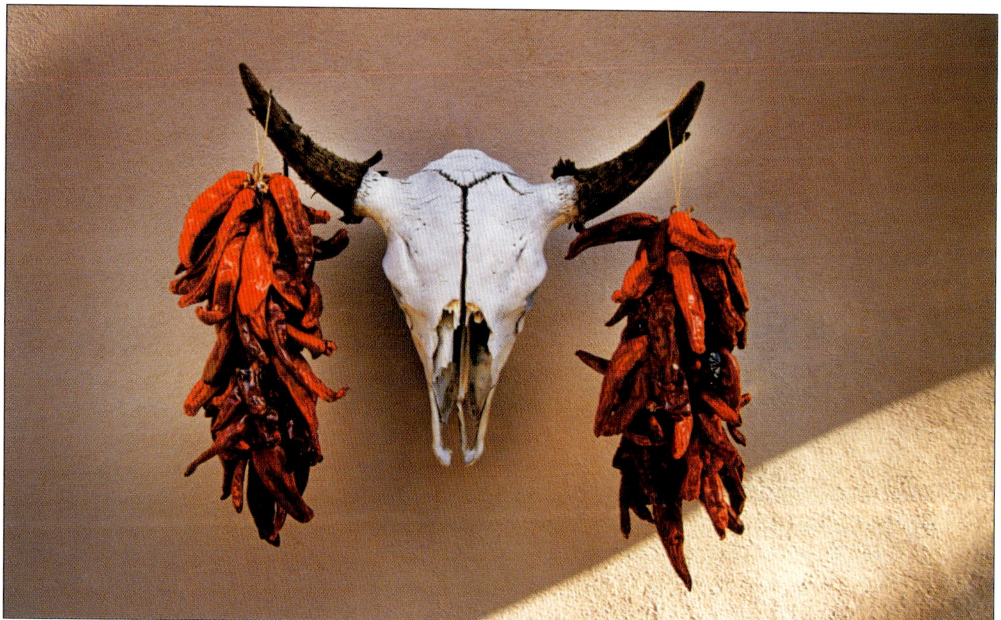

Bleached cow skulls have served as popular Santa Fe home and garden decor since the late 1970s. New Mexico artist Georgia O'Keeffe (see page 43) was perhaps the foremost instigator of the "cow skull craze," often using bleached skulls in her paintings. Her famous canvas *Cow's Skull: Red, White, and Blue* hangs in the permanent collection of the Metropolitan Museum of Art in New York City.

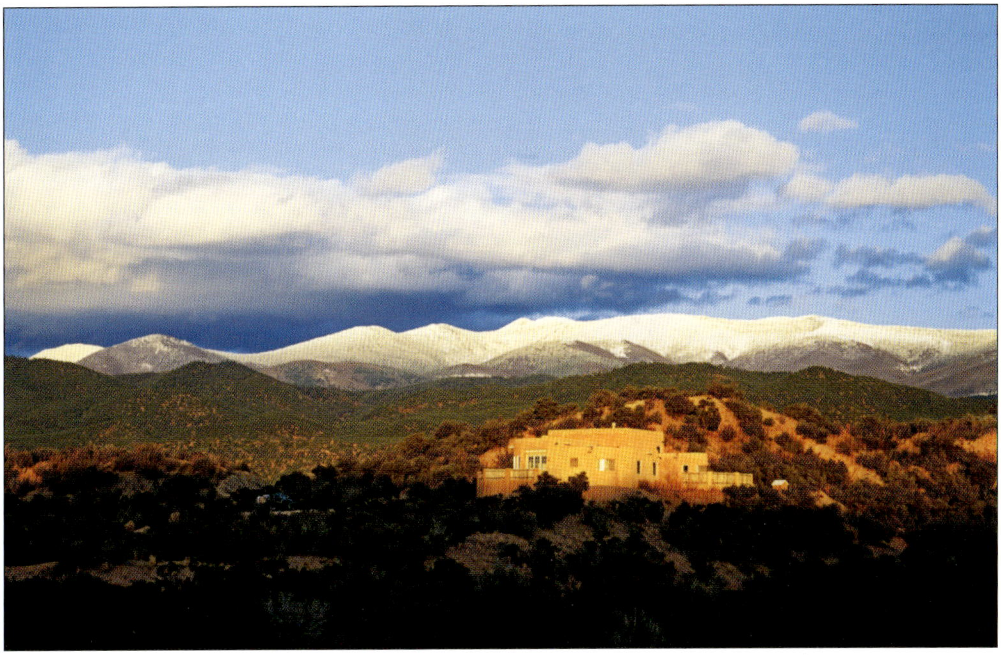

Frosty with an early autumn snowfall, the piñon-covered foothills of the Sangre de Cristo Mountains hover like a protective spirit over homes built in Santa Fe's rural and hilly east side. Since the city was founded in the early 1600s, the nearby mountains have provided residents with everything from firewood and food to building materials and outdoor recreation.

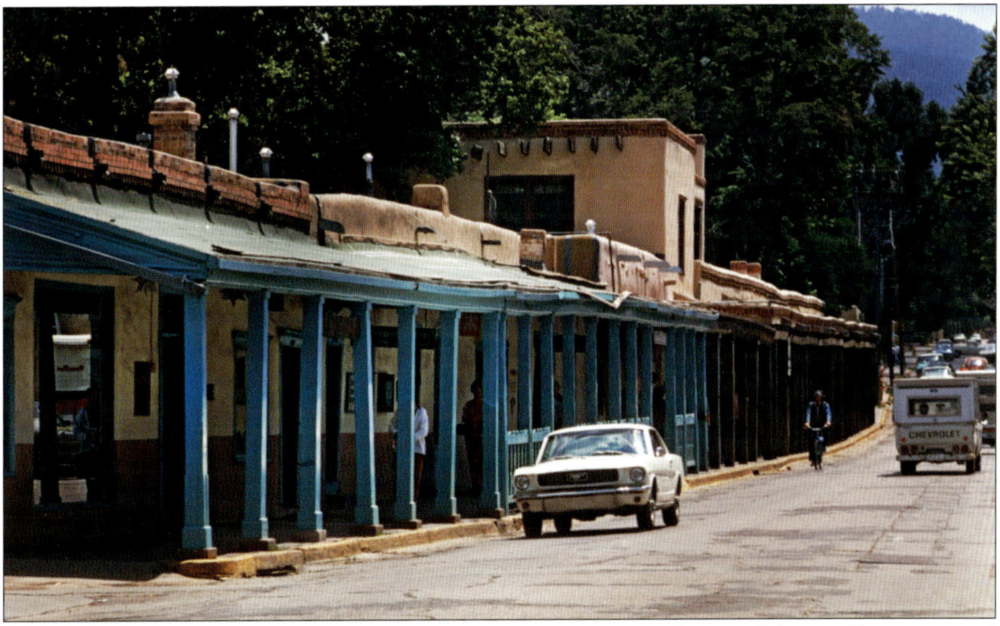

Most streets in the older sections of Santa Fe originally were designed for small wagons and oxcarts, and they have not changed much in the past four centuries. Many of these narrow thoroughfares—like East Palace Avenue, shown here about 1970—were poorly paved and filled with cracks and potholes until the late 1980s, when the City, spurred to action by protesting residents and tourists, allotted funds for a major repaving project.

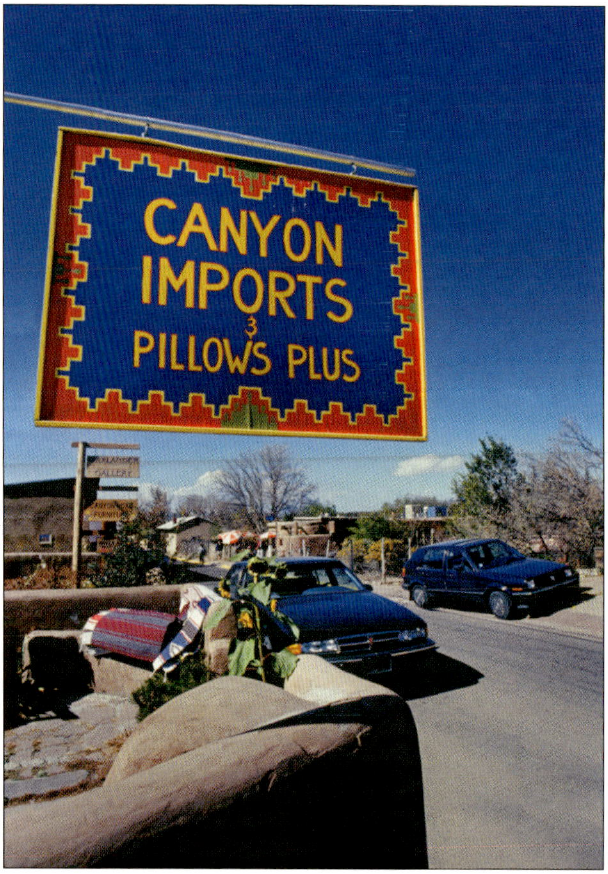

In colonial times, Canyon Road was a narrow dirt path that led directly to the nearby mountains, providing firewood gatherers and their donkeys access to nearby piñon and pine forests. More recently, Canyon Road has become the center of Santa Fe's thriving art world. In the early to mid-20th century, scores of painters, potters, and sculptors—both famous and starving—lived and worked along the street, displaying and selling artwork from their homes and studios. As Santa Fe became a more popular tourist destination, however, many of these artists' abodes were purchased by developers, renovated, and reborn as upscale shops, galleries, and restaurants that catered to the wealthy.

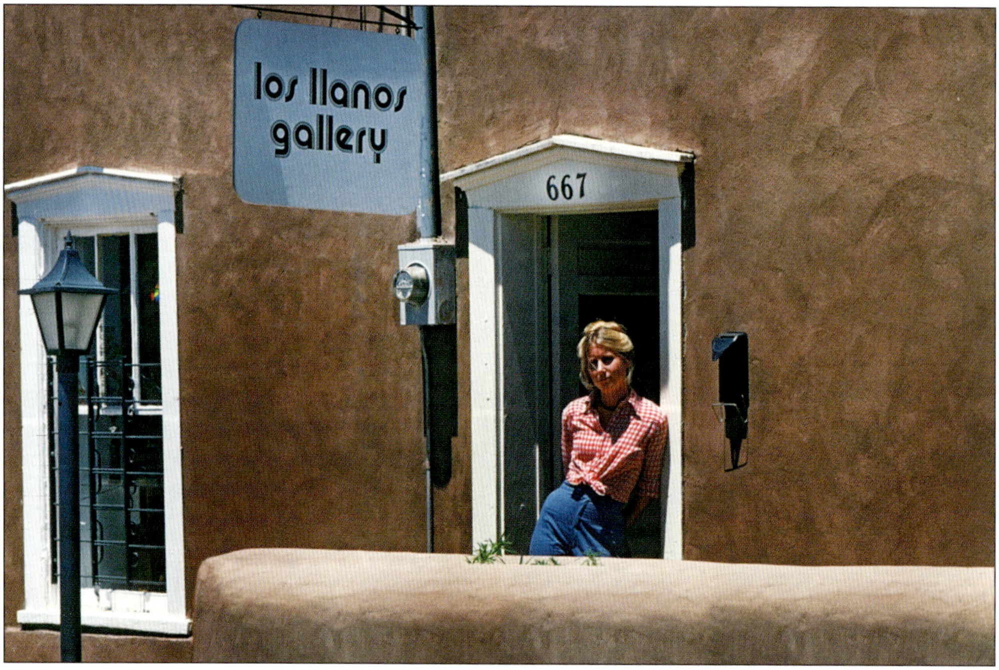

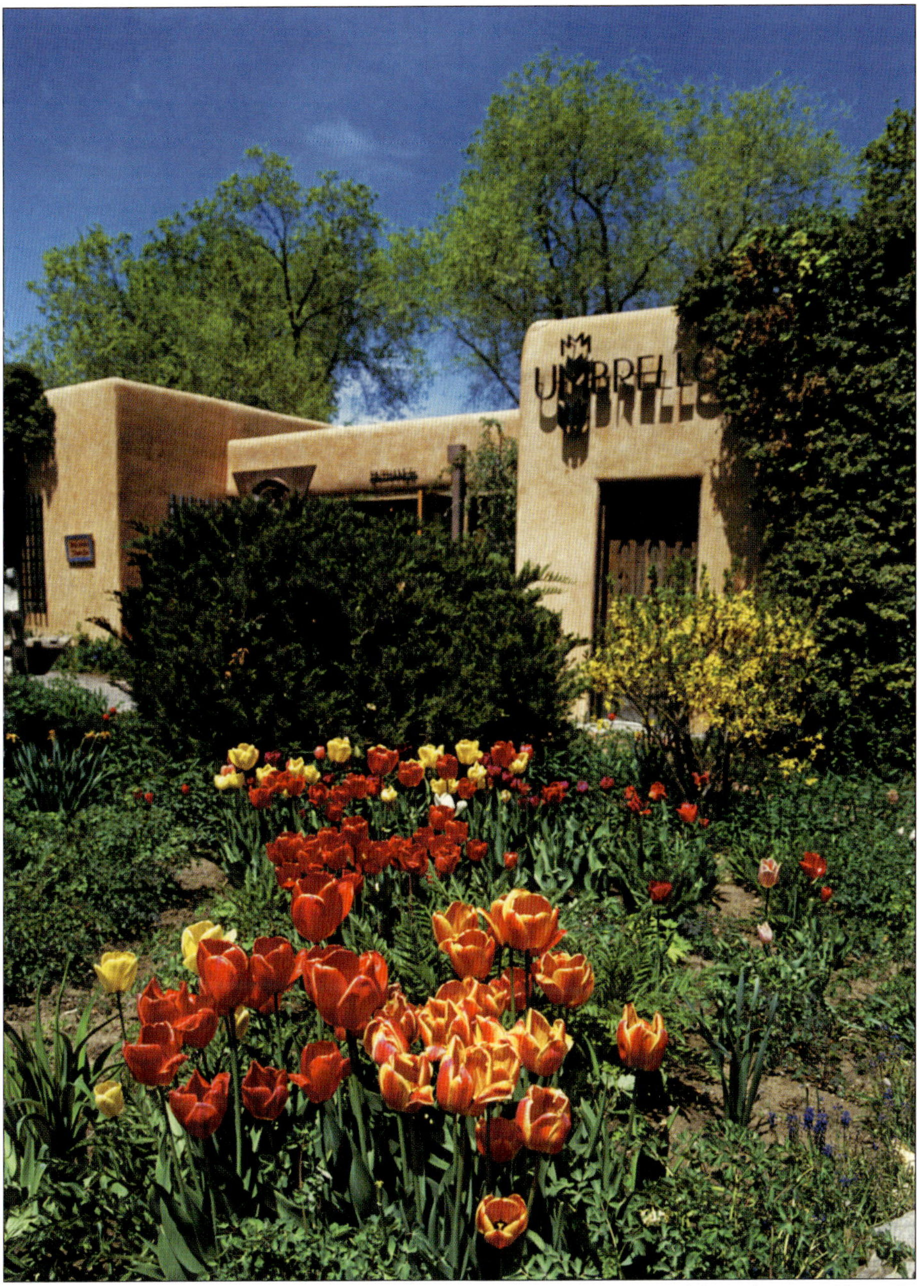

Canyon Road was not paved along its entire length until 1964. Today, although it is still rough and narrow in places (and often a bit formidable for out-of-town motorists), Canyon Road is publicized as Santa Fe's most famous thoroughfare. Most of the street's buildings were constructed between 1895 and 1950, but a few date from the mid-1700s, when homesites along the dusty woodcutters' path were typically small farms surrounded by corn and chile fields. Like many other neighborhoods in Santa Fe, however, the Canyon Road area was overdeveloped in the 1980s and early 1990s, a process which, many locals say, destroyed much of its traditional ambiance and charm. Shown here in 1989 after an extensive renovation, the upscale Umbrello Art Gallery, with its colorful flower gardens and outdoor sculpture, was symbolic of Canyon Road's brand-new "Old World Modern" face.

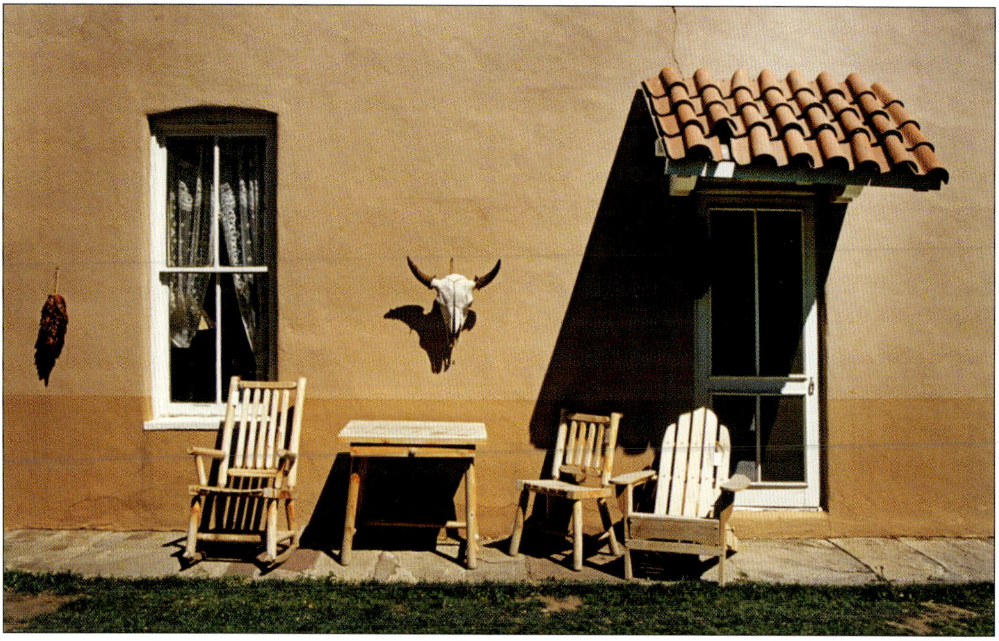

The petite Canyon Road apartment seen above was probably an artist's studio in a much larger family compound during the early part of the 20th century. The cow skull and chile ristra used to adorn the exterior wall are part of what has become known as the Santa Fe Style—a term attributed to the unique appearance of the Pueblo, Spanish, and Anglo architecture and attitude that have melded together in the American Southwest. Below, a similar apartment, with its beautiful north-facing windows, also could have been an artist's studio at the time of its construction. When the photograph was taken in 1990, however, it had become part of the well-established Santa Fe School of Cooking.

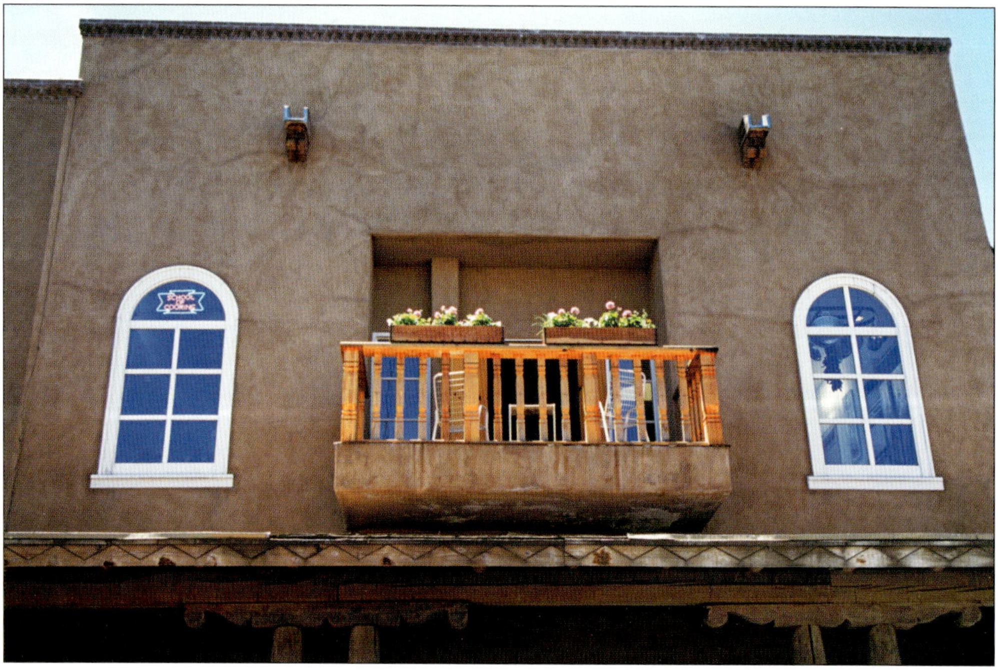

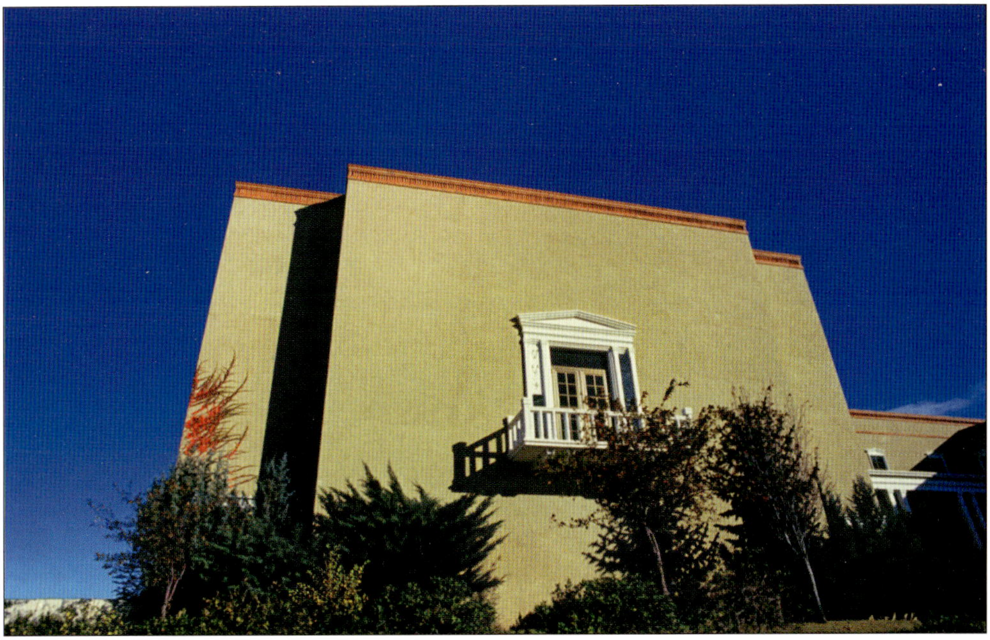

The Bataan Memorial Building, designed by architect Isaac Rapp, was completed in 1900. It served as the Territorial Capitol building until New Mexico achieved statehood in 1912, then as the state capitol building until the Roundhouse replaced it in 1966. Originally known as simply the Capitol Building, it was renamed after World War II in honor of the New Mexico army regiment that made the infamous 1942 Death March in the Philippines.

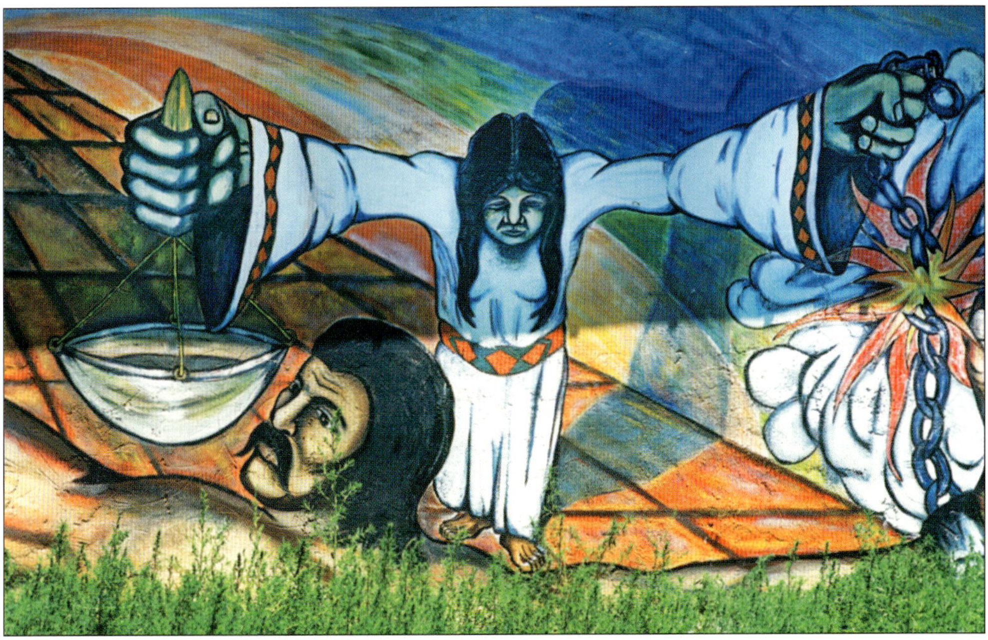

Painted on the side of a Santa Fe shed around 1975, this colorful mural was probably created by an artist from La Raza (The Race), an advocacy group working to improve opportunities for Hispanic Americans. During the late 1960s and early 1970s, La Raza joined other civil rights groups in an unsuccessful attempt to restore colonial Spanish land grants to the heirs of their original owners.

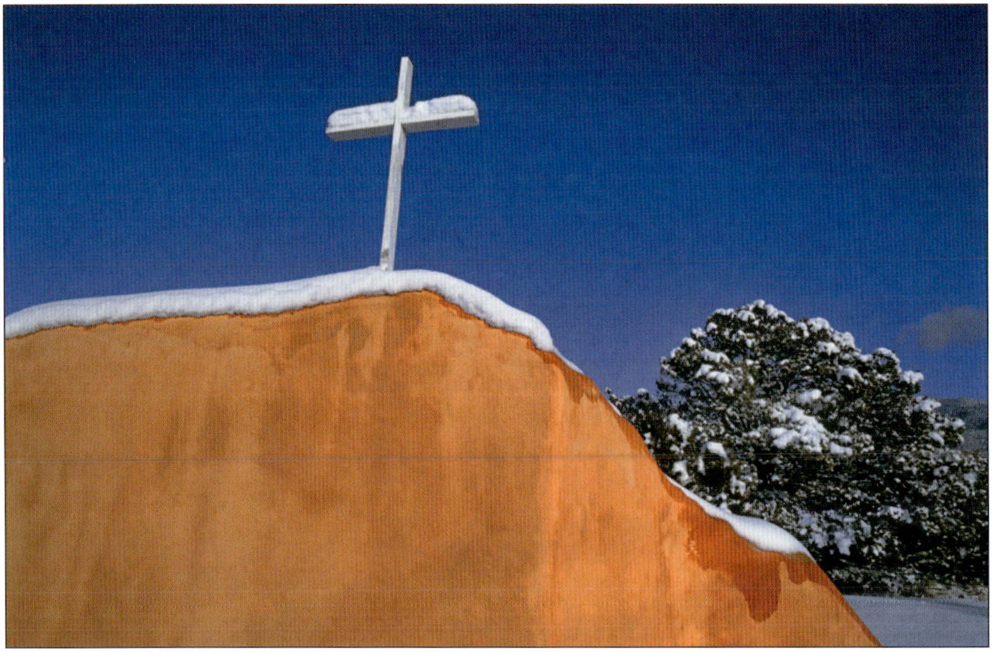

A fluffy blanket of snow atop an adobe wall near the Carmelite Monastery on Santa Fe's east side (above) and on a walled family compound near the plaza (below) marks the passage of a major winter snowstorm in January 1989. Santa Fe sits at an elevation of 7,000 feet but only receives an average annual snowfall of 26 inches. The city's mild winters and 300 days of sunshine a year have always been a large part of Santa Fe's allure, especially in the early 20th century when visiting artists from the East Coast discovered that they could paint year-round en plein air, or outside in the open air.

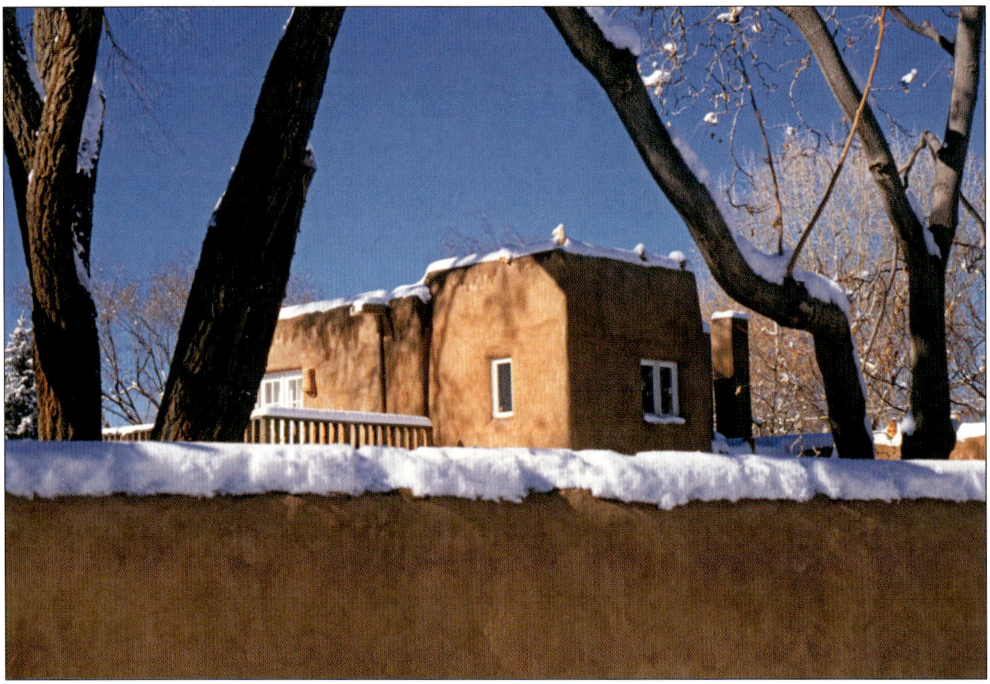

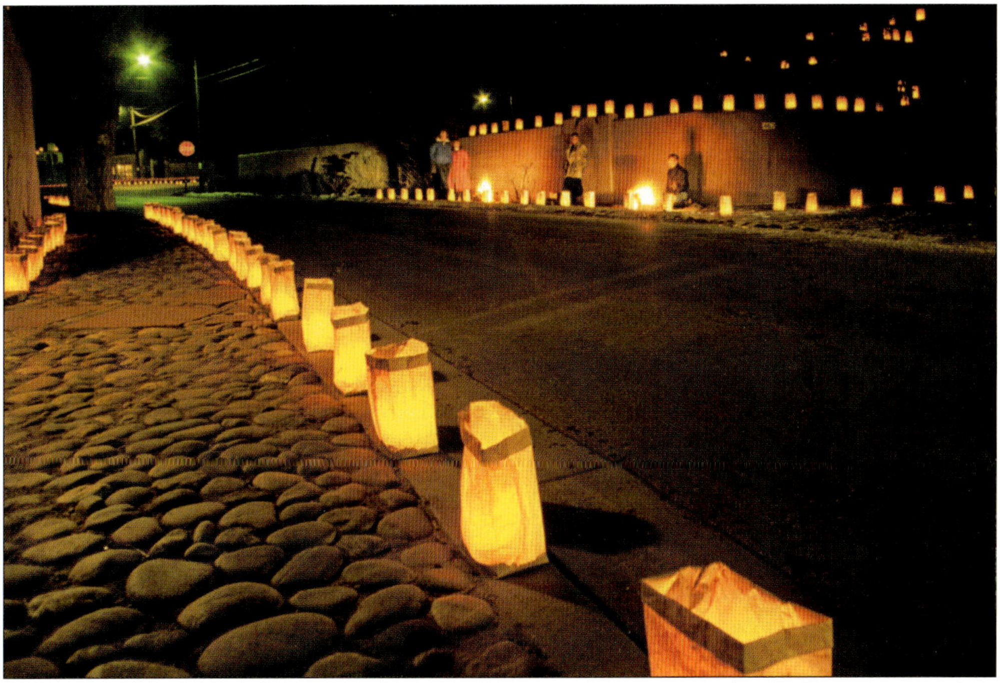

The holiday season has always been a special time in Santa Fe, particularly on Christmas Eve, when residents place thousands of *farolitos*—small sand-filled paper bags with candles inside—along many of the city's streets and sidewalks. The tradition of lighting farolitos originated during New Mexico's Spanish Colonial period, when small bonfires or luminarias, like these on Acequia Madre Street (above), were burned alongside roads and churchyards to commemorate the birth of Jesus and guide local residents to and from midnight mass at the end of the Las Posadas celebration. The farolito and luminaria lighting on Christmas Eve attracts thousands of holiday visitors who participate in what has become known as the Farolito Walk, a free self-guided walking tour of the candlelit streets.

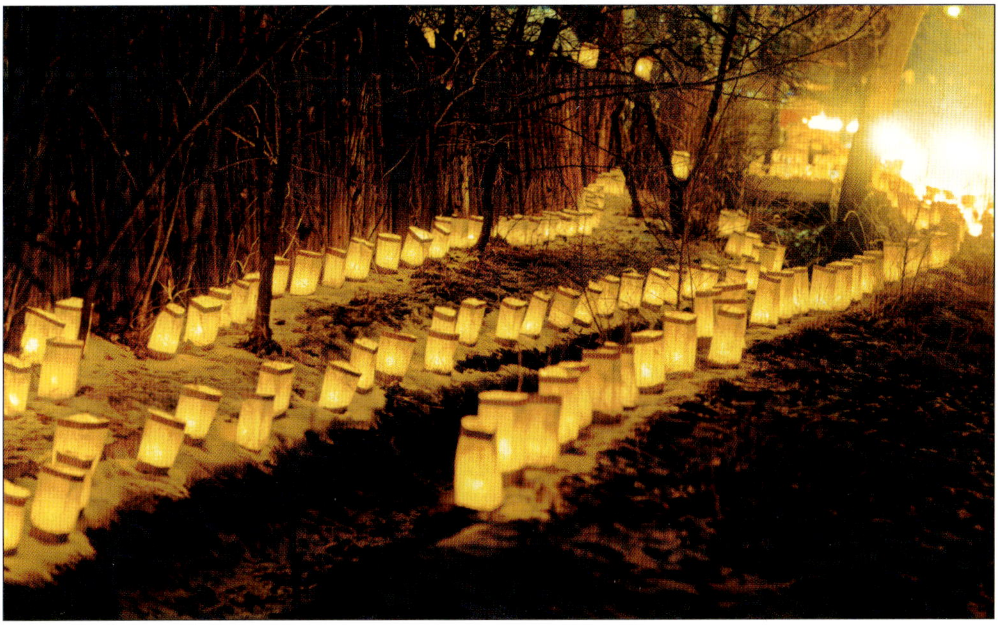

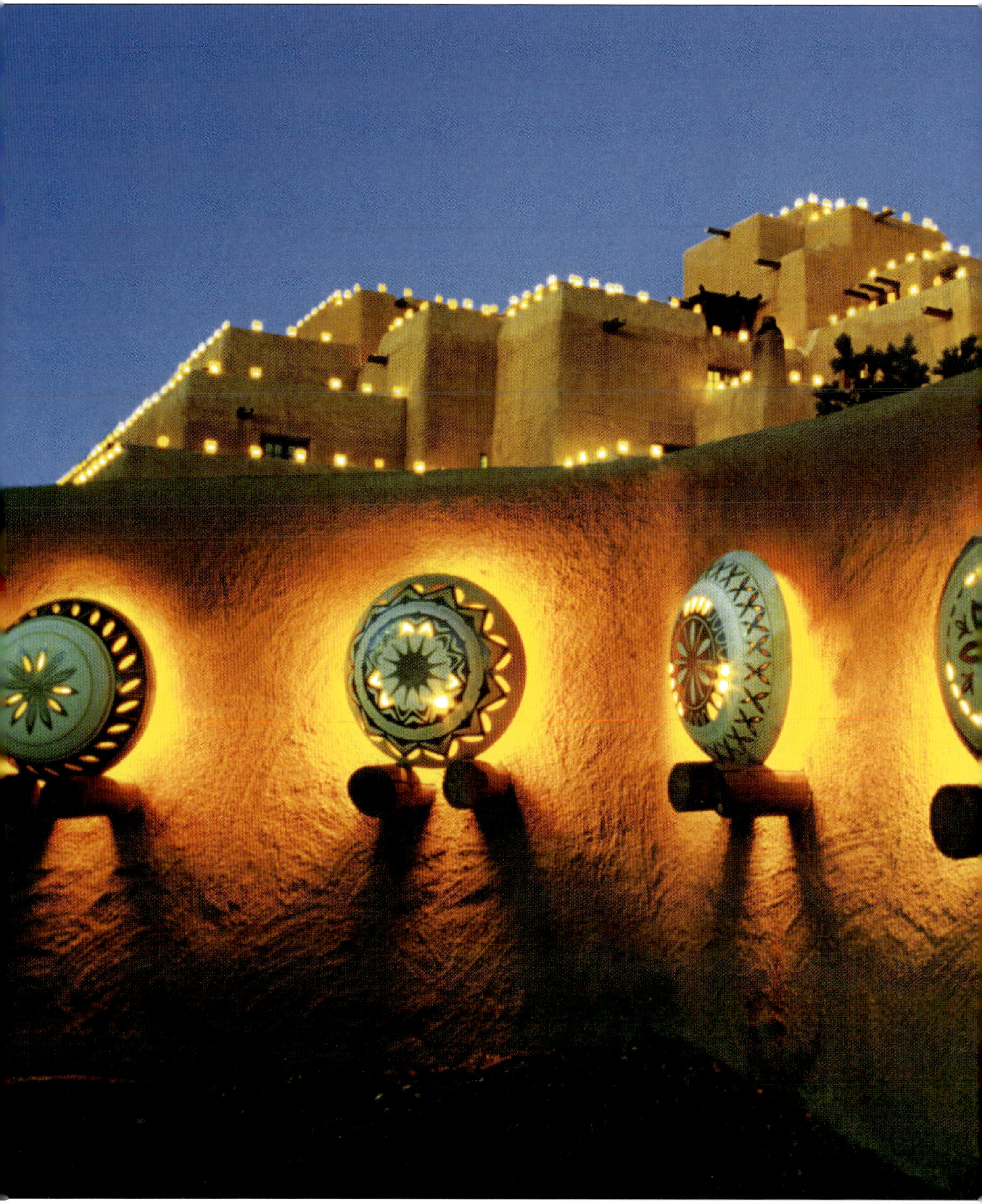

Built on the former site of the Sisters of Loretto Academy girl's school, the Inn at Loretto has been among Santa Fe's most picturesque hotels since its construction in 1975. Situated near the terminus of the historic Santa Fe Trail, just a block from the plaza, the three-story building was designed in the Pueblo Revival architectural style, which copied, up to a point, the 800-year-old

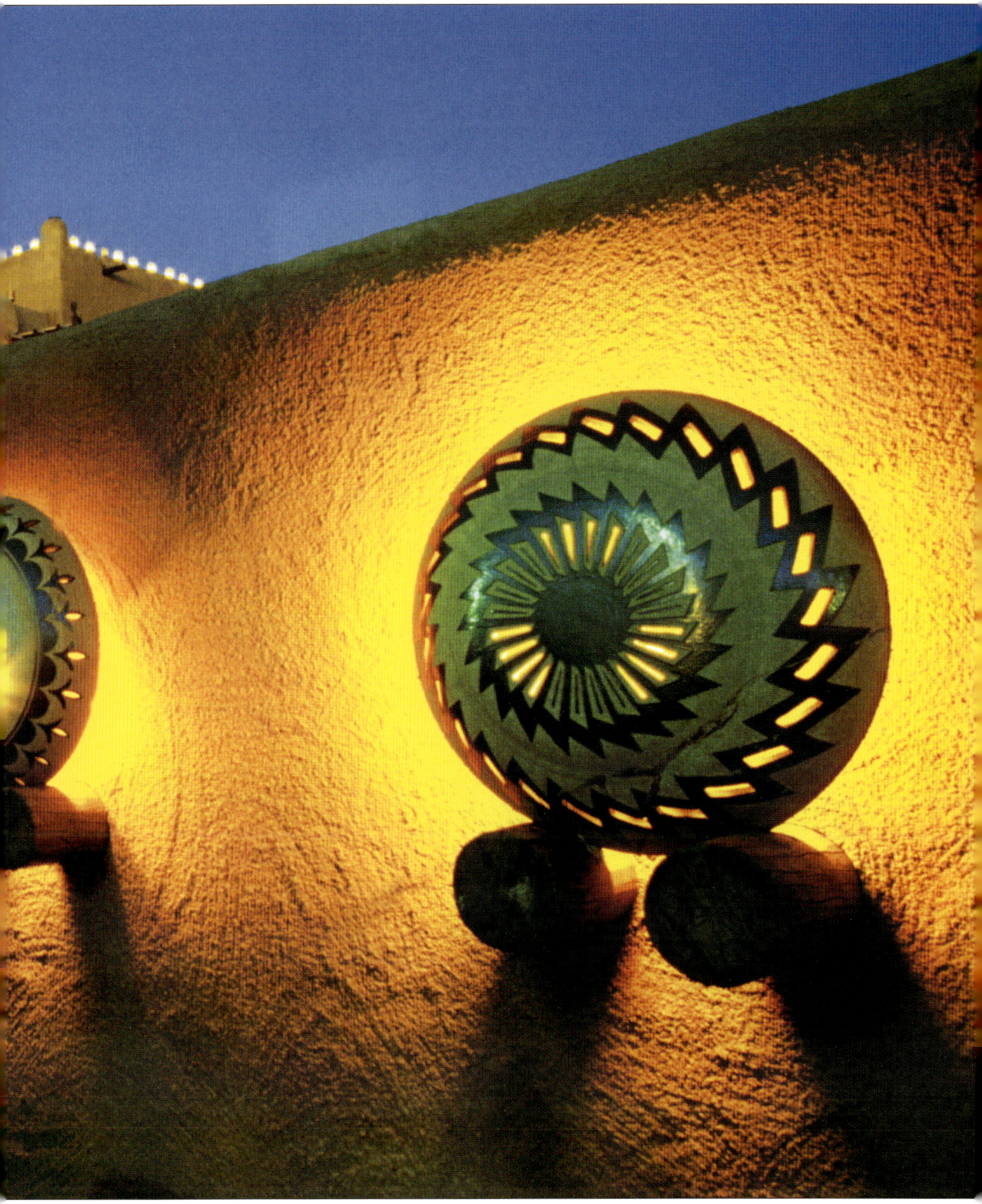

outer walls of Taos Indian Pueblo. The inn is especially appealing to photographers during the holiday season, when the walls and rooflines of the hotel are ablaze with farolitos and dotted with other decorative lights.

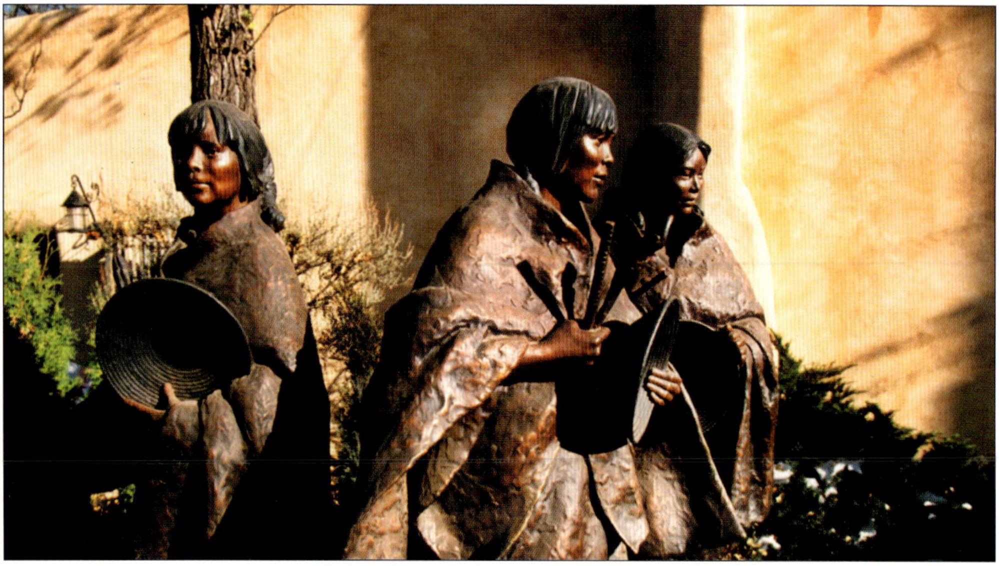

Above, the statue of Pueblo Indian women graced the grounds of the Fenn Gallery, one of Santa Fe's leading art emporiums. Owned by explorer and entrepreneur Forrest Fenn, this high-end gallery catered to wealthy customers ranging from Robert Redford and John Wayne to Jackie Kennedy and Stephen Spielberg. One of the gallery's more bizarre attractions was Beowulf, Fenn's three-foot-long pet alligator. Below, the modernist sculpture of Apache women was created by well-known Chiricahua Apache sculptor Alan Houser (1914–1994) for the exterior gardens of the Hotel Santa Fe in the 1980s. One of America's most talented native artists, Houser was a painter, wood-carver, teacher, and longtime Santa Fe resident. His estate still manages a popular gallery and sculpture garden near the Santa Fe Plaza.

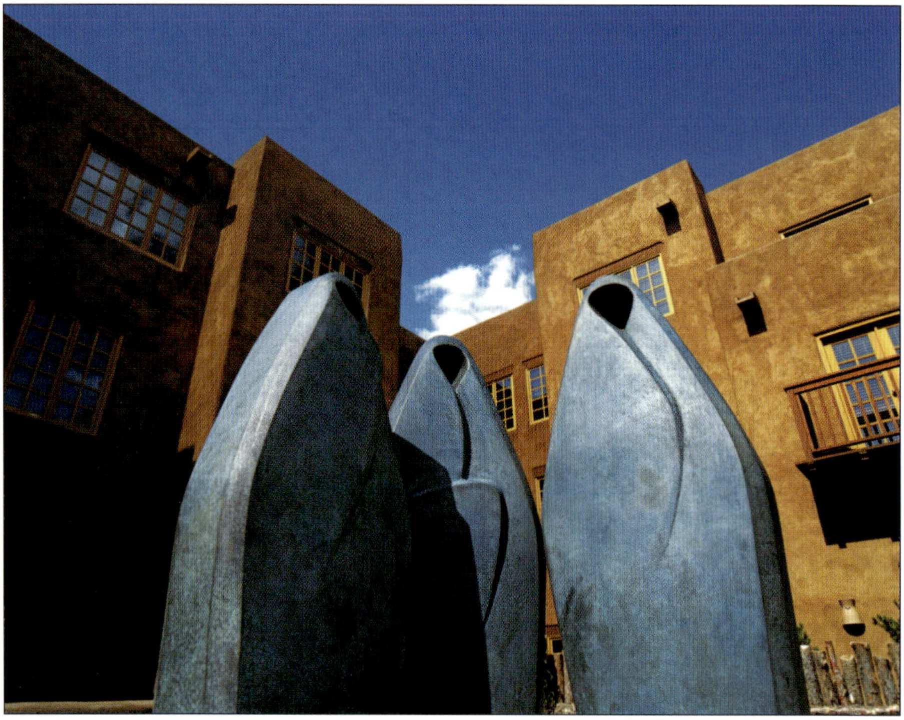

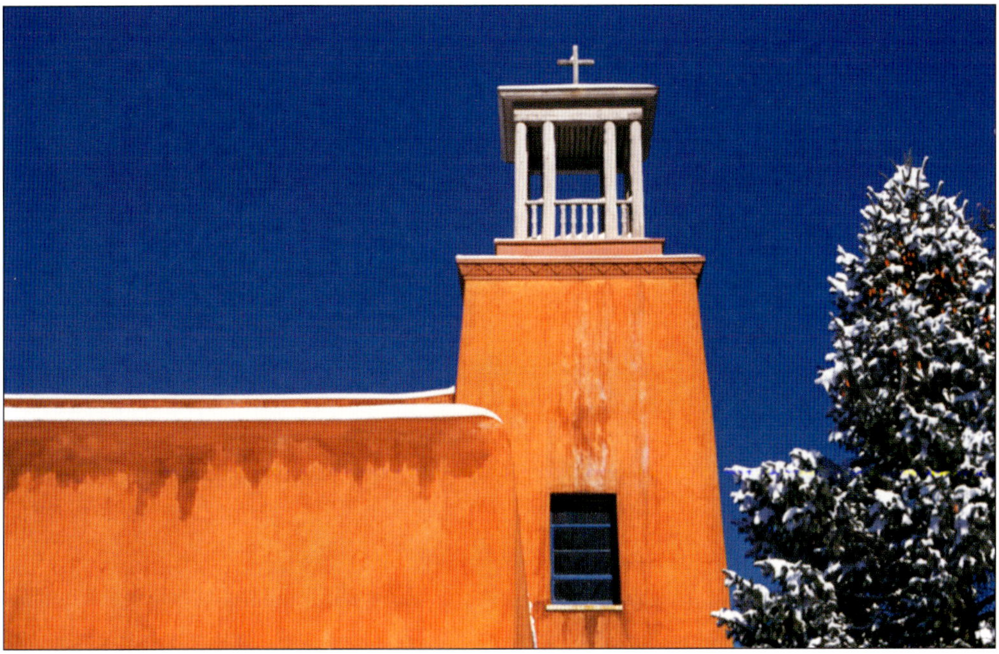

People have used adobe bricks as a building material for thousands of years, and the Spanish settlers and missionaries who established Santa Fe in the early 1600s were no exception. Most early houses, churches, and businesses in the city were constructed of adobe for two reasons: the raw materials—straw (or dung) and mud—were abundantly available, and structures made of adobe were cool in the summer and toasty in the winter. Traditional adobe architecture, as seen in the New Mexico School for the Arts building along the Santa Fe River (above) and the facade of the downtown First Presbyterian Church (below), is both aesthetically pleasing and environmentally friendly. The structures were designed by Santa Fe architect John Gaw Meem and built in the 1930s.

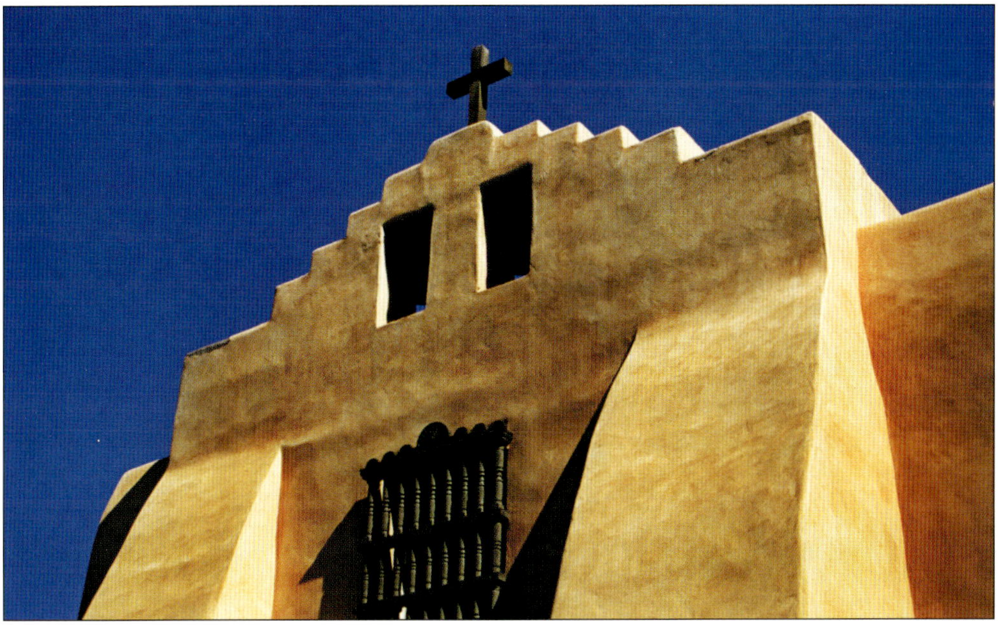

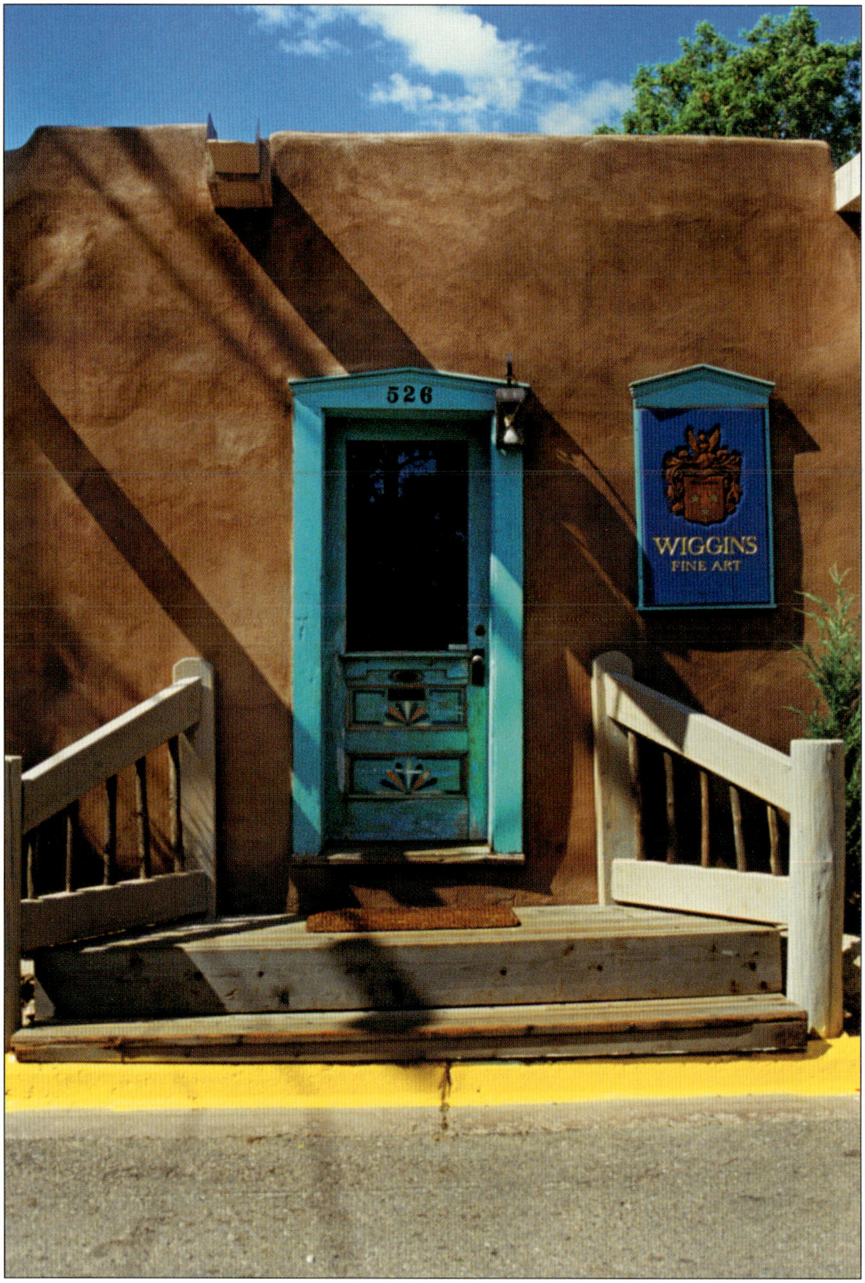

Bright-turquoise window frames and doors have been common features of Santa Fe homes and businesses for generations, especially in the city's historic district. Some historians say the practice of painting entryways this hue probably began with early colonists, many of whom strongly believed in witchcraft and thought the color blue would ward off curses and evil spirits. Another explanation is that many early families prayed daily to Nuestra Señora de Guadalupe (the patron saint of Mexico) and demonstrated their special religious devotion by painting their doors and windows the color of La Señora's robe, which the faithful regarded as blue. In recent years, the use of turquoise paint has been expanded to include garden benches, window shutters, front gates, mailboxes, bicycles, and even fences. This particular blue door belonged to an art gallery on Canyon Road.

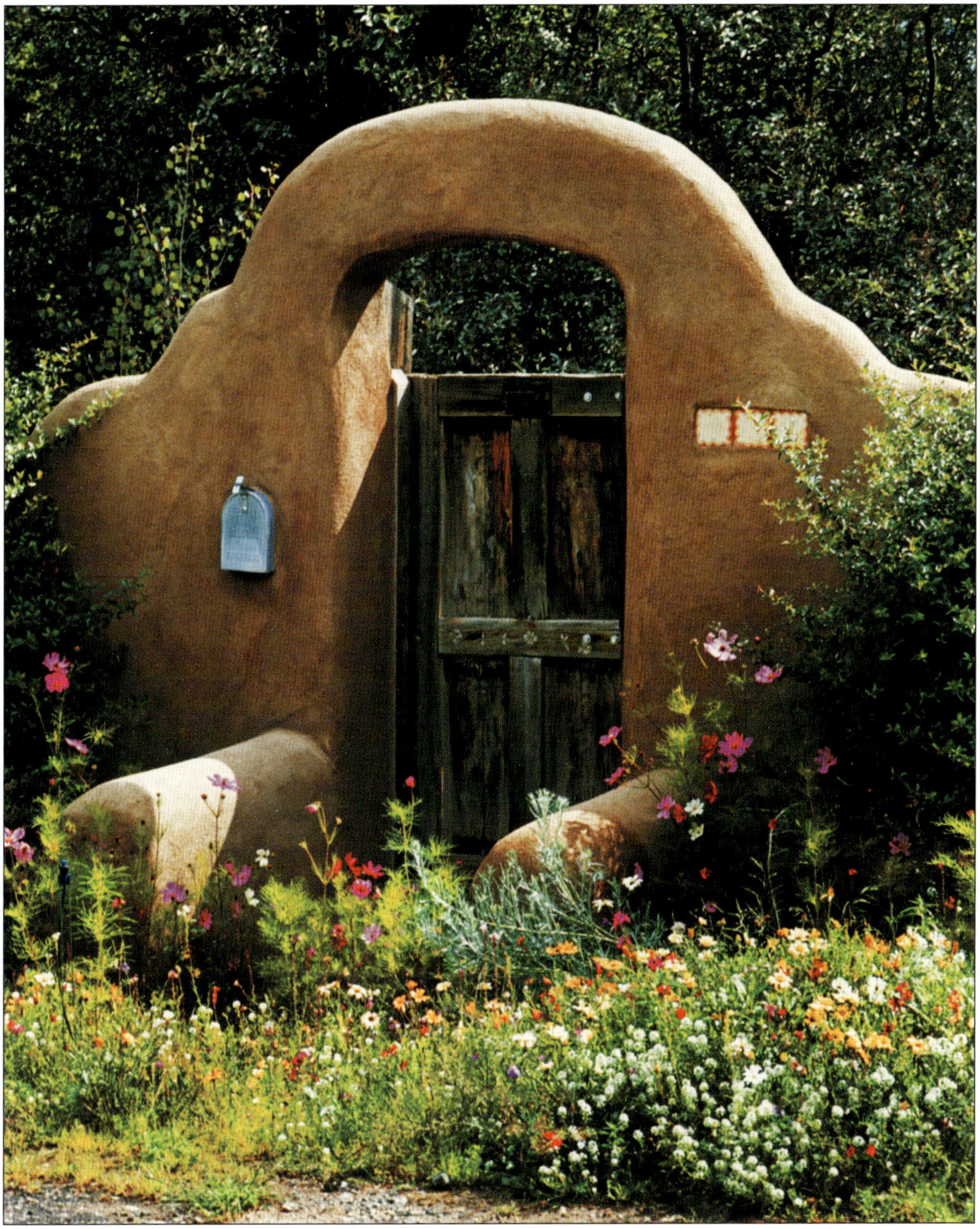

In the late 19th and early 20th centuries, concealing large Santa Fe homes and their courtyards and gardens behind high adobe walls and strong wooden gates was a widespread practice. These barriers not only provided residents with privacy from noisy neighbors and nosey passersby, they also offered protection from intruders and kept out hungry deer, stray dogs, rabid skunks, and unpleasant odors. This old adobe archway and wooden gate—adorned with a bright blanket of cosmos and daisies to appear less formidable—is typical to the practice and was probably part of the original home construction. As early as the 1930s, local companies offered guided tours—with the full cooperation of the homeowners, of course—of Santa Fe's assorted gates and walls, and sometimes of the extraordinarily grand gardens behind them. Unfortunately, a citywide water shortage, which began in the 1990s, forced many of those gardens into permanent, arid retirement.

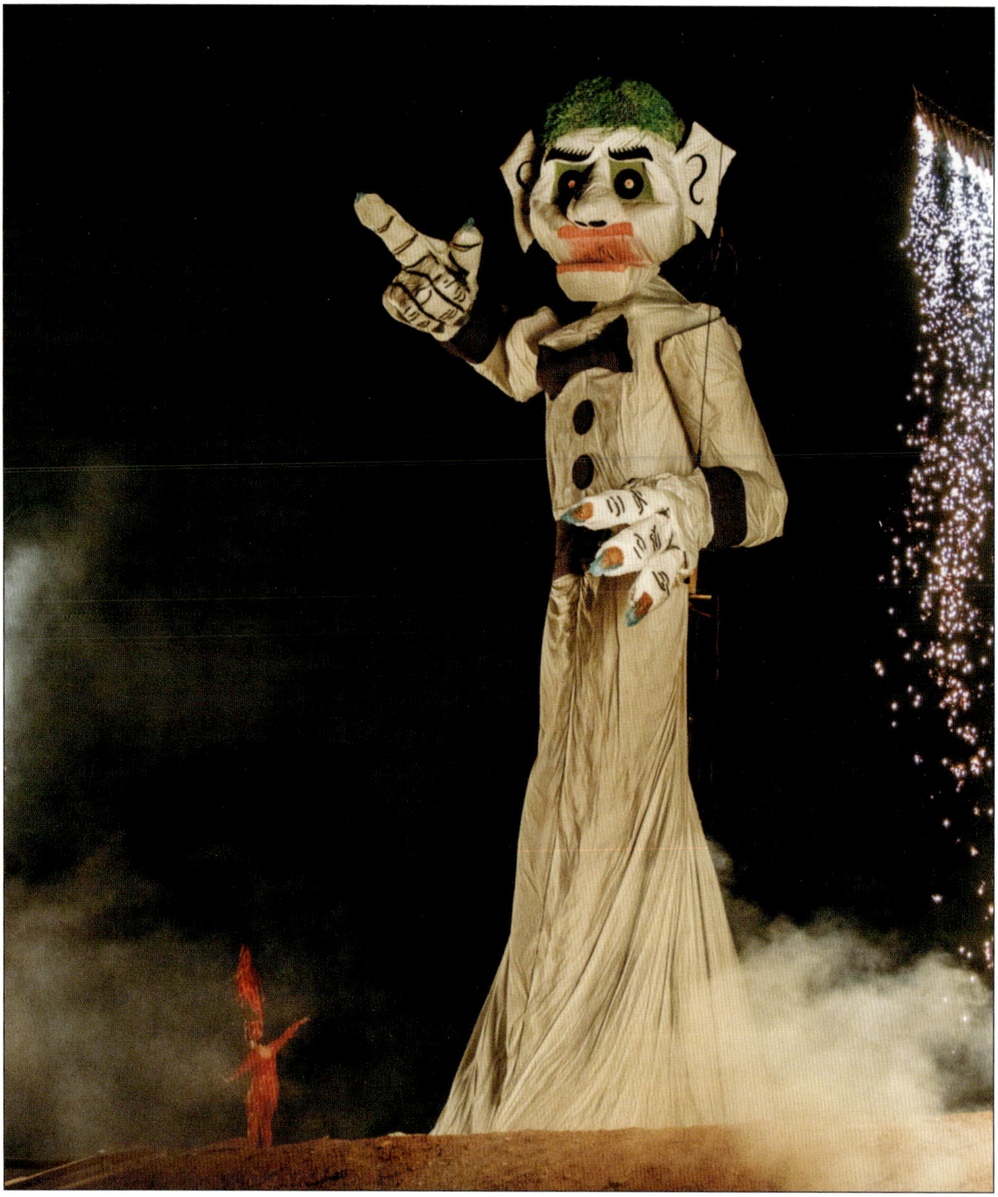

The destruction of "Old Man Gloom," better known as Zozobra, has been an annual Santa Fe ritual since 1924, when well-known artist William Shuster introduced the idea of creating and burning a giant, hideous effigy to rid Santa Feans of the troubles and anxieties of the previous year. At 50 feet tall and stuffed with thousands of notes and letters from people who write down their woes and worries and place them inside the monster's belly, Zozobra meets his fate during the Fiesta de Santa Fe each September. The moaning, groaning, swaying creature is built from chicken wire and muslin by the Kiwanis Club of Santa Fe, then set afire—accompanied by a dazzling light show—after dark in Fort Marcy Park on the first night of the Fiesta. The popular event is often attended by more than 50,000 people. (Courtesy of Melinda Herrera Photography.)

Two

The Plaza, Santa Fe's Historic Hub

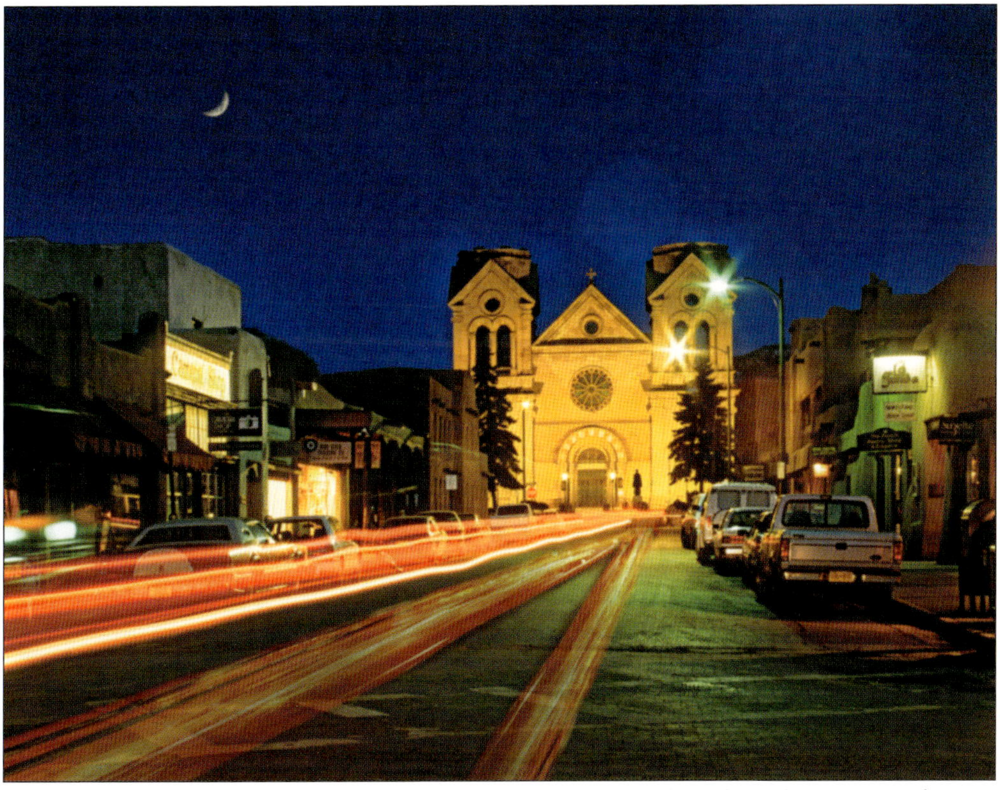

A waning moon rises over the exquisite and venerable Cathedral Basilica of St. Francis of Assisi, adjacent to the historic Santa Fe Plaza in downtown Santa Fe. Built by Archbishop Jean Baptiste Lamy between 1869 and 1886, the century-and-a half-old basilica is the mother church of the modern Archdiocese of Santa Fe.

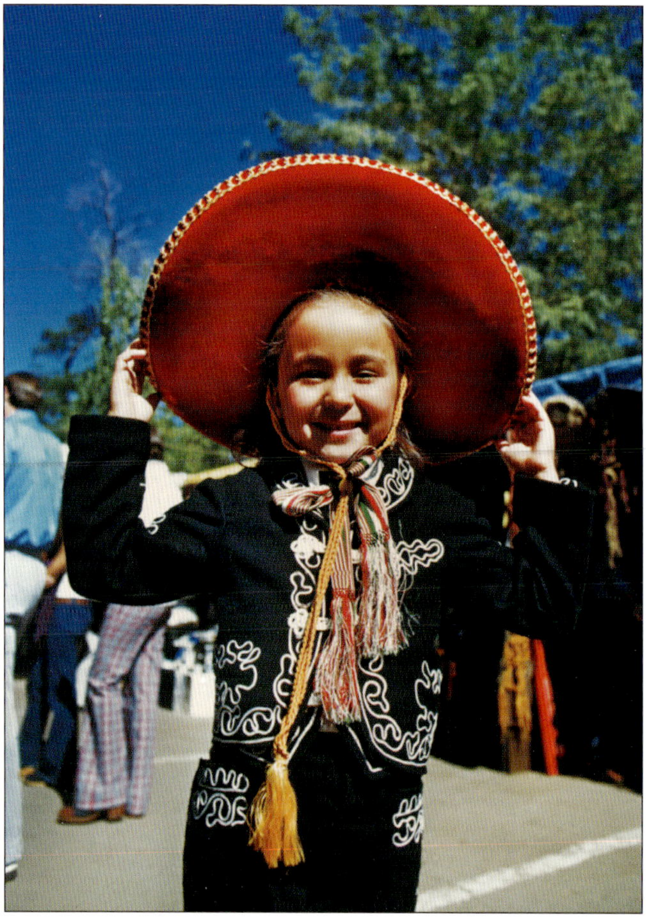

Originally surrounded by a high defensive wall, the historic Santa Fe Plaza provided early residents with a secure haven against Indian attack. Today, it is where residents and visitors go to shop, eat, drink, and soak up the city's unique ambiance, especially during the summer and early fall. From June through October, public events of some kind occur in or around the plaza nearly every weekend. The girl wearing an oversized sombrero at left was an attendee at Fiesta de Santa Fe in 1973, while the young family below could have been on the lookout for movie stars. Since the city became an in place in the early 1980s, star spotting for celebrities such as Sandra Bullock, Val Kilmer, Oprah Winfrey, and Shirley MacLaine (all of whom have owned homes or property here) has become a major pastime.

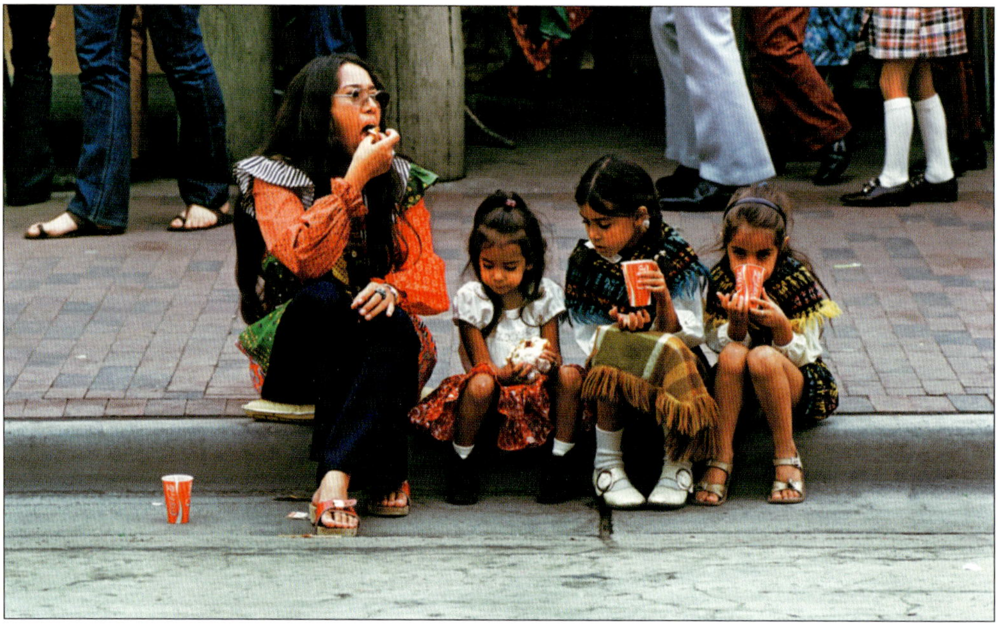

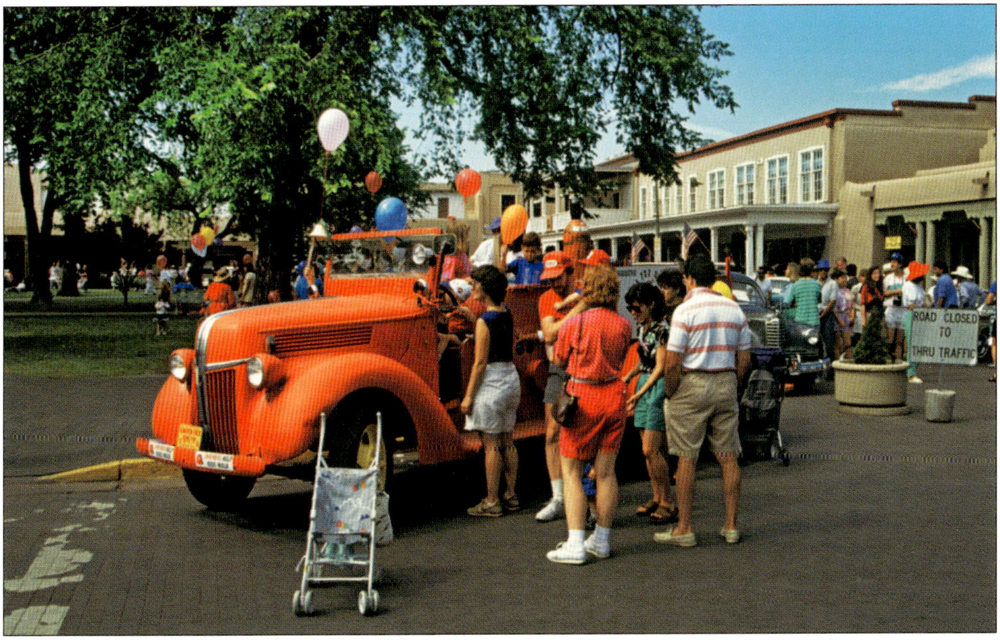

There have been considerable changes to the plaza's appearance since its initial 1608 construction as an enclosed presidio, but just as it was 400 years ago, this tree-dotted downtown square remains the vibrant and colorful hub at the heart of Santa Fe. Bordered on the south by East San Francisco Street, on the west by Lincoln Avenue, on the east by Washington Avenue, and on the north by East Palace Avenue, the square is still the social and commercial center of the city. Events such as the antique automobile show above and the open-air art market below attract thousands of visitors to the city each year.

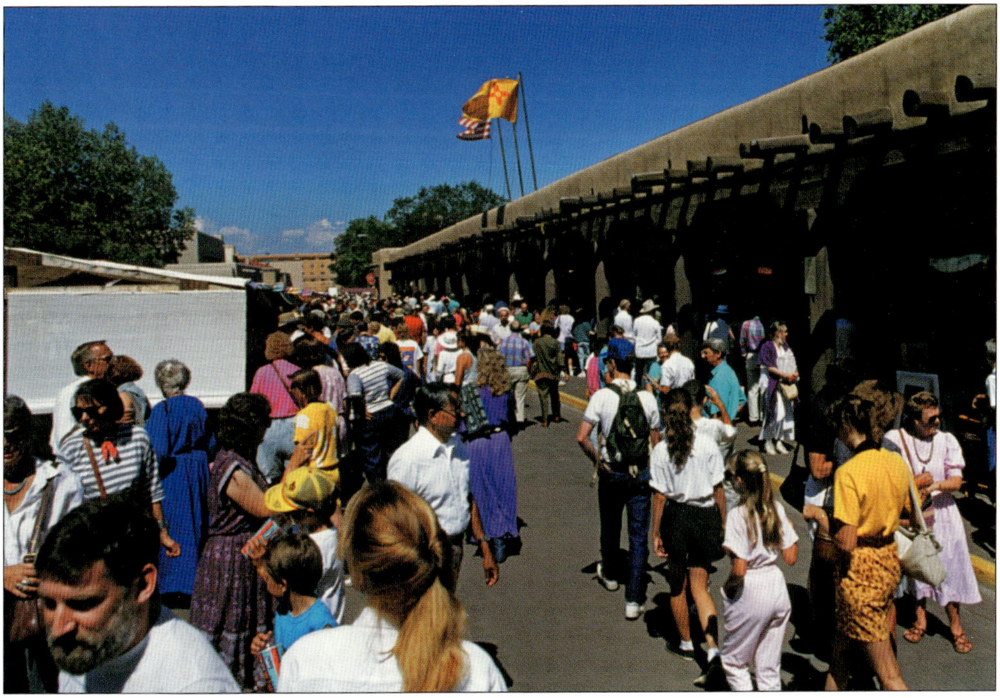

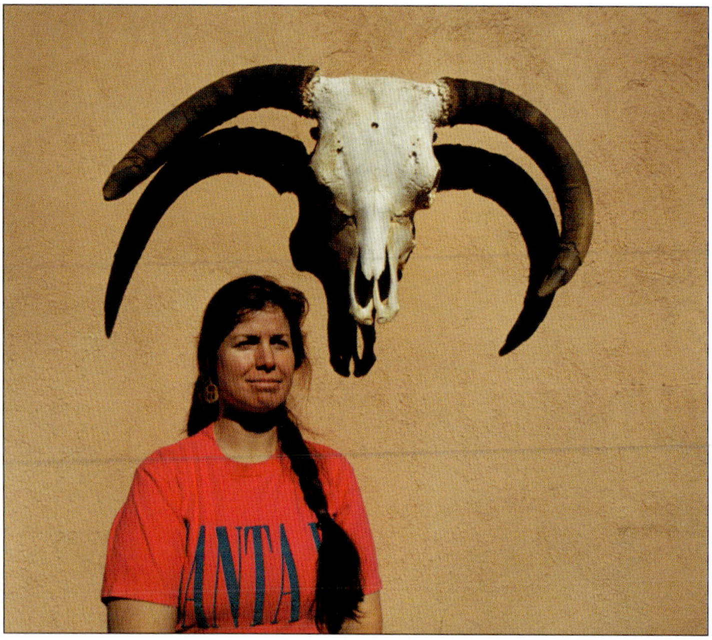

A young clerk at a busy downtown souvenir shop poses beneath one of the store's prized possessions—a giant bleached cow skull with the horns still intact. Like most Santa Fe natives in the 1980s, this young woman could not understand the intense and sudden popularity of something that had died and rotted in the desert, only to be picked up, cleaned, and placed on public exhibit with a $500 price tag.

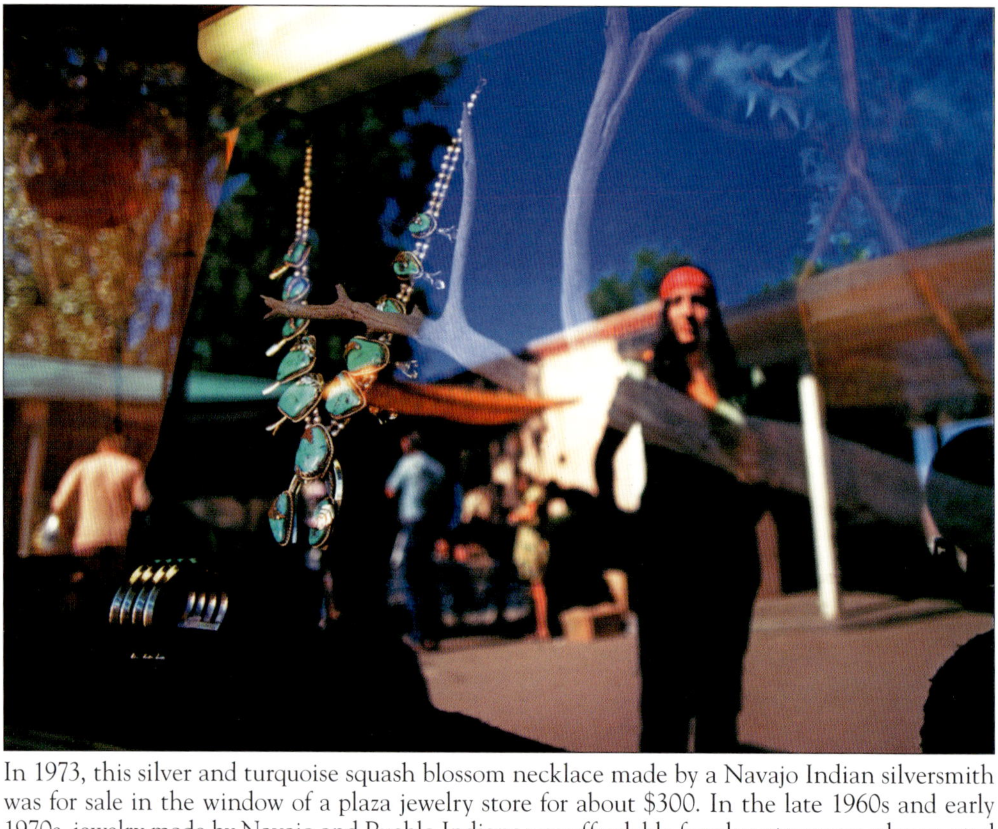

In 1973, this silver and turquoise squash blossom necklace made by a Navajo Indian silversmith was for sale in the window of a plaza jewelry store for about $300. In the late 1960s and early 1970s, jewelry made by Navajo and Pueblo Indians was affordable for almost anyone who wanted to buy it; 10 years later, however, it had become fashionable in New York and Los Angeles social circles, causing prices to soar.

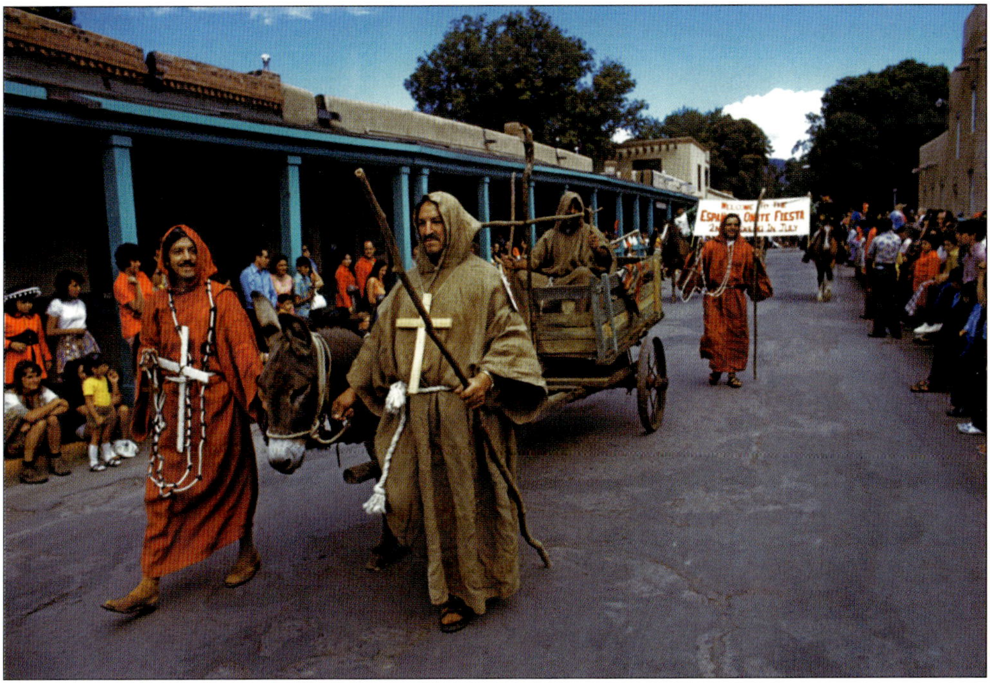

Above, Santa Feans garbed like 17th-century Franciscan friars parade through the plaza during the Fiesta de Santa Fe in the early 1970s. Held every September since 1712, the fiesta celebrates the reoccupation of the city by conquistador Diego de Vargas after Pueblo Indians—protesting inhumane sanctions imposed on them by the Spanish officials—had driven the colonists out of the region during the Pueblo Revolt of 1680. In 1693, de Vargas led a combined force of Spanish colonists and sympathetic Puebloans into the region and retook the city 13 years after Pueblo Indians had killed 400 Spaniards and forced 2,000 more to flee the province. At right, a local volunteer dressed in clothing befitting a conqueror portrays de Vargas while riding horseback in the 1973 Fiesta de Santa Fe parade.

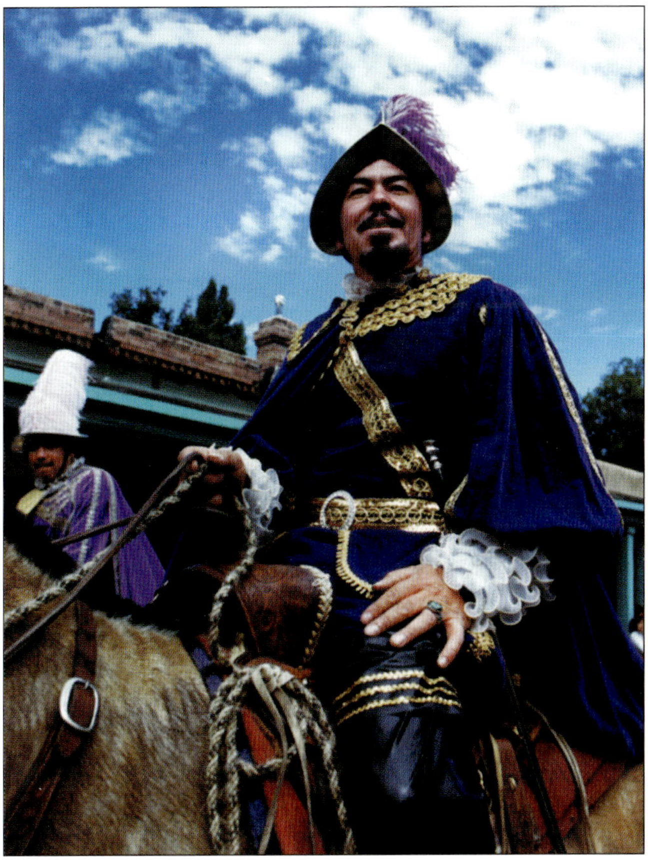

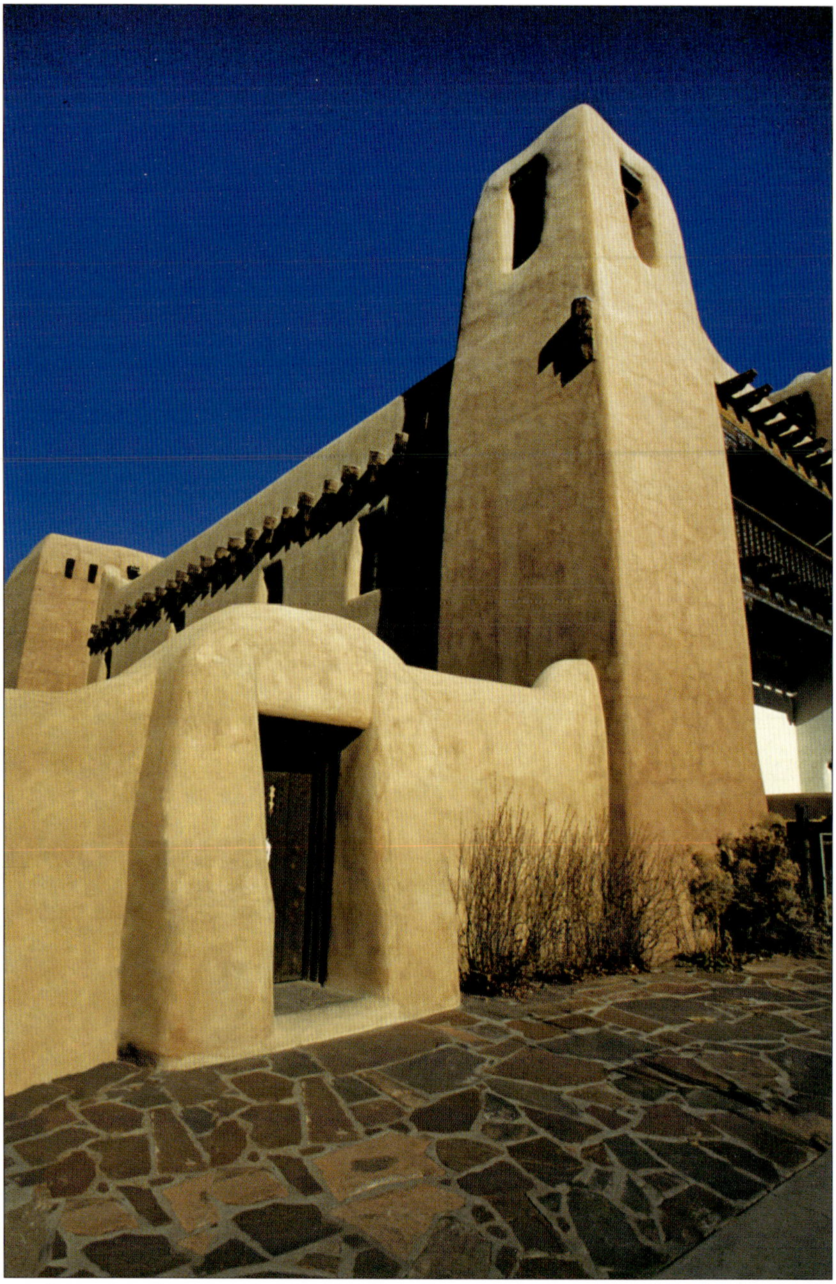

Constructed in 1917, the New Mexico Museum of Art (formerly the Museum of Fine Arts) on West Palace Avenue is perhaps the city's best example of Pueblo Revival architecture—a design style that imitates the traditional adobe construction found in New Mexico's centuries-old Indian Pueblos and early Spanish mission churches. Early on, the museum's policy was to encourage artists and craftsmen who lived in New Mexico to exhibit their work publicly. This policy did much to establish Santa Fe's early art scene and transform the city into the third-largest art market in the United States. The museum, which sits on the northwest corner of the plaza, was originally built as the art gallery for the Museum of New Mexico and features more than 20,000 works of art and photography from the Southwest alone.

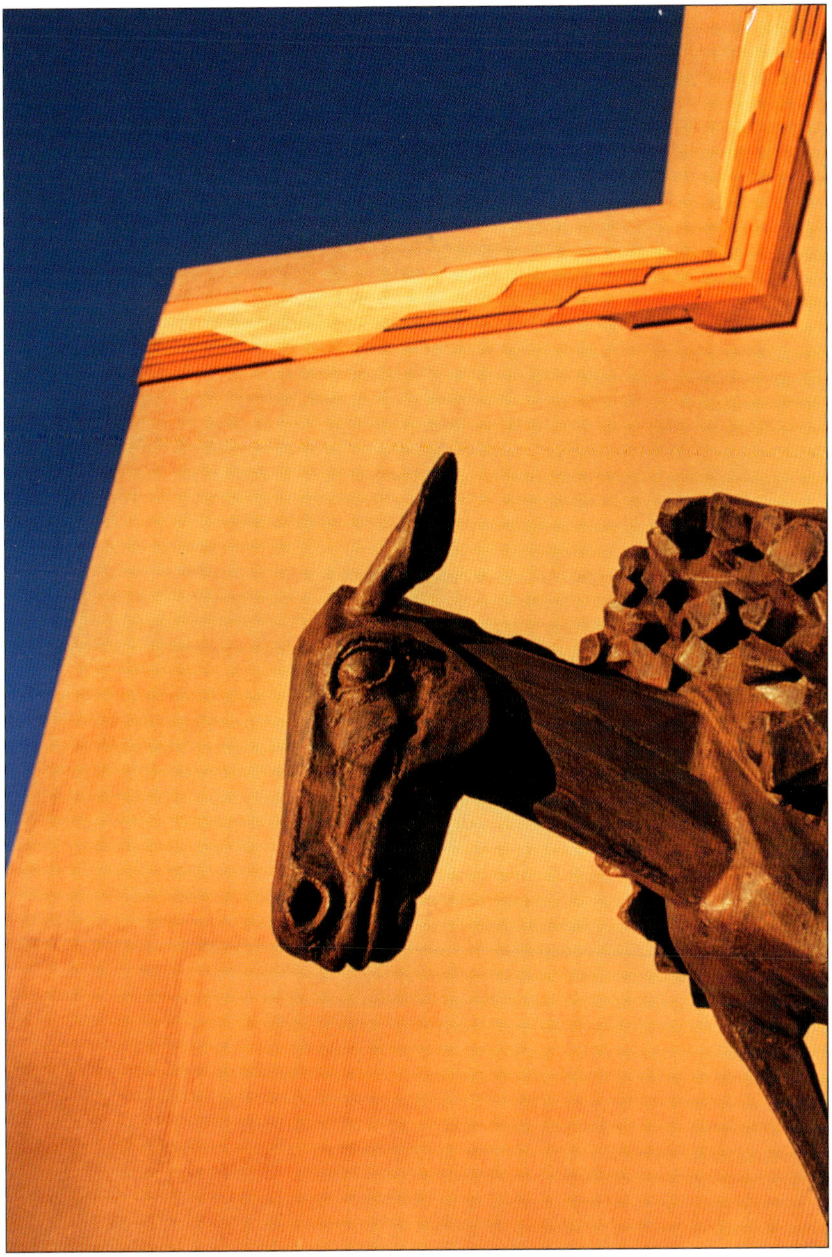

As part of Santa Fe's Art in Public Places (AIPP) program, artist Charles Southard was commissioned in 1988 to create this metal sculpture of a burro that stands patiently at the entrance to Burro Alley, the breezeway between San Francisco Street and Palace Avenue, just a short distance west of the plaza. Once the center of Santa Fe's notorious red light district, Burro Alley was lined with brothels, cantinas, and gambling establishments in the 1880s. Charles Southard's sculpture pays homage to the dozens of heavily loaded burros that were often tethered along Santa Fe streets near Burro Alley while their woodcutter owners, after a day of chopping wood in the mountains, partook of the local entertainment. The Burro Alley burro made national headlines in 2014 when its tail mysteriously disappeared, probably torn off by a vandal. A local newspaper dubbed the culprit Santa Fe's "tail bandit."

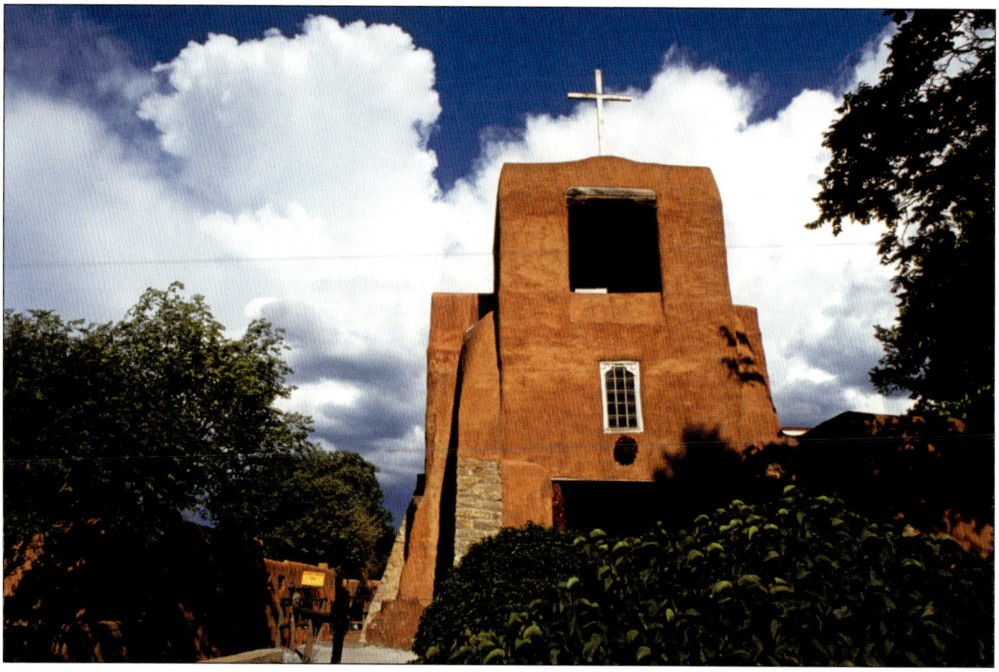

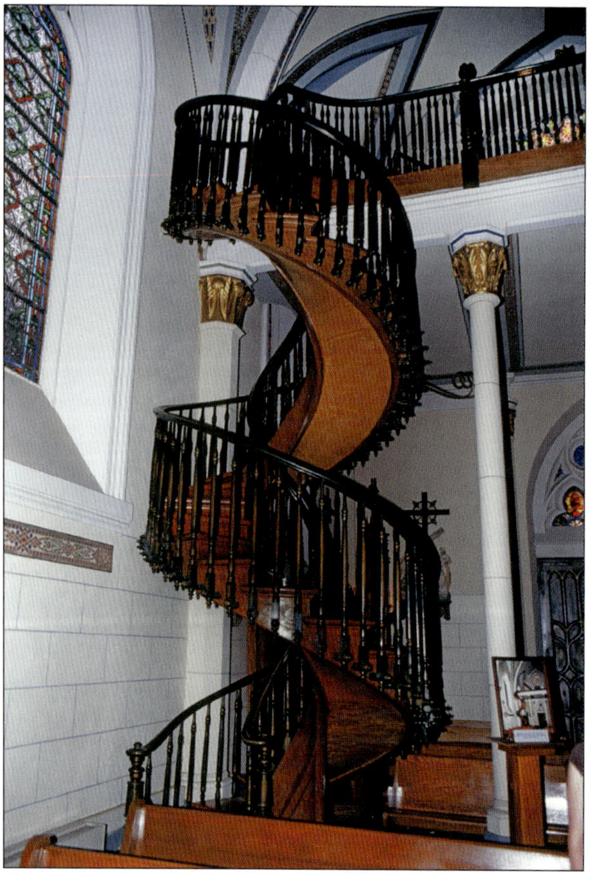

Built shortly after Santa Fe was founded in 1608, the San Miguel Chapel is probably the oldest church in the United States. Constructed to serve soldiers, Indians, and Santa Fe's poor, it was heavily damaged during the Pueblo Revolt in 1680, then rebuilt in 1710.

Legends claim that the graceful spiral staircase in the nearby Loretto Chapel was built by Joseph, the father of Jesus Christ. In 1878, the chapel's designer was murdered before a staircase leading to the choir loft could be built. When local nuns prayed to St. Joseph for a carpenter who could complete the task, a stranger appeared at their door a few days later looking for work. The circular wooden staircase he created was built without nails or glue and seems to defy gravity. When the job was finished, the stranger disappeared without saying good-bye or being paid for his trouble.

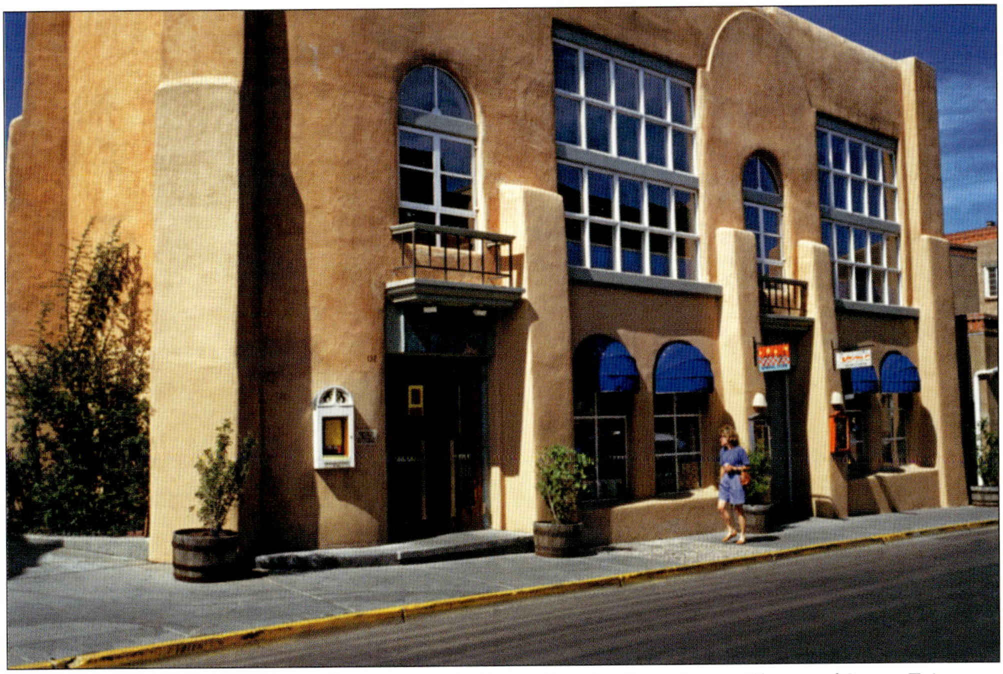

The Coyote Café opened in 1987, and nearly three decades later, it is still one of Santa Fe's most popular restaurants. Chef Eric DiStefano, who has owned the eatery since 2008, is considered one of the top chefs in the American Southwest. Most of his signature recipes include the liberal use of green chile.

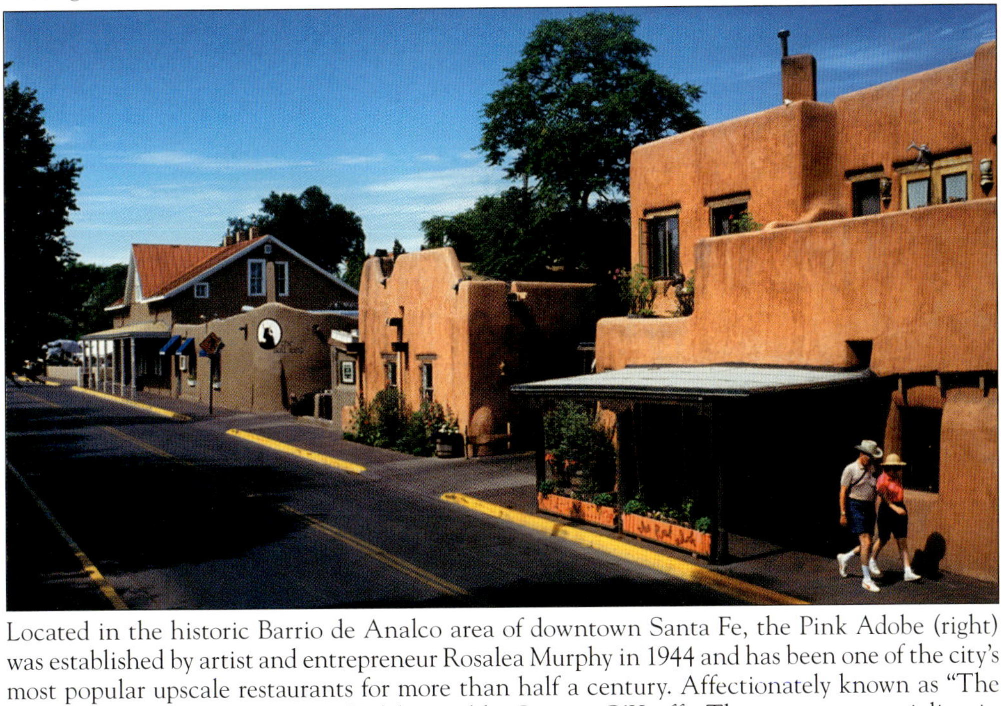

Located in the historic Barrio de Analco area of downtown Santa Fe, the Pink Adobe (right) was established by artist and entrepreneur Rosalea Murphy in 1944 and has been one of the city's most popular upscale restaurants for more than half a century. Affectionately known as "The Pink," it was once the hangout of celebrities like Georgia O'Keeffe. The restaurant specializes in traditional New Mexican food and is considered a Santa Fe institution.

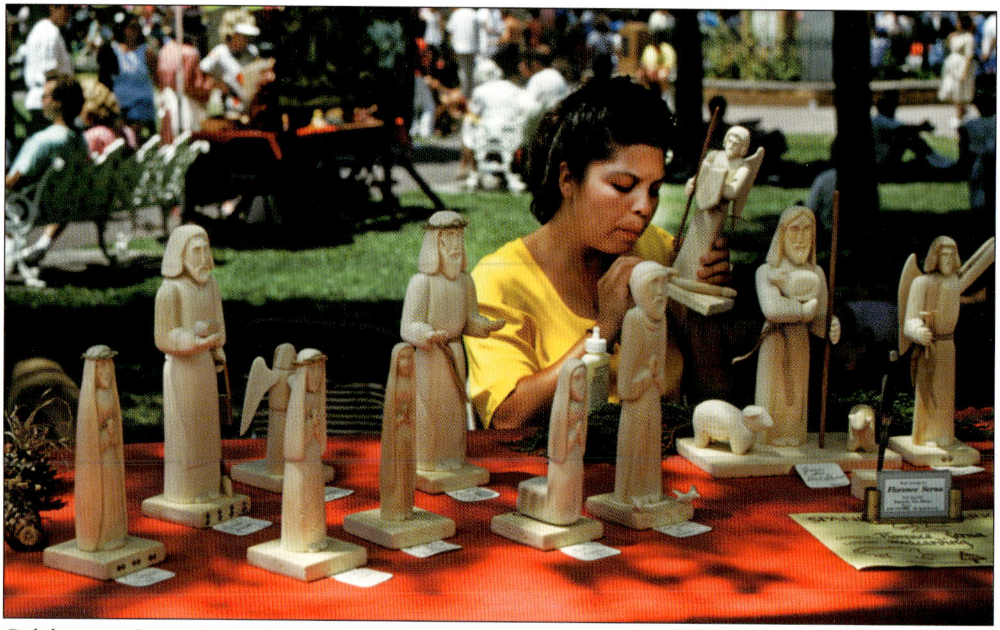

Celebrating Santa Fe's colorful Spanish and Mexican heritage, the annual Spanish Market is a popular two-day-long affair held in the downtown area in late July. Woodcarvings, such as these santos created by carver Florence Serna, are among the numerous kinds of folk art that skilled Hispanic artisans exhibit during the event. Hundreds of booths display examples of traditional Spanish handicrafts, such as tinwork, furniture making, silversmithing, and weaving.

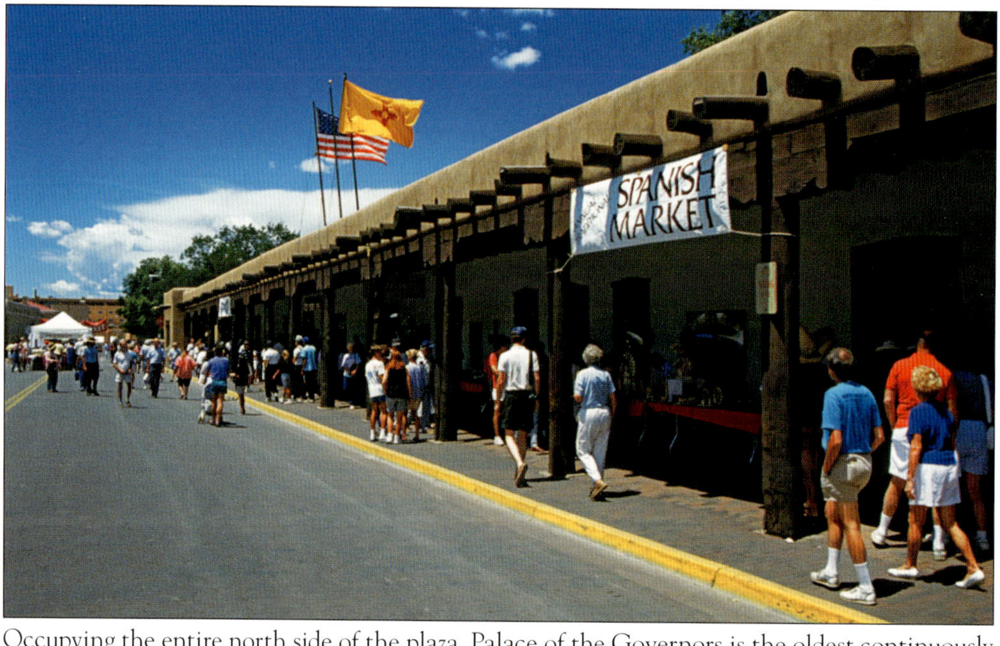

Occupying the entire north side of the plaza, Palace of the Governors is the oldest continuously inhabited public building in the United States. Built sometime between 1610 and 1618, the beautiful old building is a US National Historic Landmark and, today, houses the Museum of New Mexico. In 1870, territorial New Mexico governor and author Lew Wallace wrote the final chapters of *Ben Hur* while residing in the palace.

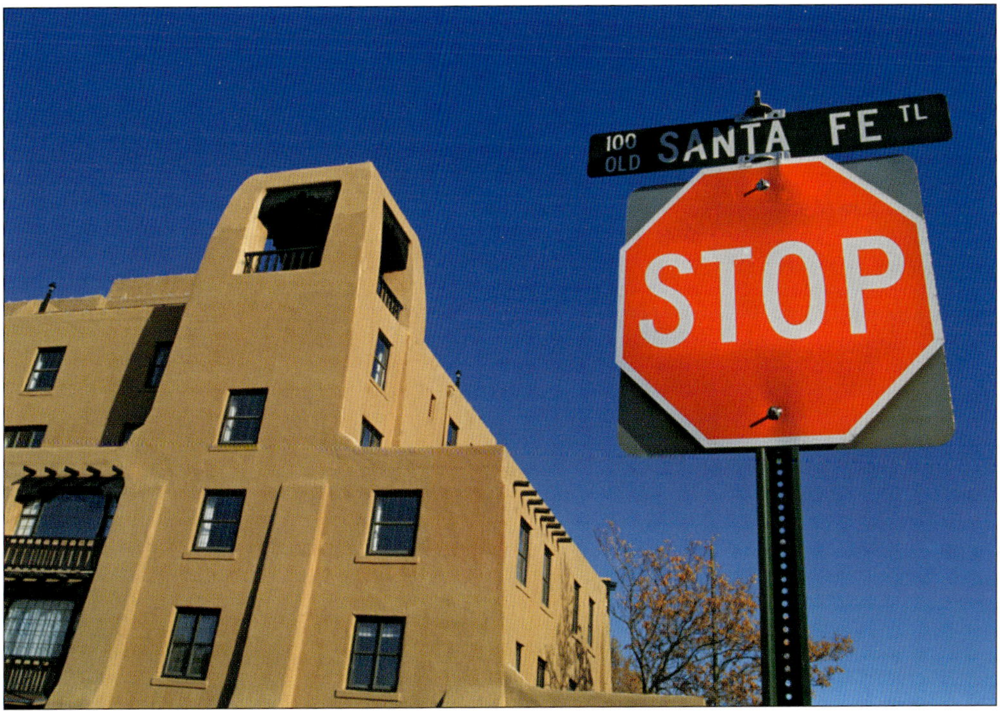

Perched like an adobe palace on the plaza's southeast corner, the La Fonda Hotel has been a Santa Fe landmark for decades. Built by architect John Gaw Meem and designer Elizabeth Colter in 1922, the six-story structure was purchased by the Atchison, Topeka & Santa Fe Railway three years later, then leased to the Fred Harvey Company, which operated La Fonda as one of its legendary Harvey House Hotels for nearly 40 years.

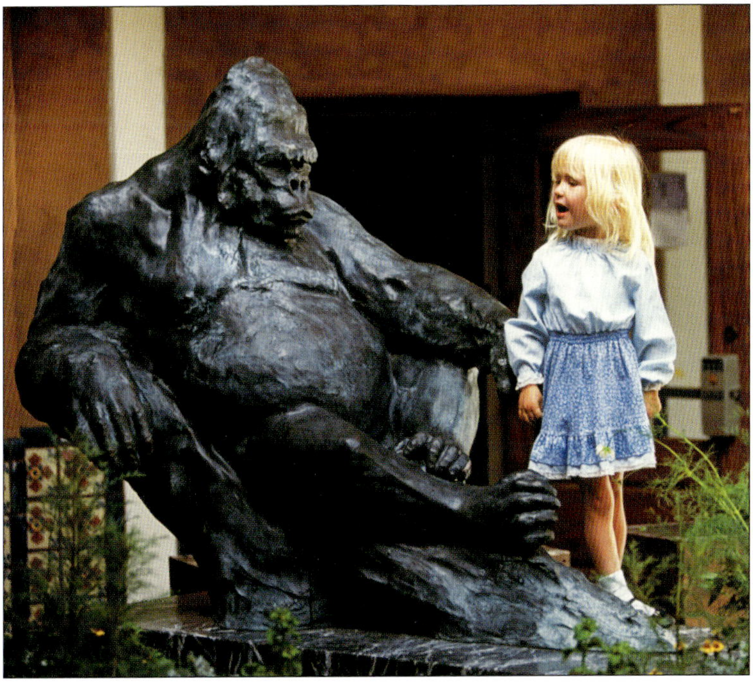

On a cozy covered patio adjacent to East Palace Avenue, this little girl enjoys a quiet chat with a large bronze gorilla by well-known wildlife sculptress Sherry Sander. The gorilla, along with dozens of other pieces of art scattered around the community, was part of the city's Art in Public Places (AIPP) program, initiated by the Santa Fe Arts Commission in 1985 and still in full swing today.

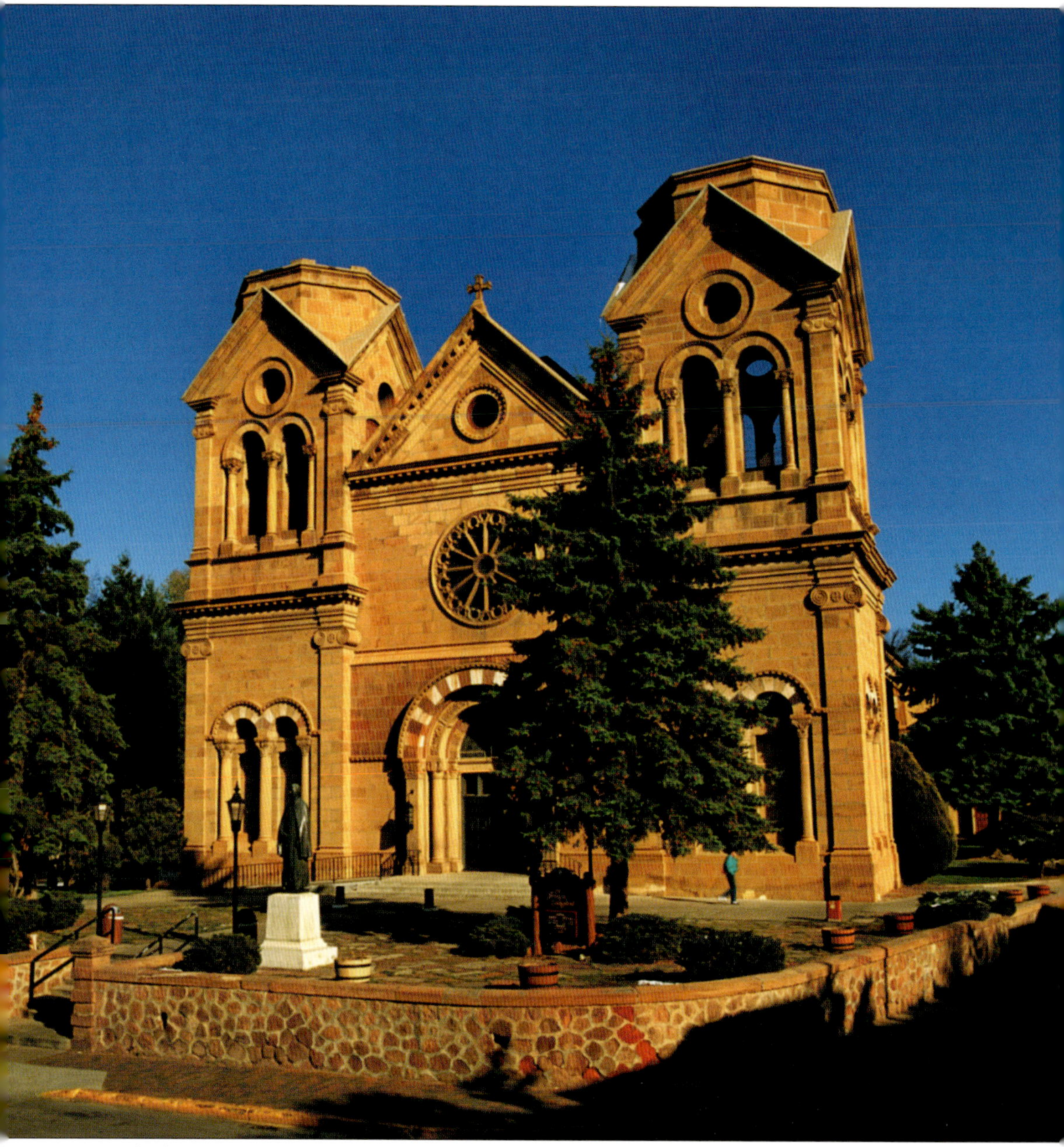

Easily the most conspicuous building in downtown Santa Fe, the beautiful Cathedral Basilica of St. Francis was built between 1869 and 1886 by Archbishop Jean Baptiste Lamy, the first archbishop of Santa Fe. (The famous novel *Death Comes for the Archbishop*, by American writer Willa Cather, is based on Lamy's life and career.) Designed and built in the Romanesque Revival architectural style—popular in Europe in the mid-1800s but unusual in the United States—the church is made of thousands of heavy yellow limestone blocks, hauled in by wagon from a quarry 18 miles away. The towers were supposed to have been capped with 160-foot-high steeples, but they were never finished because the church ran out of money. The basilica contains relics from the early 1600s, including the 30-inch-high carving of Our Lady of the Rosary, or *La Conquistadora*, the oldest statue of the Virgin Mary in the United States.

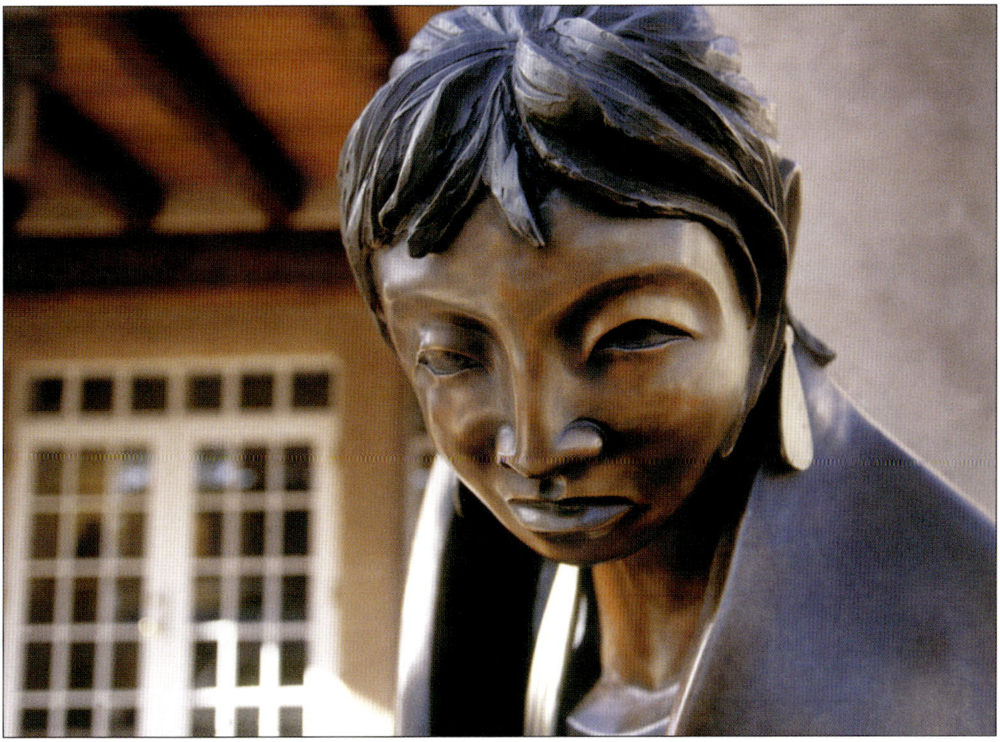

Visitors to the Frank Howell Gallery in downtown Santa Fe were greeted by a large bronze sculpture of an American Indian woman wearing a traditional hand-woven blanket, as seen above in 1989. (Indian women were a popular subject for many Santa Fe sculptors in the 1980s.) Frank Howell (1937–1997) was a Lakota Sioux, not a Puebloan, but he was among the cornerstone artists of the Southwest Native American Fine Art Movement. Below, the large bronze deer sculpture, by Texas sculptor Bill Worrell, was also on display outside a plaza gallery. Many of Worrell's sculptures are interpretations of Indian pictographs from the Lower Pecos River.

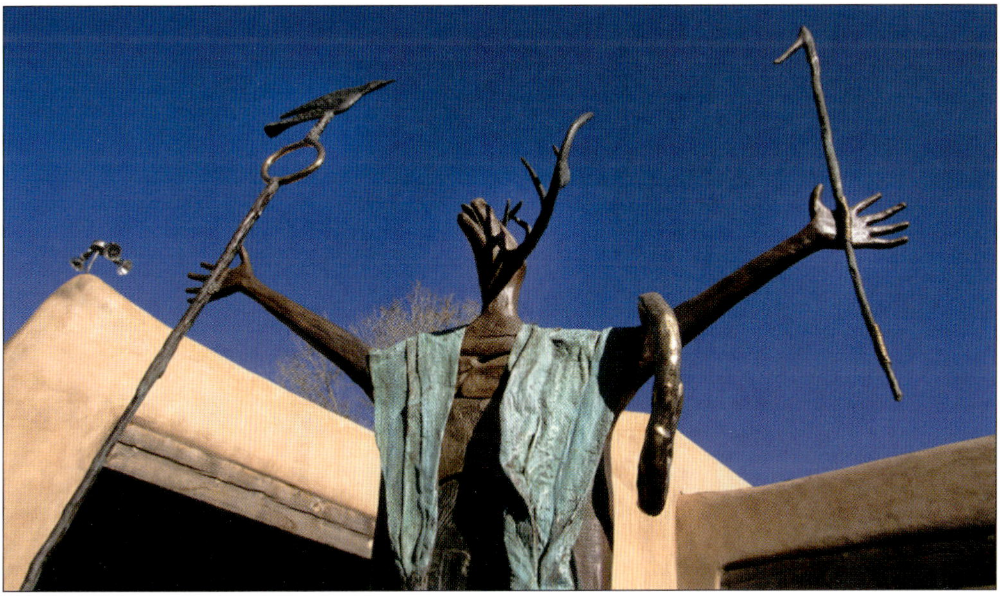

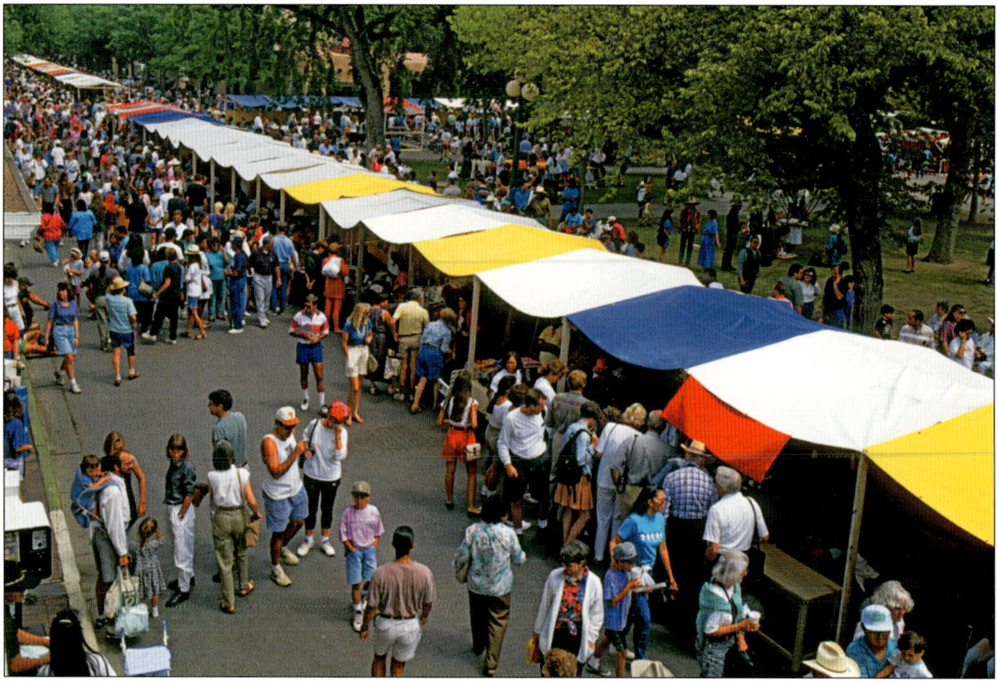

Tens of thousands of visitors pack the Santa Fe Plaza and surrounding streets during the famous Indian Market, a two-day event held annually in mid-August. Artists and craftsmen from 100 different American Indian tribes crowd into the downtown area, selling everything from jewelry, textiles, and baskets to beadwork, leather goods, sculpture, and pottery. Traditional American Indian food is popular fare at the Indian Market and plays an important role in attracting visitors to the event. One of the most sought-after dishes offered by food vendors is skillet-made Indian fried bread, eaten either plain or drizzled with any combination of honey, sugar, and cinnamon. This giant bazaar has been held in one form or another since 1922. Originally part of the Fiesta de Santa Fe, it became an entirely separate event in 1962.

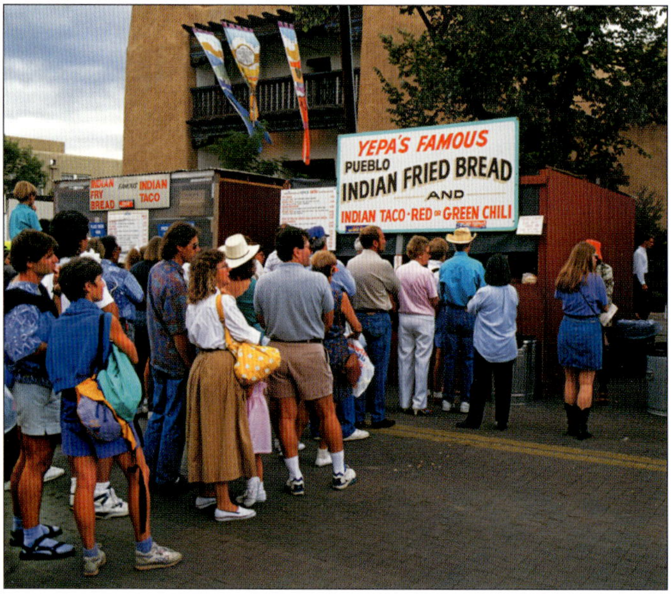

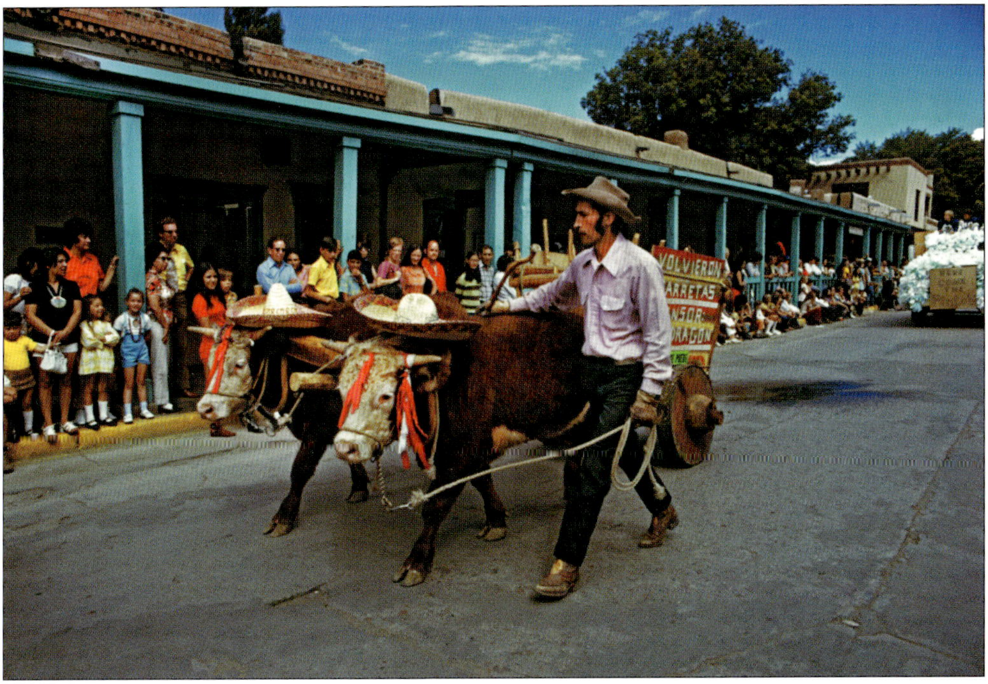

During the 17th and 18th centuries, the early Spanish settlers and merchants who navigated the long and dangerous El Camino Real de Tierra Adentro (The Royal Road of the Interior Land) from Mexico City to Santa Fe sometimes used wooden-wheeled oxcarts called *carretas* to transport their worldly belongings. Carretas were also used around town to haul firewood, lumber, adobes, or cobblestones. The cart above, along with its traditionally dressed driver, was part of the Fiesta de Santa Fe Parade around 1972.

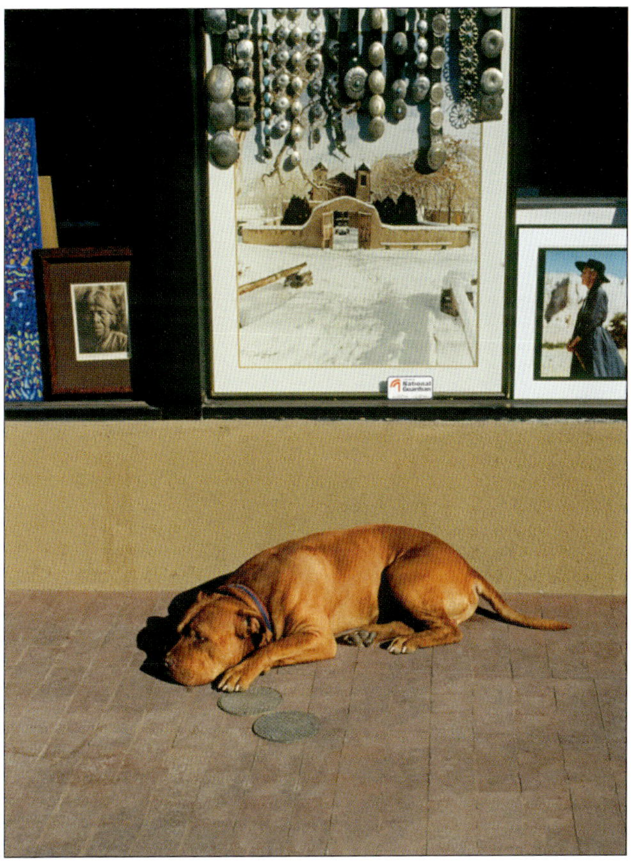

Enjoying a siesta, the large furry fellow at right patiently spent a pleasant winter afternoon on the warm sidewalk in front of a plaza art gallery while his master did some last-minute Christmas shopping.

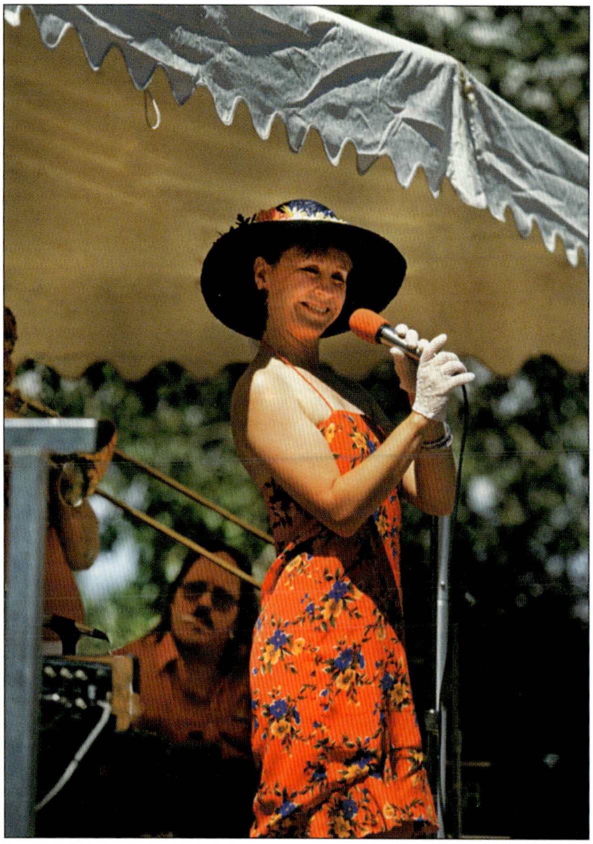

Live music is one of many attractions that has always made the Santa Fe Plaza an enjoyable place to hang out, especially during the warmer months. The jazz ensemble at left entertained a standing room–only crowd with old favorites on a Saturday afternoon, while the professional young Mariachi band below, dressed in charro outfits, played traditional folk music from Central Mexico. Since 2003, the plaza has been home to a free 10-week summer music festival called Santa Fe Bandstand, which provides music lovers with everything from Afrobeat to zydeco. Starting in late June and continuing through late August, the bandstand features both local and nationally known musicians and offers about 100 performances each year.

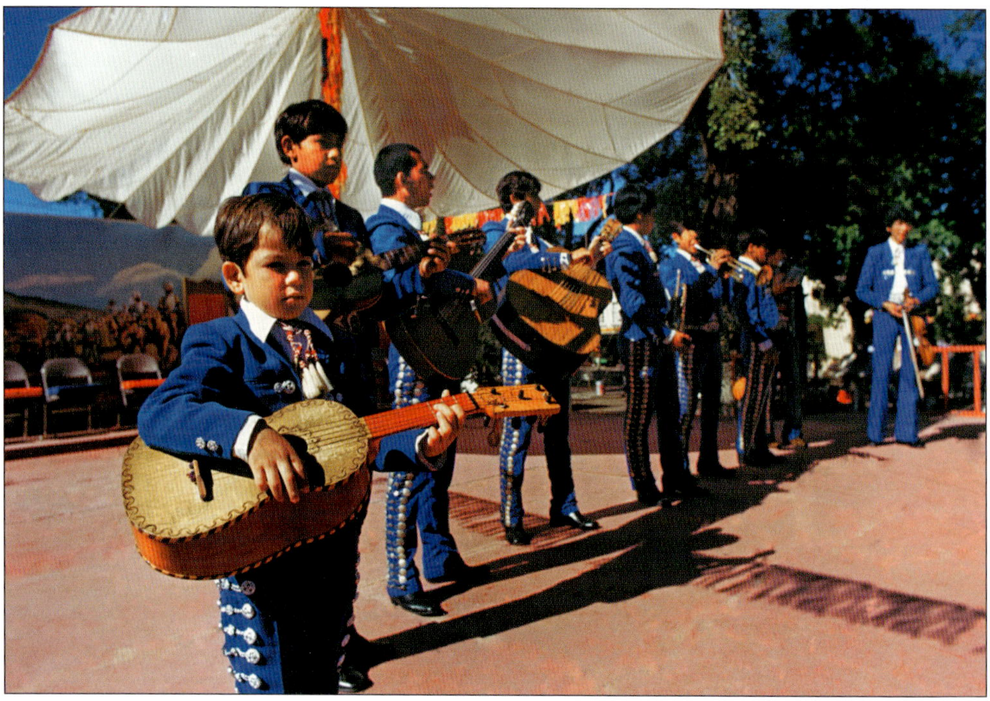

Three

Some Memorable Santa Feans

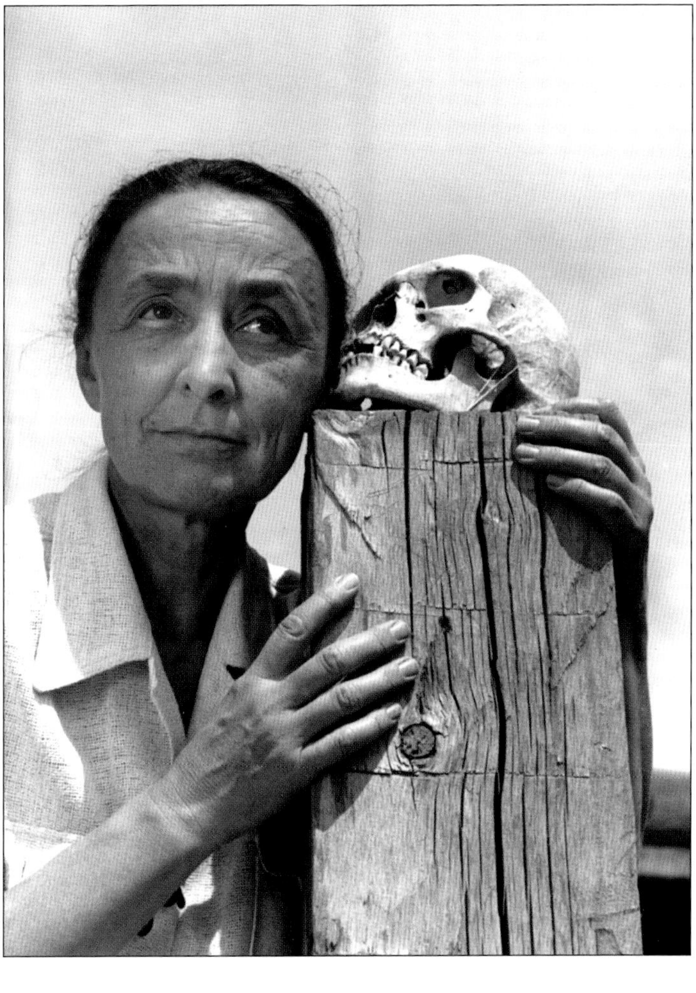

Painter Georgia O'Keeffe (1887–1986) visited Santa Fe in 1929, then permanently moved to nearby Abiquiu from New York in 1949. Among the most significant and influential painters of the 20th century, O'Keeffe spent her final years in Santa Fe, where she died at age 98. The Georgia O'Keeffe Museum, which opened in Santa Fe in 1997, is the only museum in America dedicated solely to an internationally known female artist. (Photograph by John Candelario; courtesy of Palace of the Governors Photo Archives, 165652.)

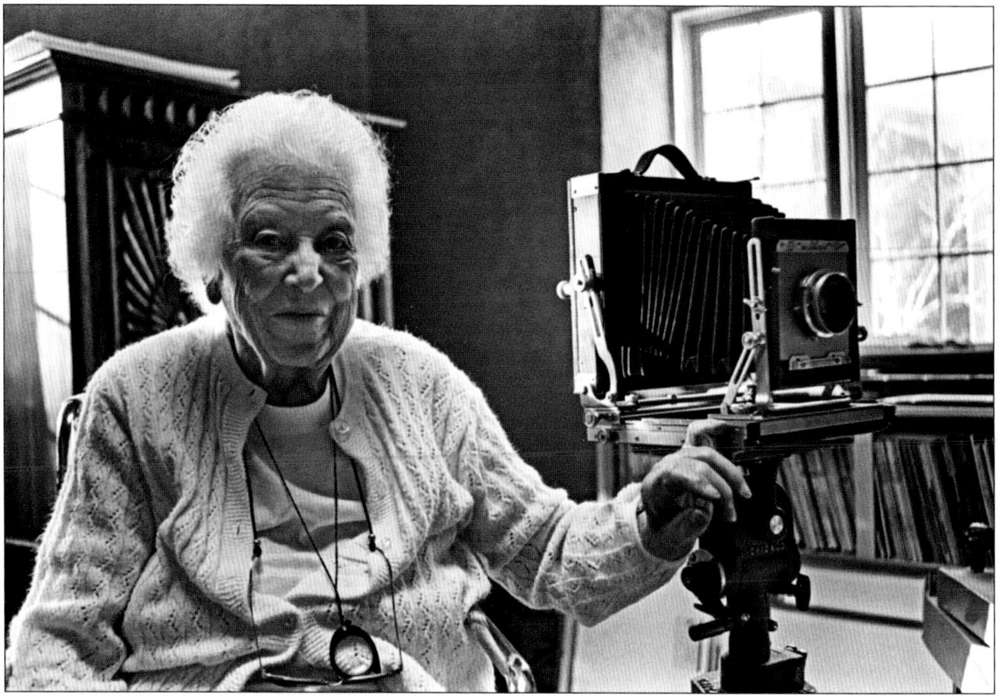

Longtime Santa Fe resident Laura Gilpin (1891–1979) was one of the best-known women photographers in America. Her favorite subjects were the Navajo Indians, who occupy the remote high-desert regions of eastern Arizona and northwestern New Mexico. Using a heavy 4x5 field camera, Gilpin documented the culture and timeless, arid world of the Navajo more vividly and accurately than any other photographer.

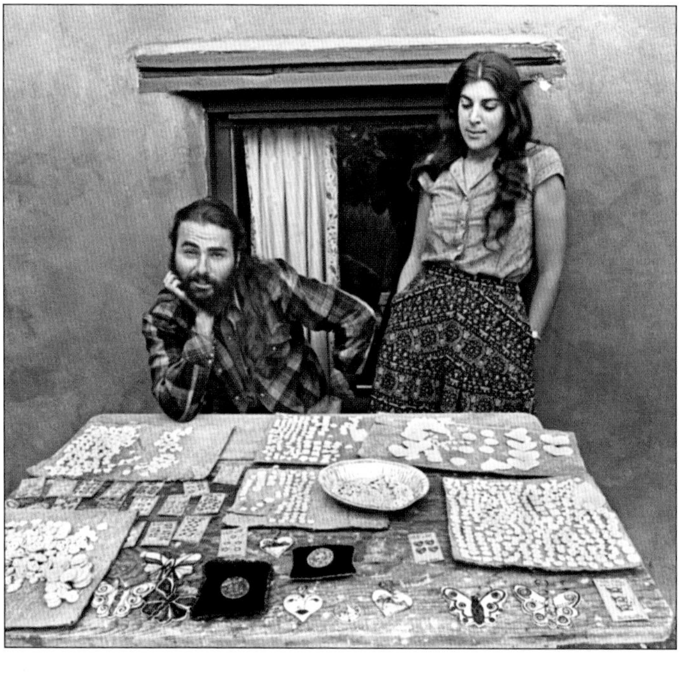

Entrepreneurs Mark Mishory and Arel Heilman traveled through Europe and the Mideast for many years before moving to Santa Fe in the mid-1970s and starting a button studio. Neighbors thought they were just hippies looking for a crash pad, but by 1978, each week, the husband-and-wife team was shipping more than 3,000 individual handmade porcelain buttons, combs, earrings, and brooches to clients in 10 states and several foreign countries.

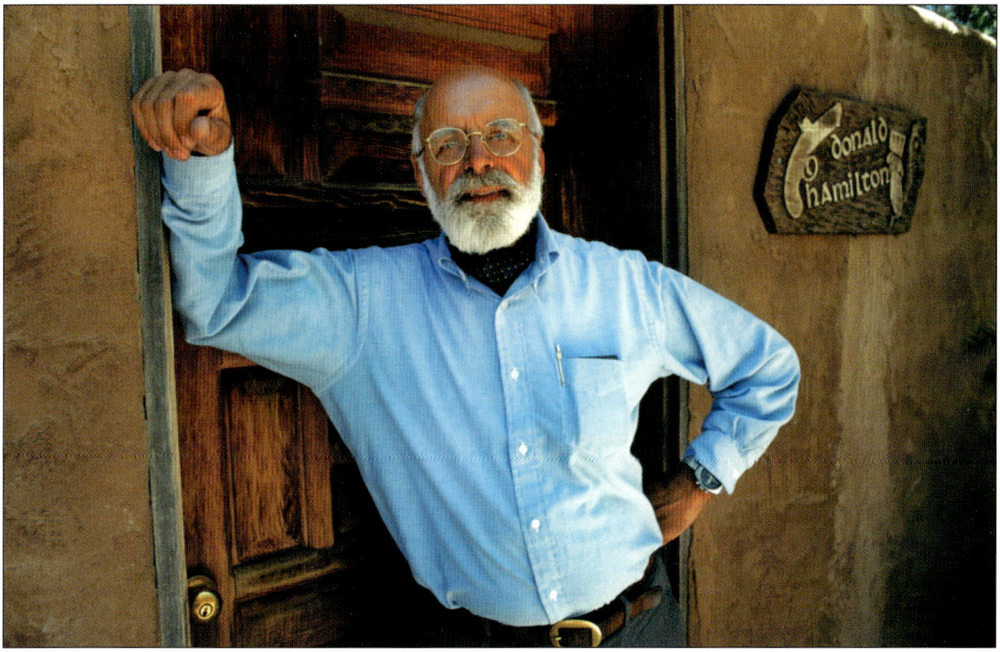

Above, novelist Donald Hamilton (1916–2006) was the author of *The Big Country* (with a movie adaptation starring Gregory Peck and Jean Simmons) and several other classic Western novels, but he was far better known to the reading public for creating Matt Helm, a cold-blooded government assassin who shot, stabbed, and exploded his way through 27 best-selling novels. Hamilton is seen here in 1977, posing in front of his writing casita in east Santa Fe. Below, award-winning novelist John Wadleigh (1927–2013) penned 13 highly acclaimed novels, including the blockbuster *Vandenberg*, but wrote under the pseudonym Oliver Lange. Wadleigh seldom used his real name in public, allegedly because one of his ex-wives was suing him for child support.

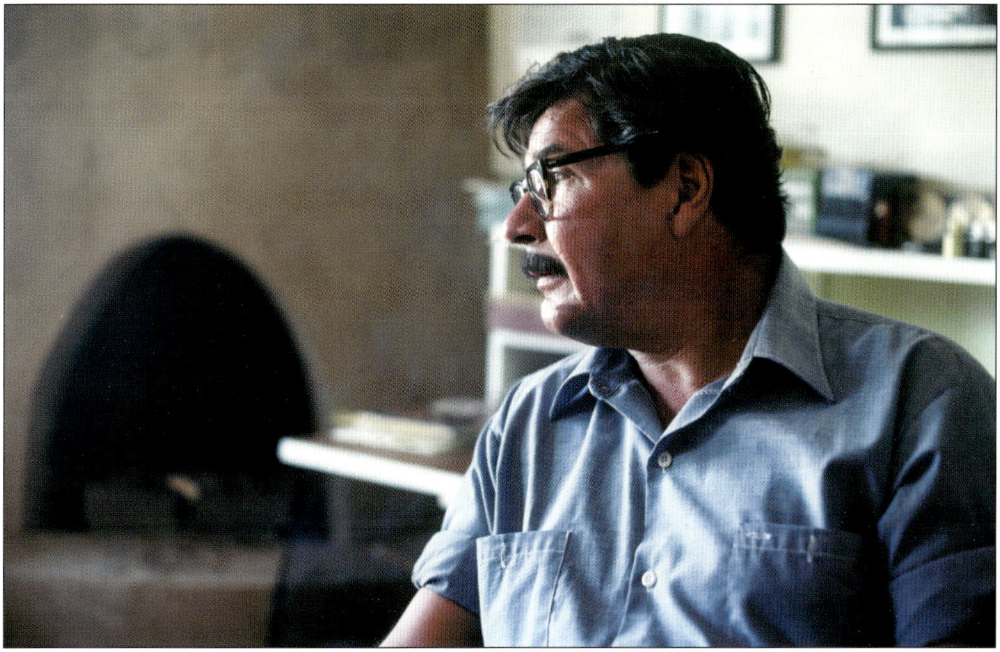

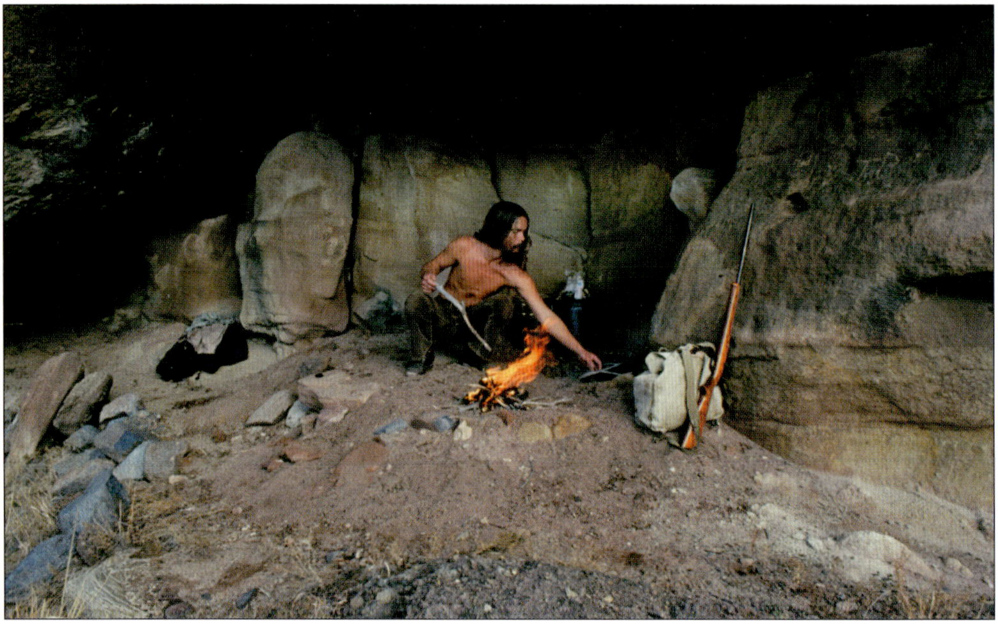

Known simply as "the Gypsy," northern New Mexico locals often encountered Jeffery Salkeld as he wandered barefoot through the high desert. Salkeld was not a hippie, and he was not a bum; he was simply someone who preferred his own company to that of other humans. In warm weather, Jeff rambled around the juniper-dotted canyon country of the Galisteo Basin near the village of Cerrillos for weeks at a time, living off the land and sleeping in whatever natural shelters he could find. When Salkeld was not "roaming," as he called it, he occupied a shallow walled-in cave on the slope of a dry arroyo, in which he had placed a homemade wood-burning stove and a sleeping bag.

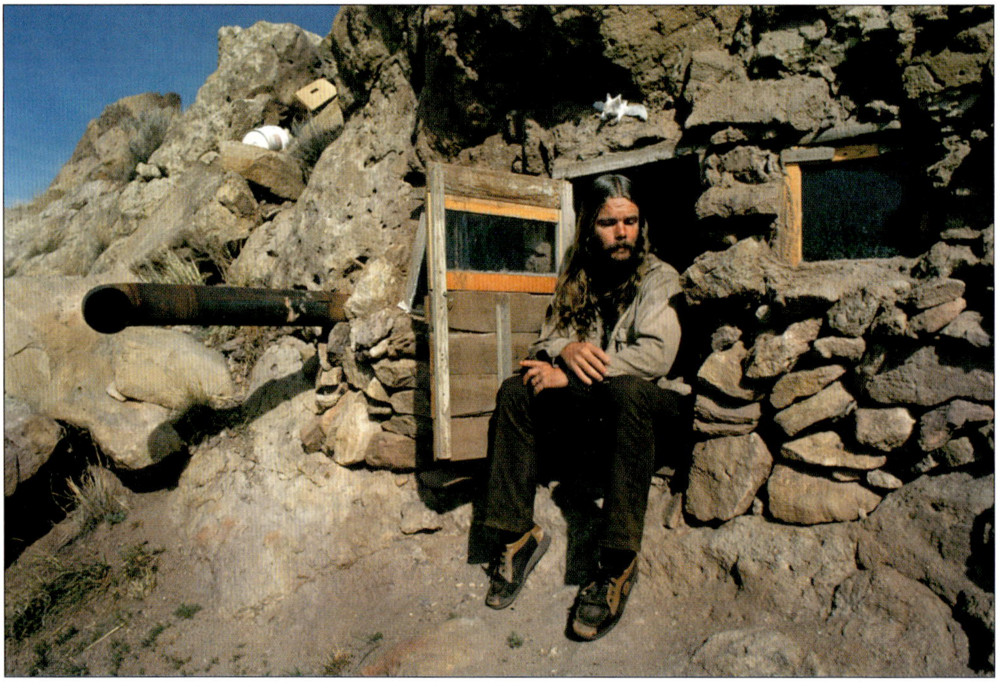

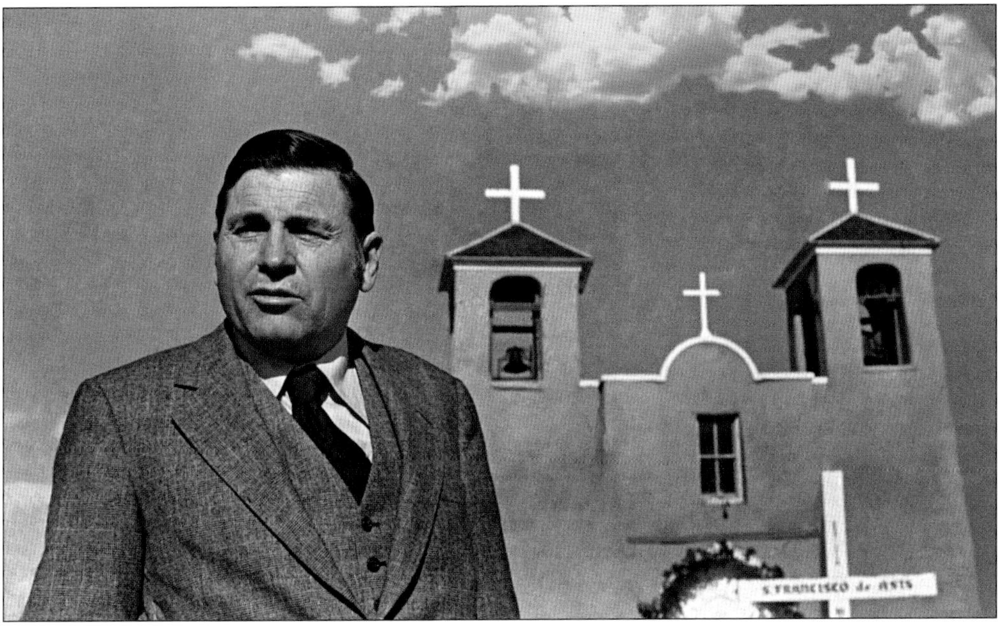

Gov. Bruce King (1924–2009) was perhaps New Mexico's most inimitable governor, elected three times during the 1970s, 1980s, and 1990s. A rancher by trade when he was not taking care of the state's business, King spent much of his time on his cattle ranch, just south of Santa Fe. A local newspaper once described the governor as a "pleasant, outgoing, no nonsense, rural-bred people's representative with a lot of horse sense."

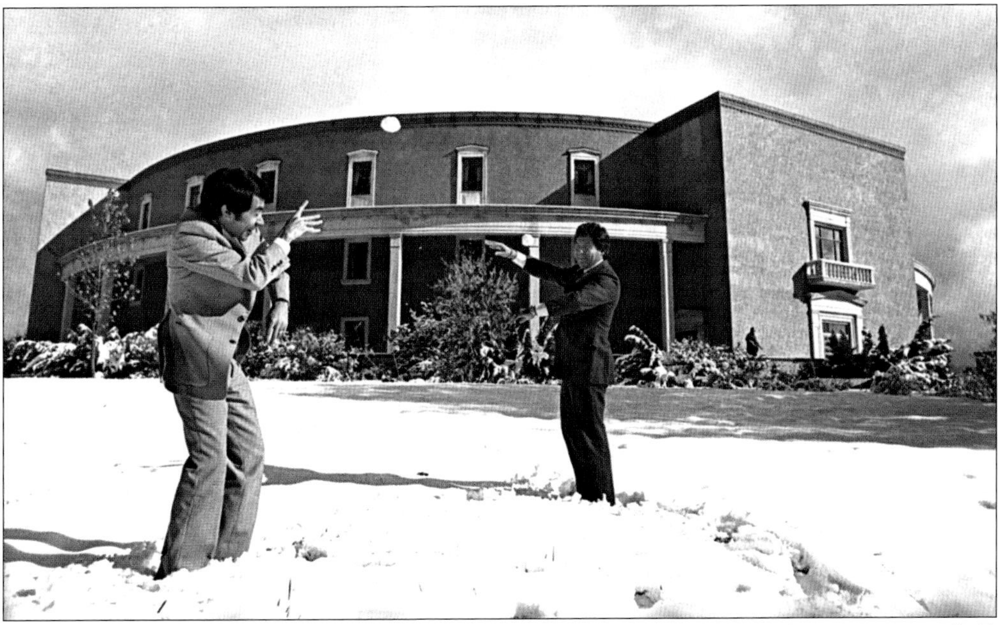

It was a slow December day in state government when state attorney general Toney Anaya (left) and New Mexico governor Jerry Apodaca (right) took time away from their official duties to have a snowball fight outside the state capitol in 1976. The sight of two popular politicians in business suits standing in six inches of new snow and flinging snowballs at each other did not even attract a crowd. Anaya later became the state's 26th governor.

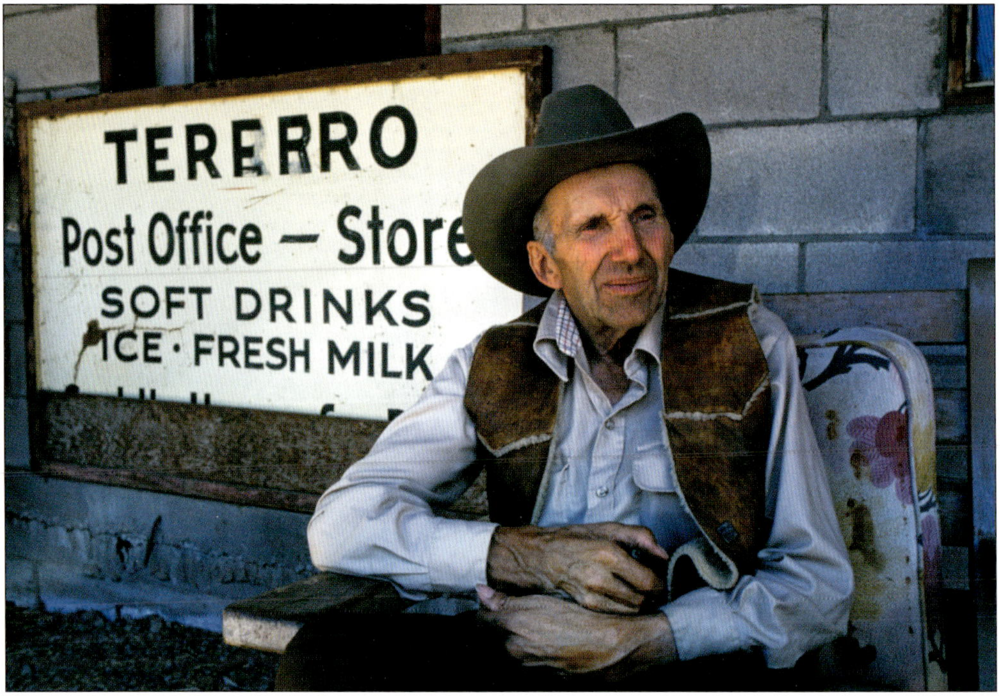

Happy Ley (1909–1999) was a hunting guide, outfitter, and the owner of the rustic Terrero General Store, east of Santa Fe. For more than 70 years, his workspace was the 230,000-acre Pecos Wilderness. Known as the best guide in the Pecos, and a legend among elk and bear hunters, Happy probably knew more about the terrain and big game animals of the Pecos Wilderness region than anyone alive.

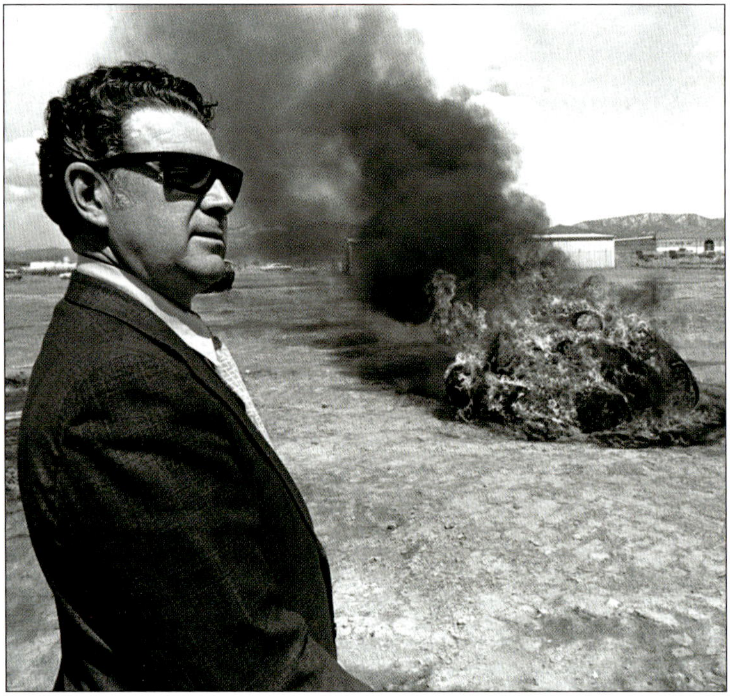

New Mexico State Police deputy chief Tranquilino Chavez, head of the Narcotics Squad in 1974, looks extremely pleased as he oversees the incineration of a massive pile of confiscated marijuana. Pot was everywhere in the Southwest in the 1970s, but it was especially abundant in Santa Fe and northern New Mexico because of the area's large and growing population of commune hippies.

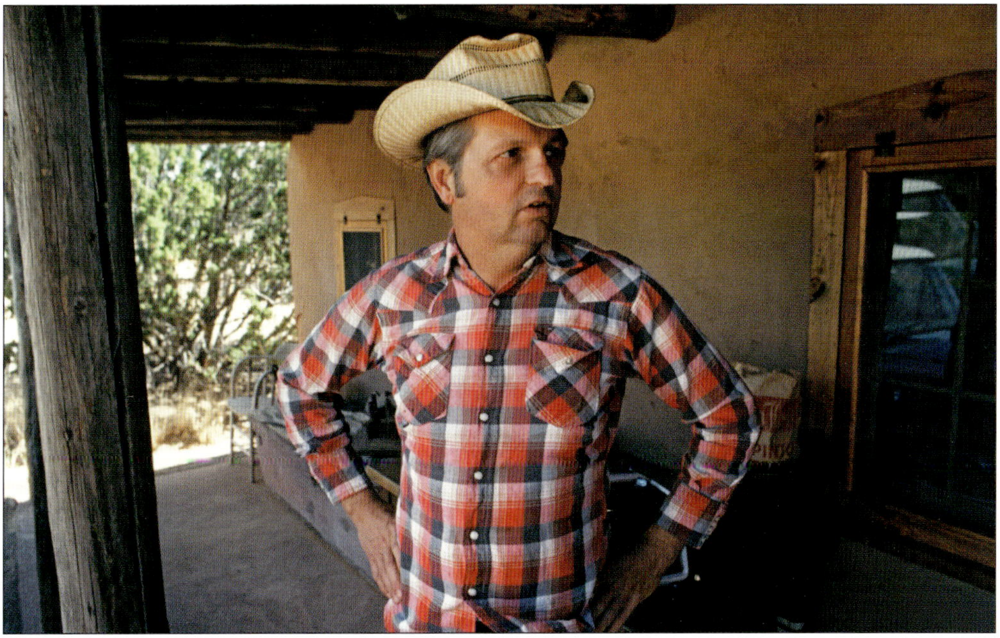

Southwest historian, writer, and teacher Dr. Marc Simmons has lived in a tiny hand-built adobe compound, located a few miles south of Santa Fe in the Galisteo Basin, for more than 50 years. When these photographs were taken in 1978, his rural residence had no running water, electricity, or telephone, and his nearest neighbor was three miles away. A fireplace and woodstove provided heat, and he hauled his drinking water in by the tankful from a distant well and bathed in a galvanized "cowboy tub." The author of more than 40 nonfiction books and innumerable academic articles, Dr. Simmons often worked by lamplight and typed his manuscripts on a manual typewriter.

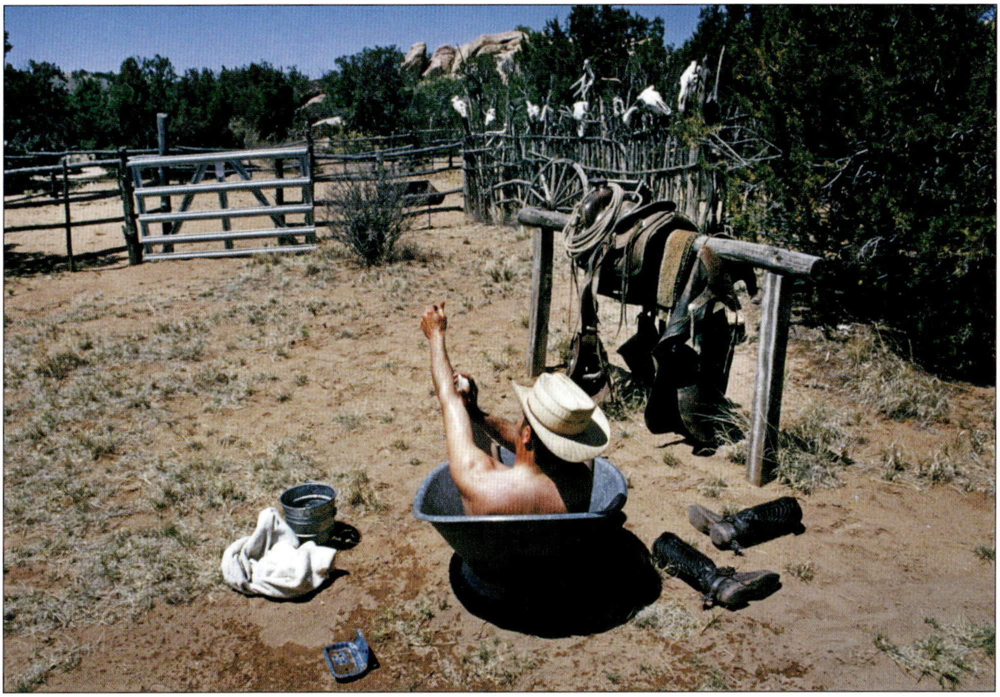

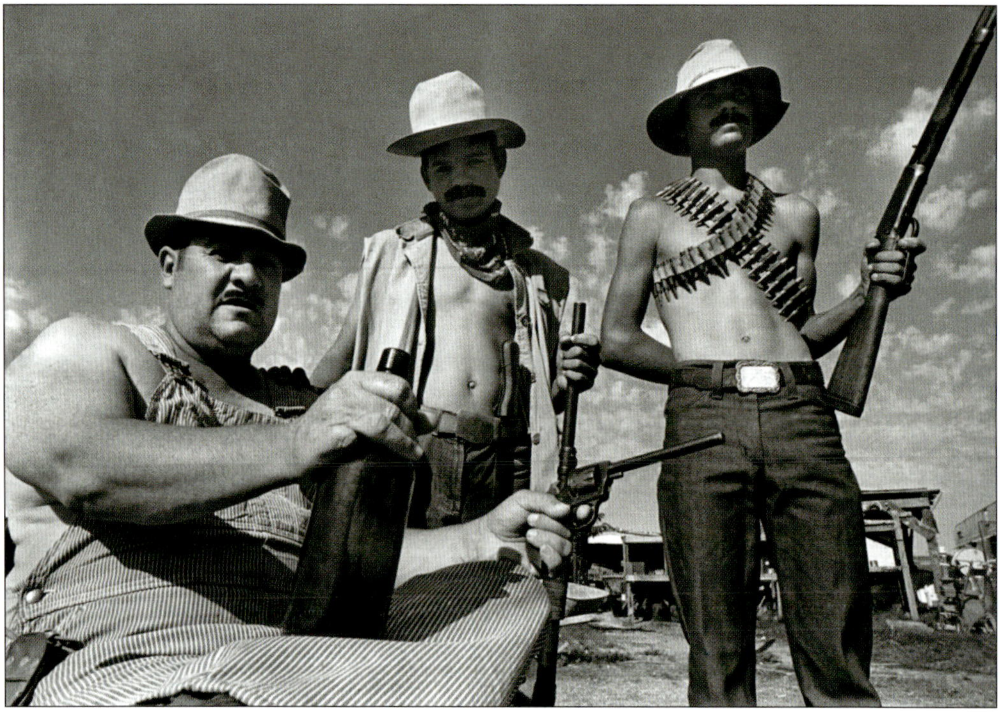

In the late 1960s, many homesites in the rolling juniper-covered hills on Santa Fe's southwestern outskirts were occupied by nonconformist rural families like this who enjoyed the privacy that rough dirt roads and a lack of telephones and other utilities could provide. By the mid-1980s, most of those homesites had been purchased by real estate developers and replaced with sprawling housing developments.

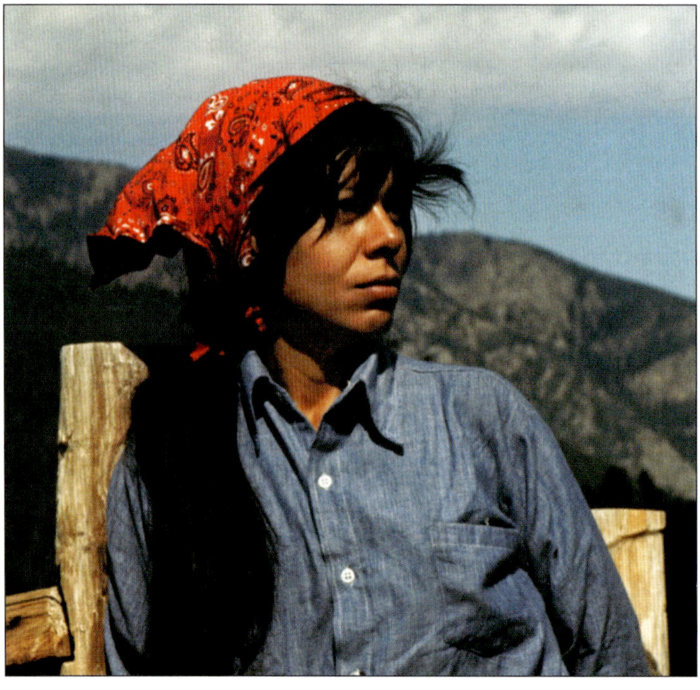

Half Santa Clara Indian and half Anglo, Helen Hardin (1943–1984) was among the most talented and prominent figures in the American Indian art world during the 20th century. Her meticulously crafted paintings were often intricate abstract interpretations of traditional Pueblo and Navajo cultural practices and ceremonies. In the early 1970s, when this photograph was taken, Hardin's shows and gallery exhibits often sold out within a few hours.

Part-time rancher, wrangler, cook, fashion model, and hermit, Susie Henderson (1927–2002) was a woman for all seasons. She lived alone for nearly 40 years on an isolated ranch in the high desert of the Galisteo Basin, south of Santa Fe. Her home and property, which she called her "sacred land," had no telephone, running water, or electricity. She is posing here in 1977 for a magazine story on western ranch women.

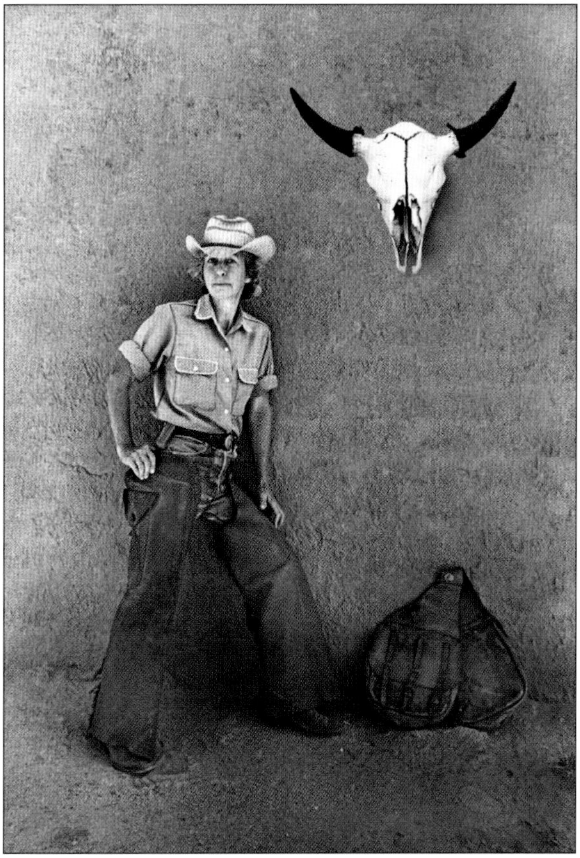

A colleague of Isaac Asimov and Robert Heinlein, acclaimed science fiction writer Roger Zelazny (1937–1995) was a three-time winner of the Nebula Award and six-time winner of the Hugo Award—science fiction's two highest literary honors. Seen here in his Santa Fe writing studio around 1980, Zelazny wrote more than 30 novels and hundreds of short stories during his career. Some of his best-known works were *The Changeling* and *Lord of Light*.

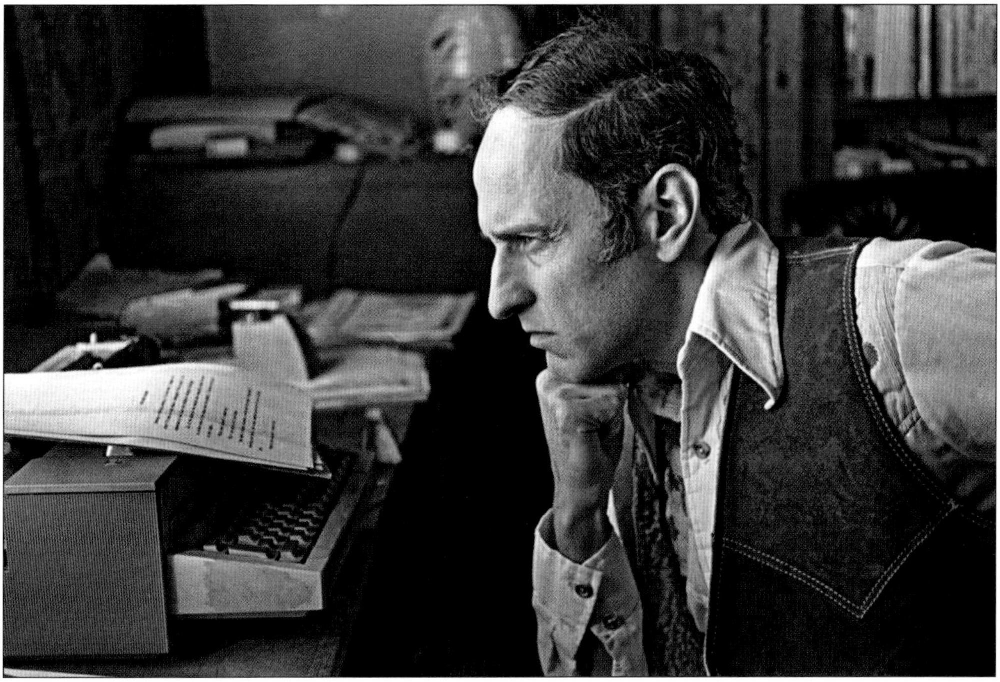

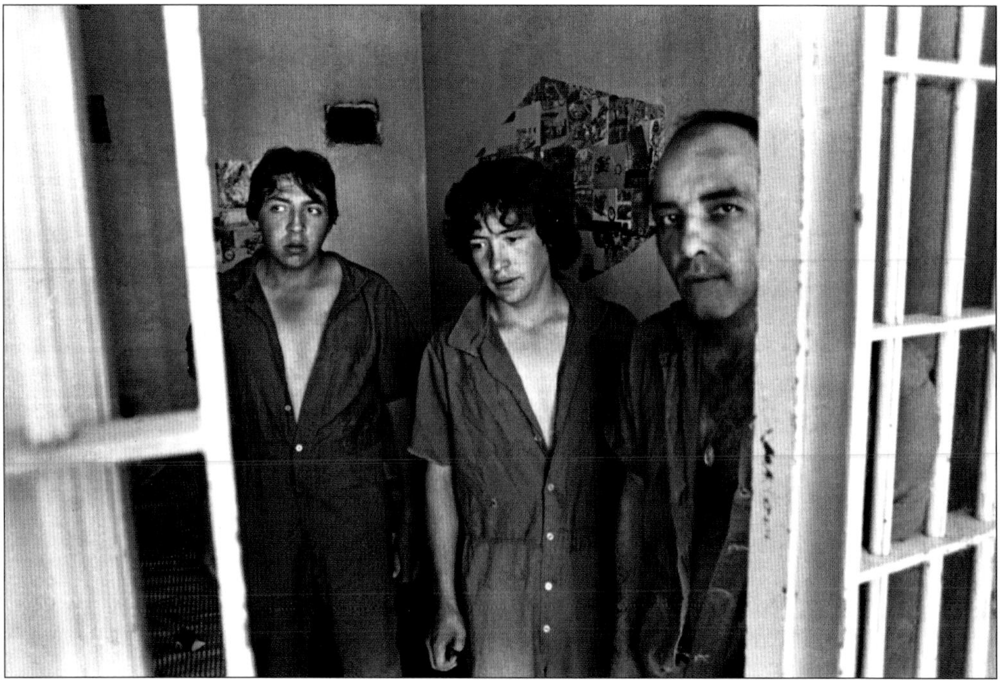

In the fall of 1979, inmates incarcerated in the maximum-security unit at the New Mexico State Penitentiary near Santa Fe complained to the press and others about the badly overcrowded conditions at the prison, and with very good reason. Many of the tiny six-foot-by-nine-foot cubicles in the cell blocks held at least three—and sometimes as many as four—prisoners. Some convicts had to sleep on the floor on thin mattresses, which were rolled up and piled in a corner during the day. Worse, the seatless toilets in the cells offered no privacy to the users, and the stench of feces, urine, and disinfectant was often overpowering.

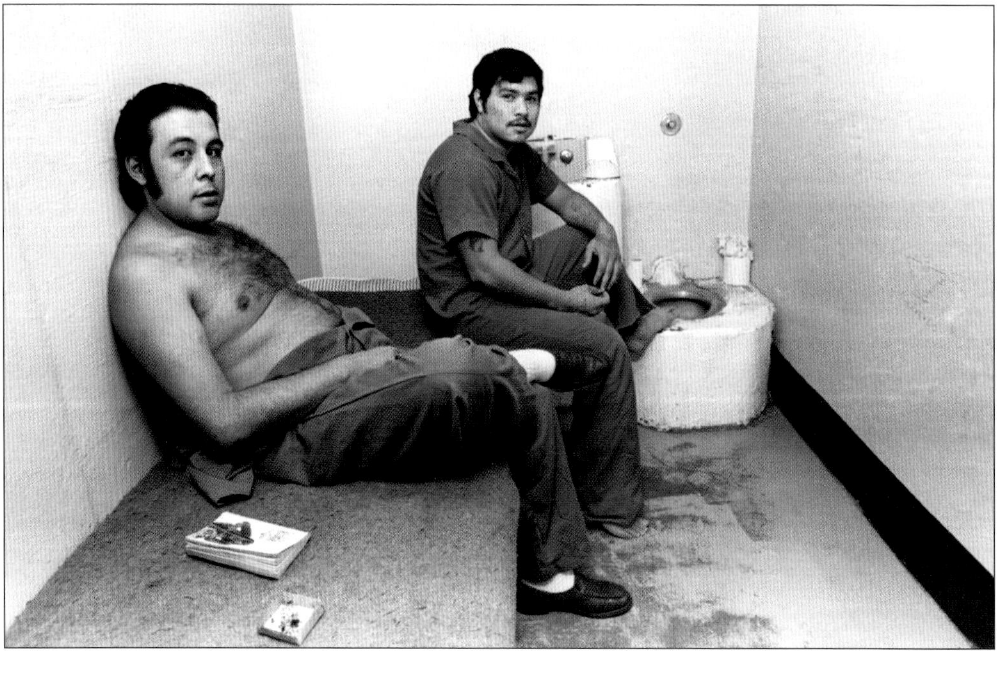

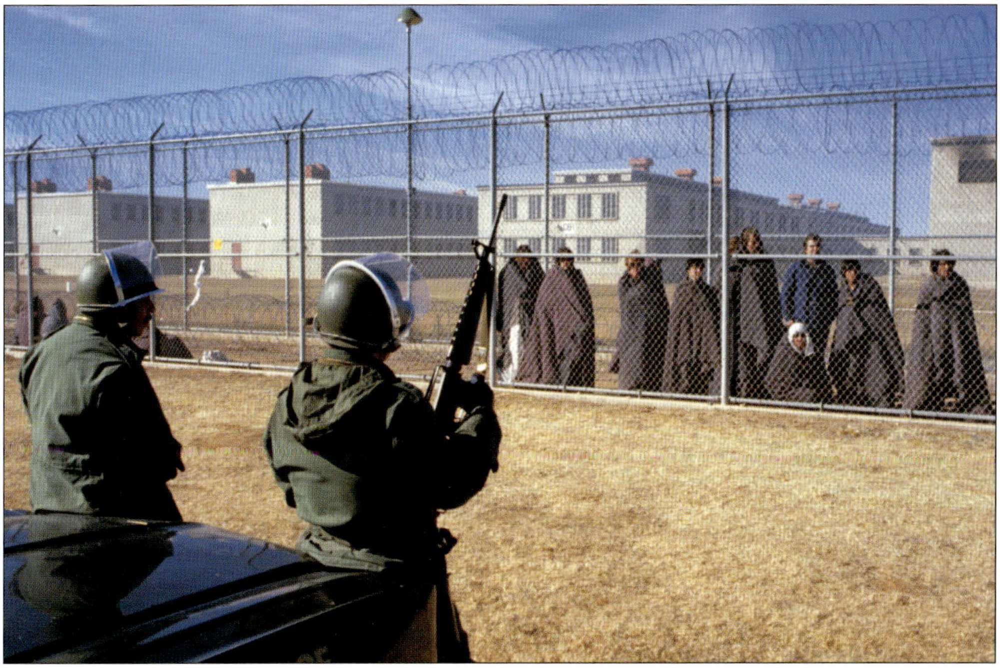

In January 1980, a few months after the complaints had been made, inmates at the penitentiary took matters into their own hands. During a 48-hour riot, 33 convicts housed in the protective custody unit of Cell Block 4 were brutally murdered by their fellow prisoners, and at least 200 others, including several guards, were injured. The barbaric scene inside Cell Block 4 was so gruesome that most national magazines did not run photographs of the carnage. Some inmates escaped the bloodbath inside by hiding in the outer prison yard, as seen here shortly after the riot ended. Wearing wool blankets to ward off an icy February chill, they are guarded by stern-faced National Guardsmen clad in riot gear and carrying loaded M16 rifles.

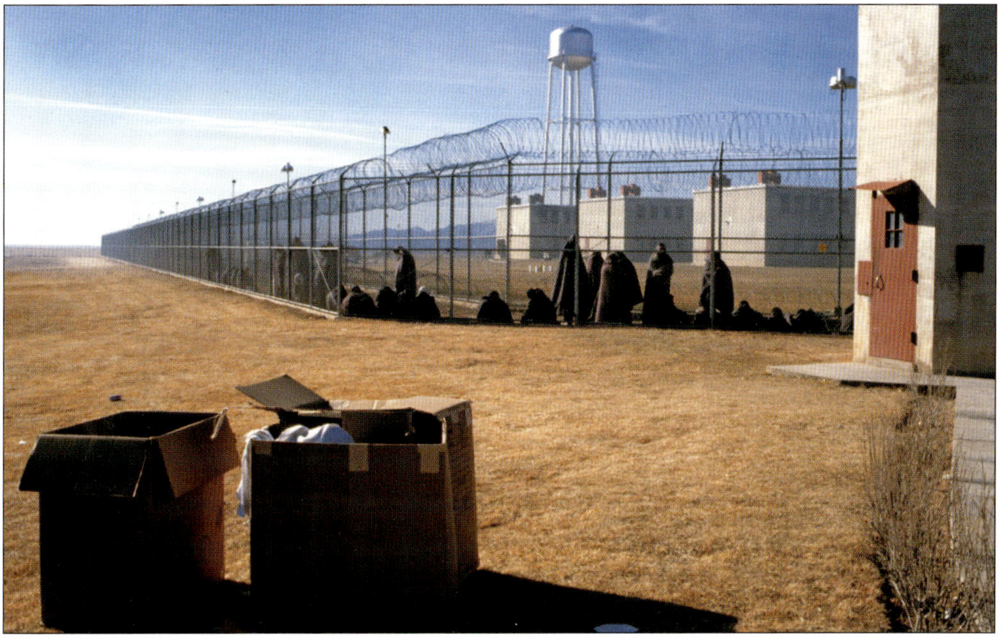

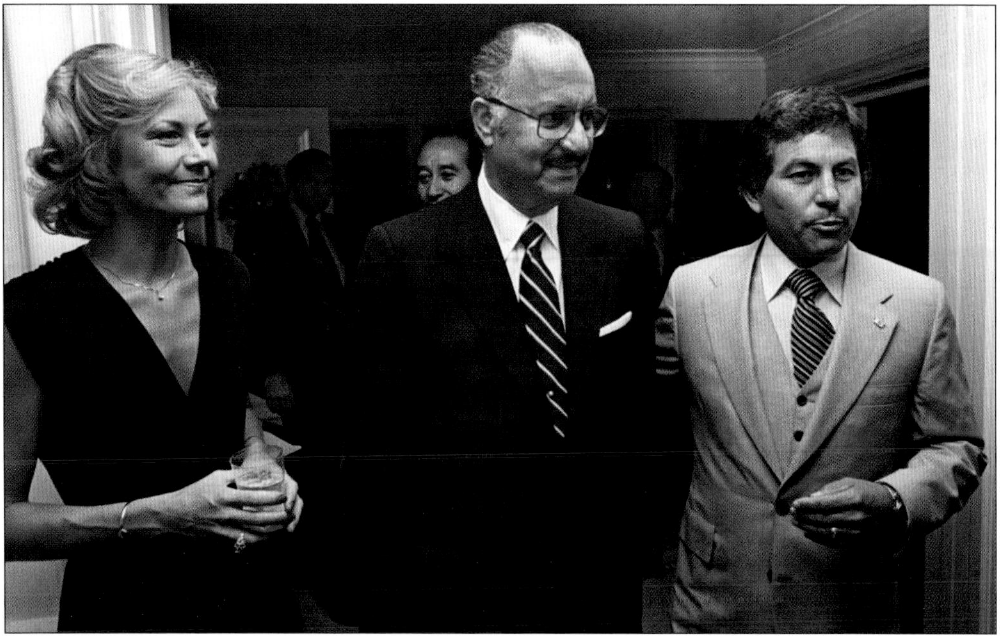

Responsible for the deaths of 50,000 Nicaraguans during his two presidential terms, Nicaraguan president Anastacio Somoza (center) was among the most infamous dictators in the western hemisphere, according to human rights organizations. Yet, in 1978, an extravagant welcome reception was held for him at the Governor's Mansion in Santa Fe, hosted by then New Mexico governor Jerry Apodaca (right) and his wife, Clara (left). Somoza was assassinated in Paraguay two years after this photograph was taken.

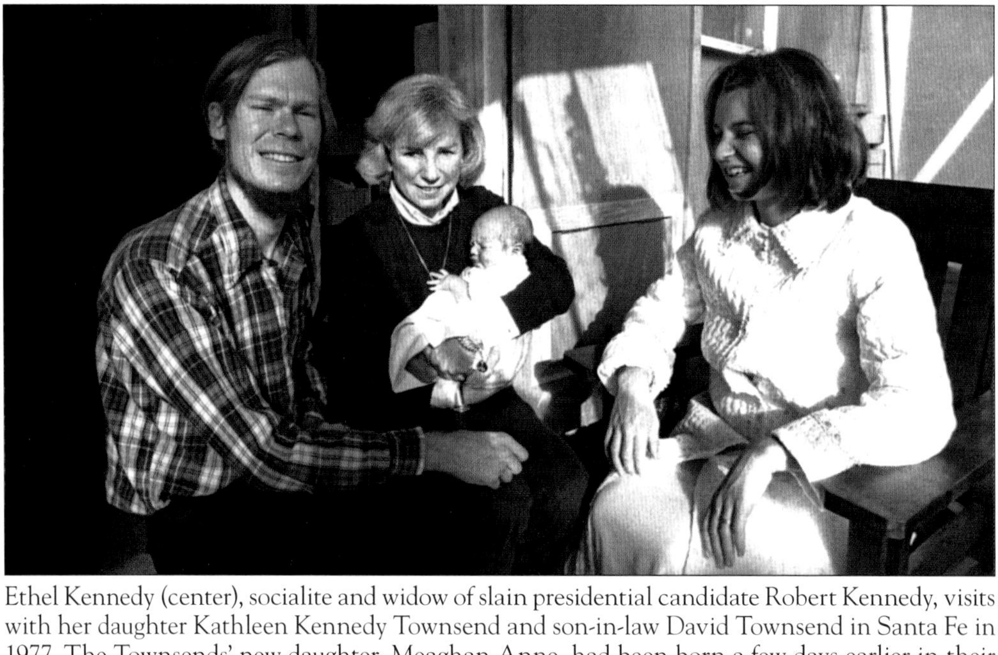

Ethel Kennedy (center), socialite and widow of slain presidential candidate Robert Kennedy, visits with her daughter Kathleen Kennedy Townsend and son-in-law David Townsend in Santa Fe in 1977. The Townsends' new daughter, Meaghan Anne, had been born a few days earlier in their home on Santa Fe's northeast side. At the time, Kathleen was a law student at the University of New Mexico.

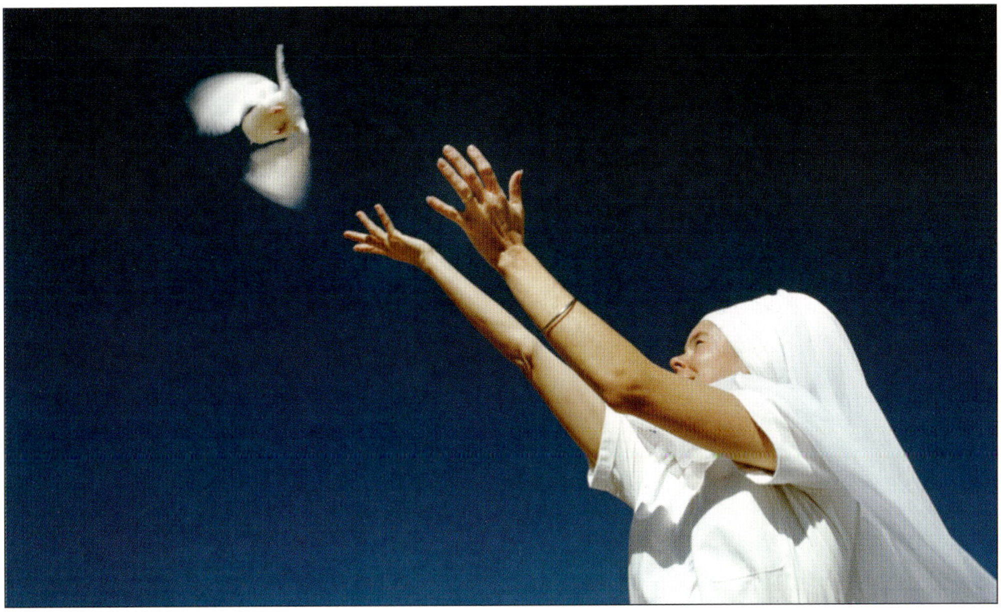

The 40-acre Sikh Dharma Ashram, north of Santa Fe, was a controversial community from the time of its establishment in 1971. The 250 American Sikhs who lived there seemed totally out of place in this mostly Hispanic region of the state. A few suspicious locals even claimed that the Sikhs were ex-felons, recovering drug addicts, or worse. Within a few years, however, Ashram members had proved themselves worthy and respected additions to the northern New Mexico community. Many were involved in successful agriculture projects on the Ashram itself, while others had joined the local business community as landscapers, security consultants, real estate agents, and restaurant owners.

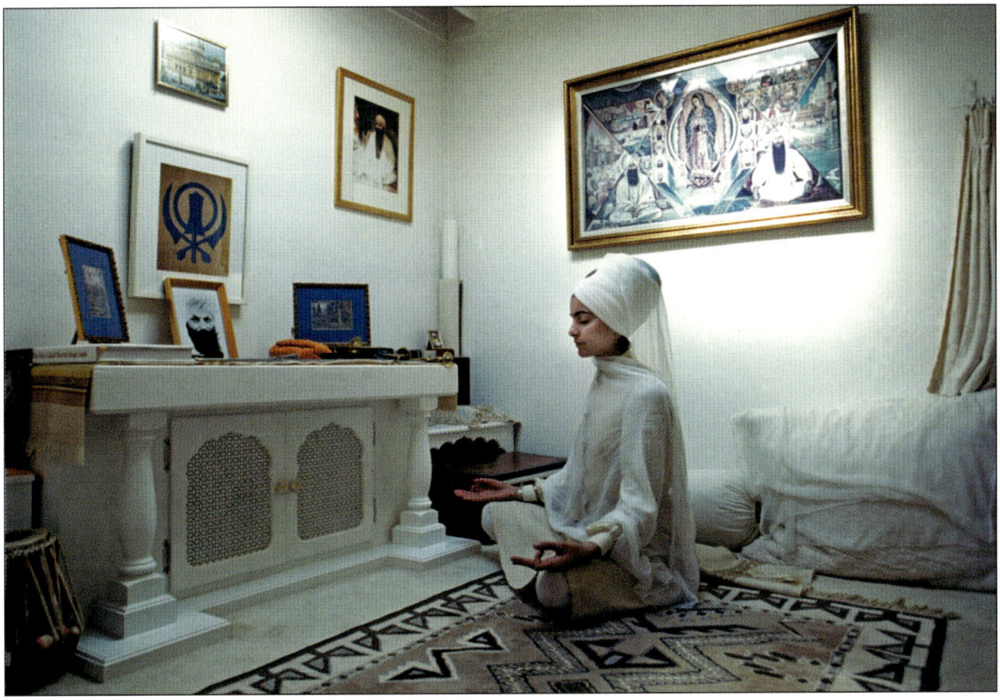

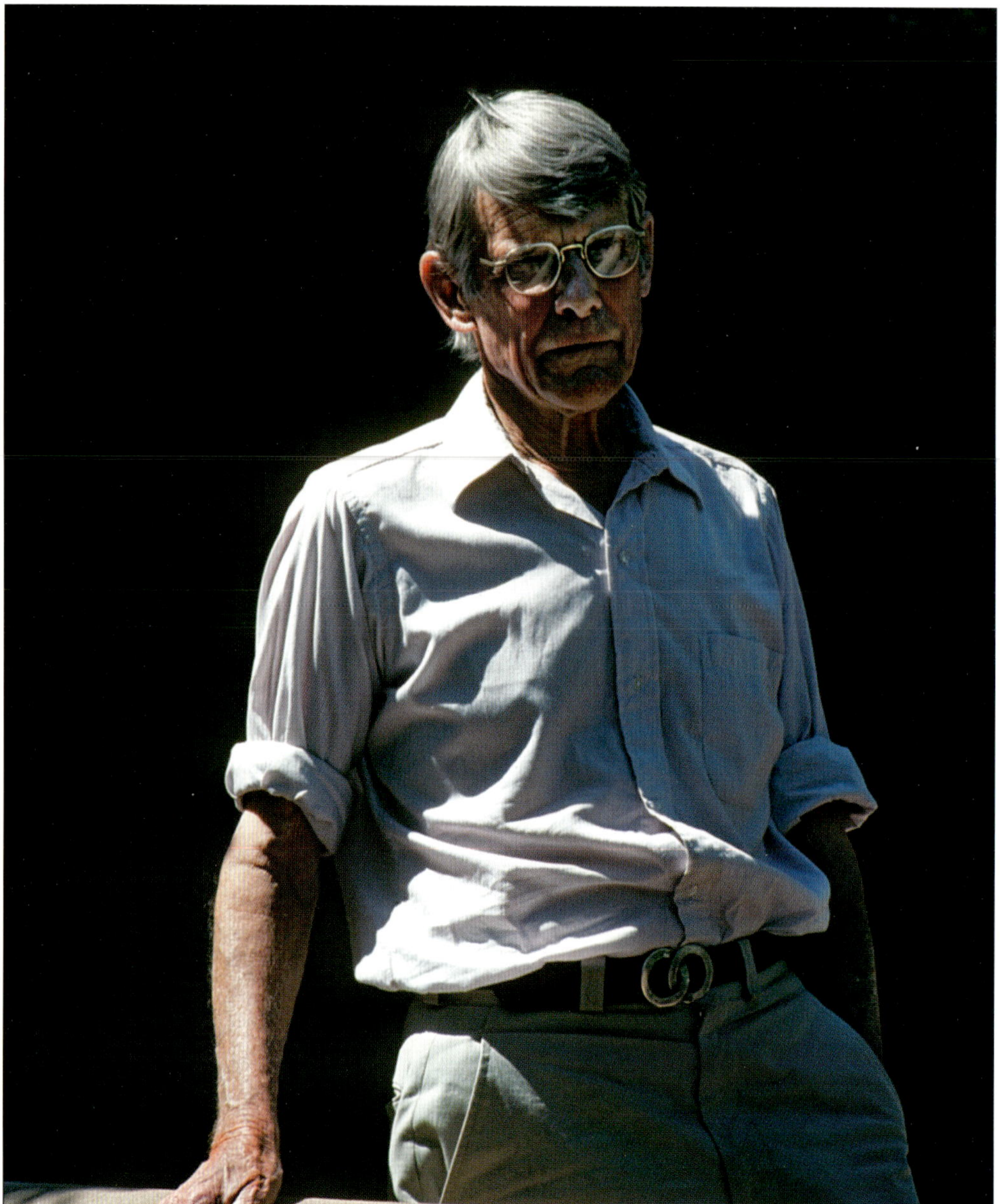

Renowned nature photographer and author Eliot Porter (1901–1990) was best known for his color landscapes and phenomenal bird photographs. Porter moved to Santa Fe from Winnetka, Illinois, in 1946. He was the author of *In Wilderness Is the Preservation of the World, The Place No One Knew: Glen Canyon on the Colorado River, Baja California and the Geography of Hope*, and several other, similar coffee table publications—many of them published by the Sierra Club. Porter was an avid proponent of color photography and worked in the medium as early as 1939, while most other American photographers were still shooting black-and-white film. A large number of his prints hang in the permanent collections of New York's Metropolitan Museum of Art and the Amon Carter Museum in Texas. This portrait was taken at his home and studio in Tesuque, near Santa Fe, around 1975.

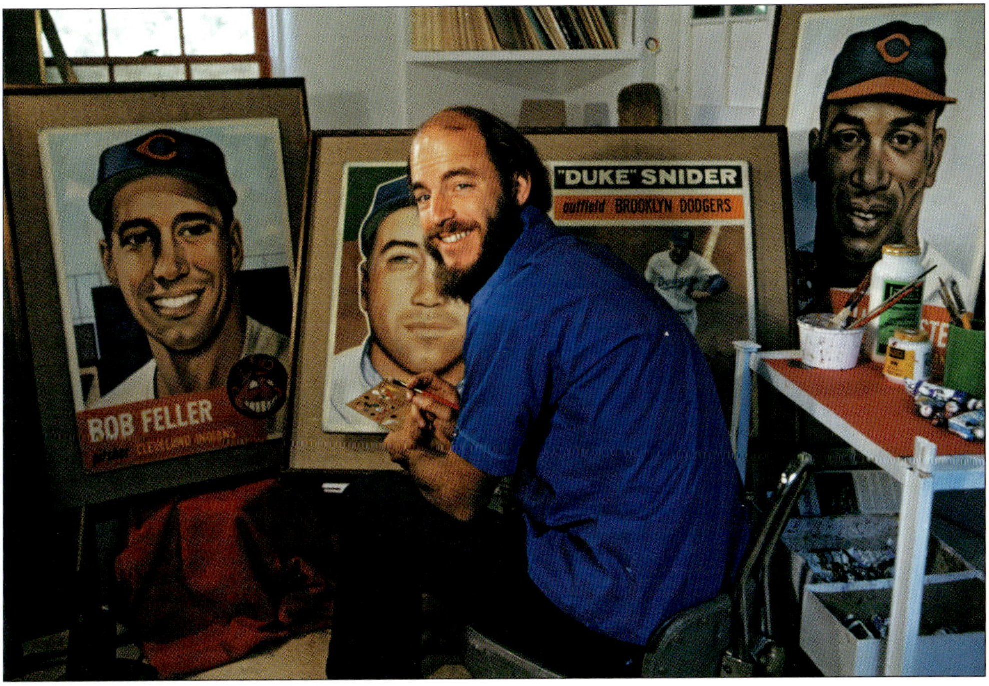

Baseball card artist Bill Forsythe was a true night owl—painting all night, sleeping all day, and seldom rising before 4:00 in the afternoon. His unique niche was the creation of exact replicas of rare baseball cards on canvas, which often sold for more than $1,000 each to collectors of baseball memorabilia. This photograph was taken in Forsythe's Pecos, New Mexico, studio in 1977.

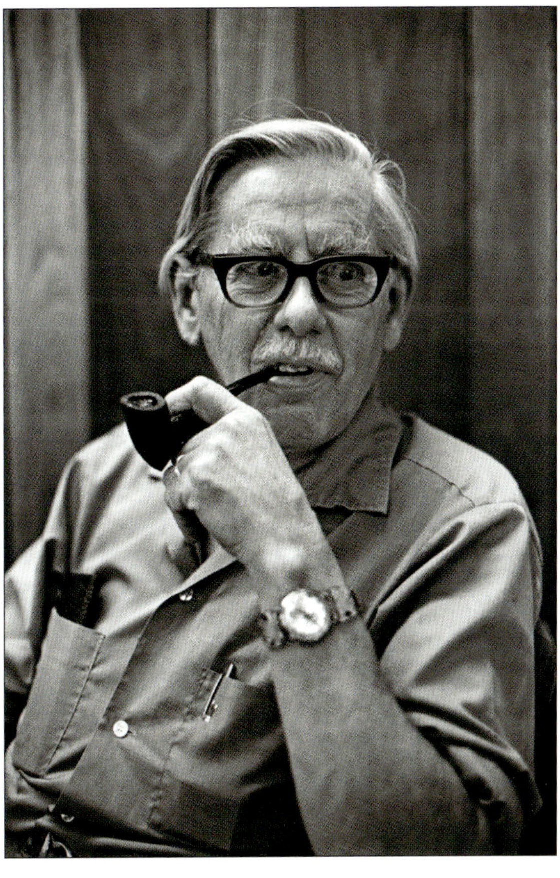

Writer Jack Schaefer (1907–1991) had never been west of the Mississippi when his celebrated Western novel *Shane* was published in 1949. Schaefer finally moved to Santa Fe in 1955, figuring that if he was going to write Westerns, he should at least live in the "Wild West." By the mid-1970s, his later books, such as *Monte Walsh* and *The Plainsmen*, had become standard reading fare for high school and college literature courses.

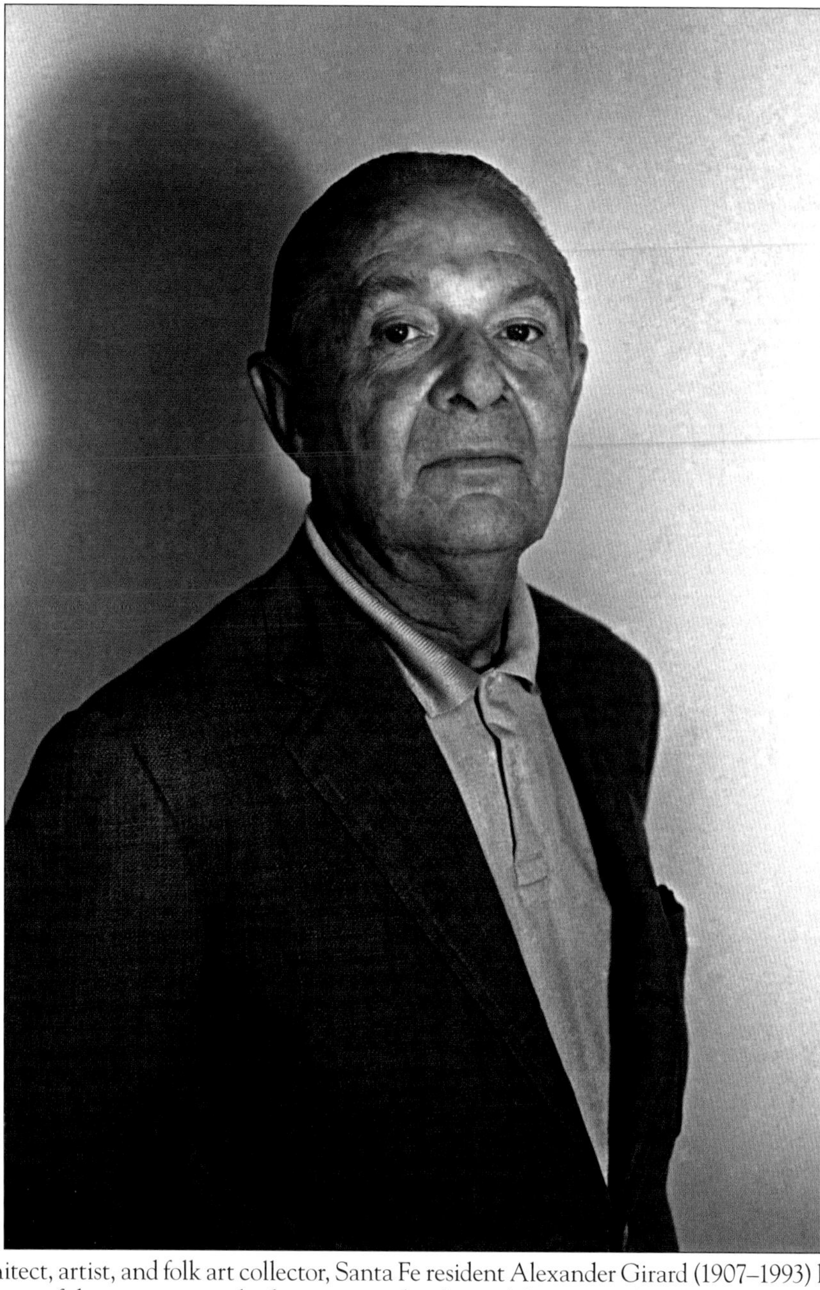

An architect, artist, and folk art collector, Santa Fe resident Alexander Girard (1907–1993) has been dubbed one of the greatest textile, furniture, and industrial designers of modern times. Among his many achievements were the establishment and expansion of the highly respected Herman Miller Textile Division in 1952 and the complete redesign of Braniff International Airways, from the size and shape of menus, napkins, and sugar packets to the color schemes of the aircraft themselves. Santa Fe residents since the early 1950s, Girard and his wife, Susan, were major collectors of folk art, and in 1962, they established the Girard Foundation to manage their huge 100,000-piece collection. They contributed the entire assemblage—the largest private collection of folk art in the world—to Santa Fe's Museum of International Folk Art 16 years later. It was necessary for the museum to construct an entirely new wing to house the collection.

Four

Native Faces, Special Places

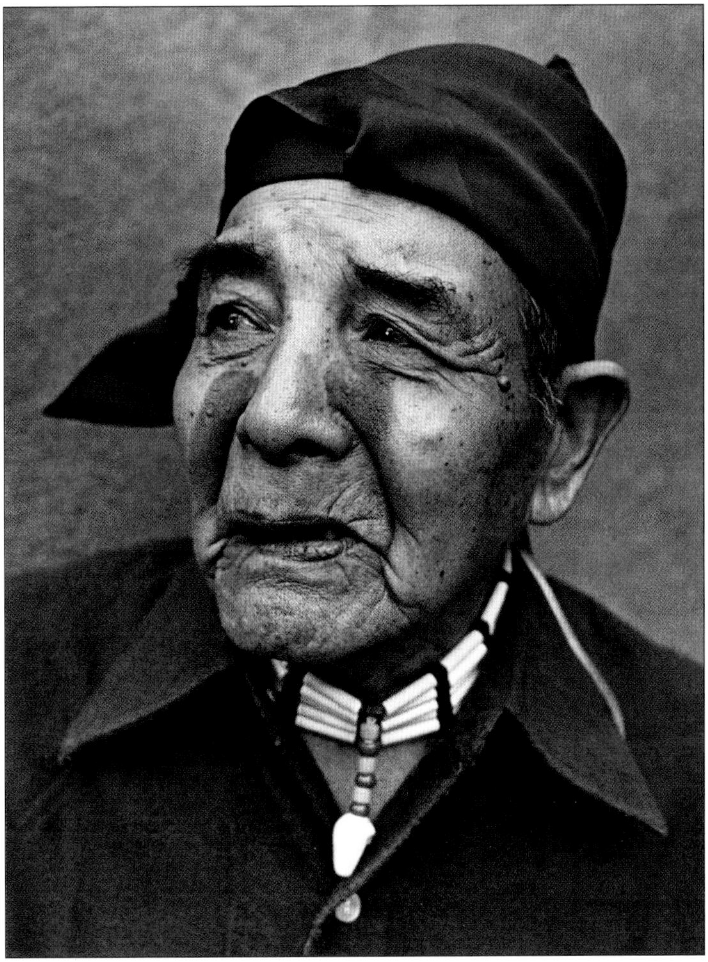

The consequences of decades spent in the dry northern New Mexico climate is clearly etched on the face of this tribal elder from Ohkay Owingeh Pueblo (formerly San Juan Pueblo), pictured in 1974. In 1598, just 10 years before Santa Fe was established 25 miles to the south, Spanish conquistador Don Juan de Oñate declared Ohkay Owingeh as New Mexico's first capital city.

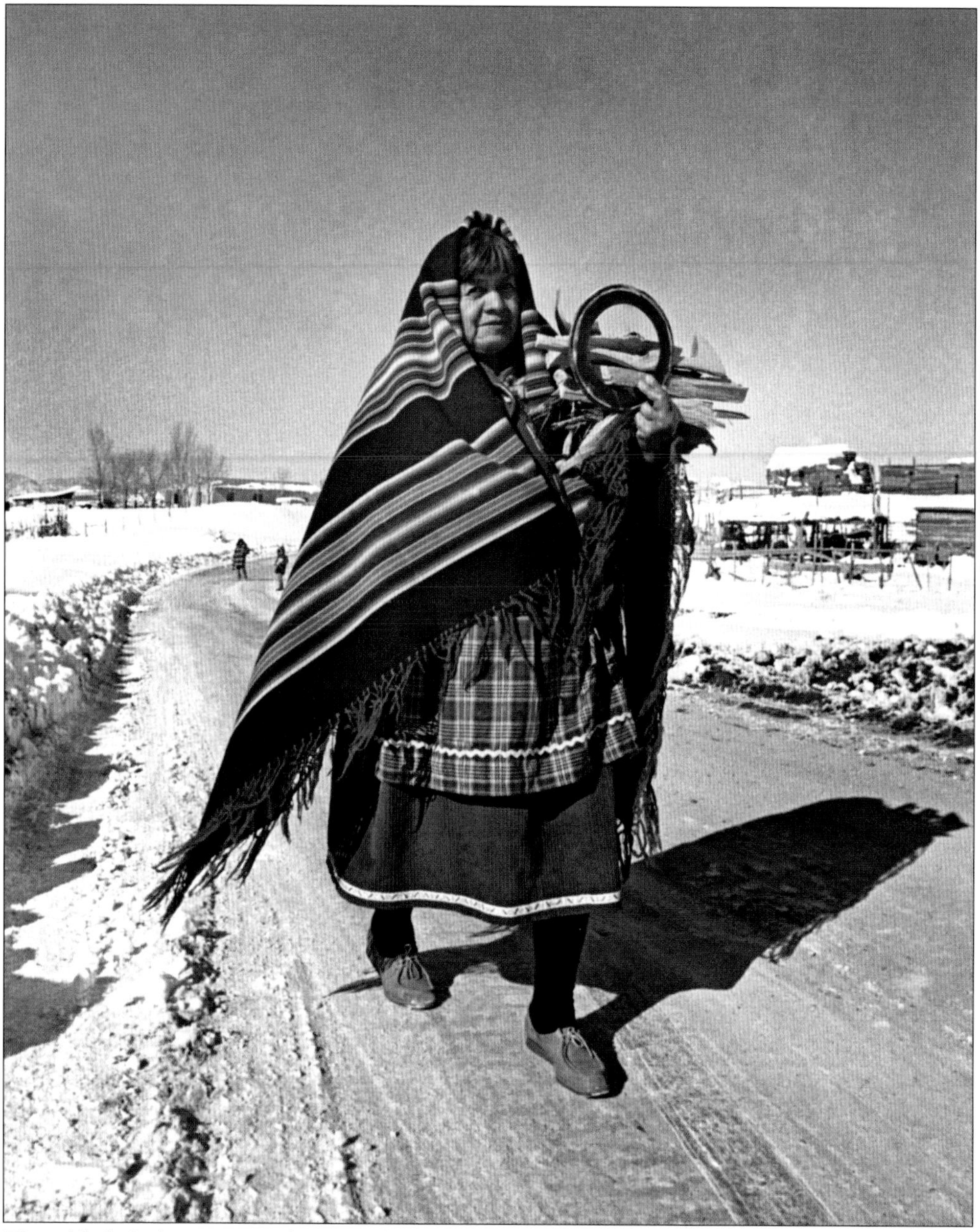

This elderly Indian woman from Cochiti Pueblo brandishes a makeshift prayer ring to ward off *brujas* (witches) and other evil spirits while she gathers firewood on a snowy January day. Belief in witchcraft and magic was still prevalent in many of New Mexico's Indian communities when this photograph was taken in 1970, and most ill fortune, even sickness and death, could be blamed on bruja activity. Evidence uncovered by archaeologists in 1,000-year-old petroglyphs and on prehistoric ceremonial objects suggests that witchcraft and magic were tangible and threatening realities, even in the earliest Anasazi societies along the Rio Grande. The Cochiti people, along with most other Puebloans in northern New Mexico, are direct descendants of Anasazi migrants who settled along the river in the late 1300s, searching for fertile farmland and a permanent source of water.

A bit shy, but flashing a mischievous smile, the adorable five-year-old Indian girl at right was attending the 1989 Indian Market with her mother. Both were residents of Kewa Pueblo (formerly Santo Domingo Pueblo), a conservative Indian community about 30 miles south of Santa Fe. Below, artist Pablita Velarde (1918–2006) was a full-blooded Santa Clara Indian known worldwide for her detailed paintings of daily pueblo life. Her most recognized works were what she called her "earth paintings," which were created with mineral pigments that she gathered, then ground into powder by hand using a traditional *mano* and *metate* (stone-grinding implements). Her children's book *Old Father Story Teller* was the first book ever published by a Pueblo Indian woman. Velarde was the mother of Helen Hardin (see page 50), also a well-known Indian painter.

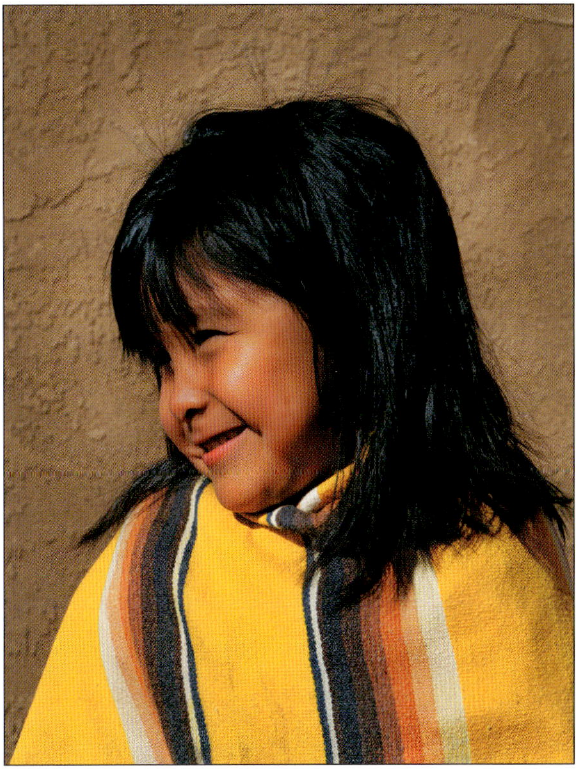

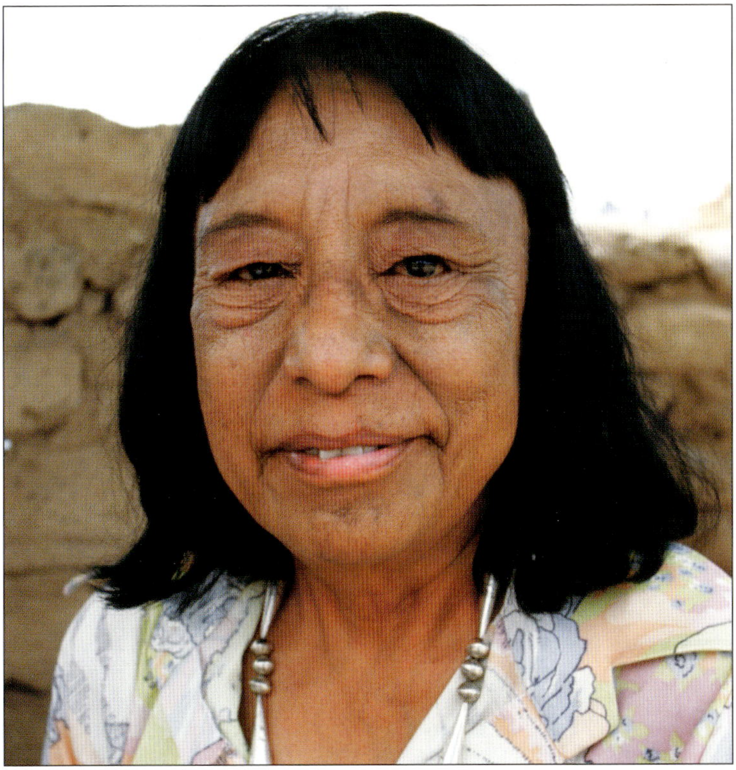

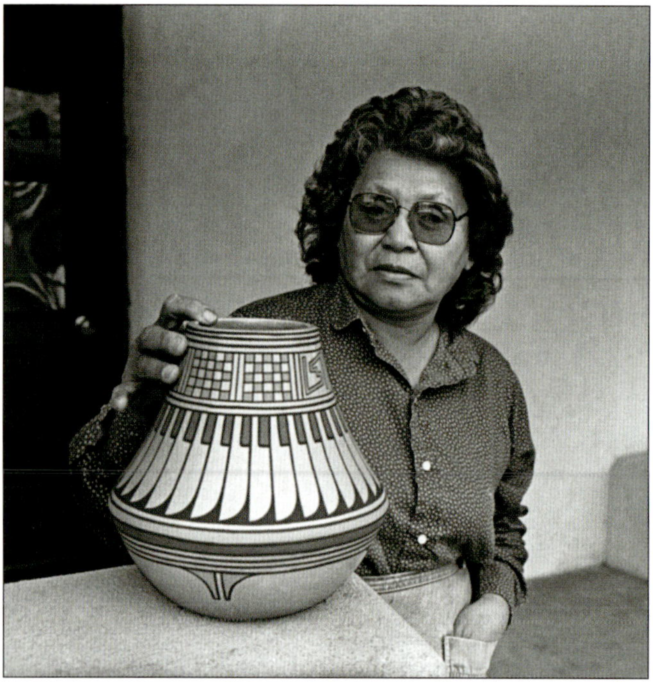

San Ildefonso Pueblo resident Blue Corn (1920–1999) learned to make pottery at age three from her grandmother. She is best known for reintroducing traditional polychrome whiteware pottery to San Ildefonso's culture and was one of the pueblo's most famous artisans—second to only renowned potter Maria Martinez. Her beautiful creations can be found in the permanent collections of the Smithsonian Institution, as well as other leading North American and European museums.

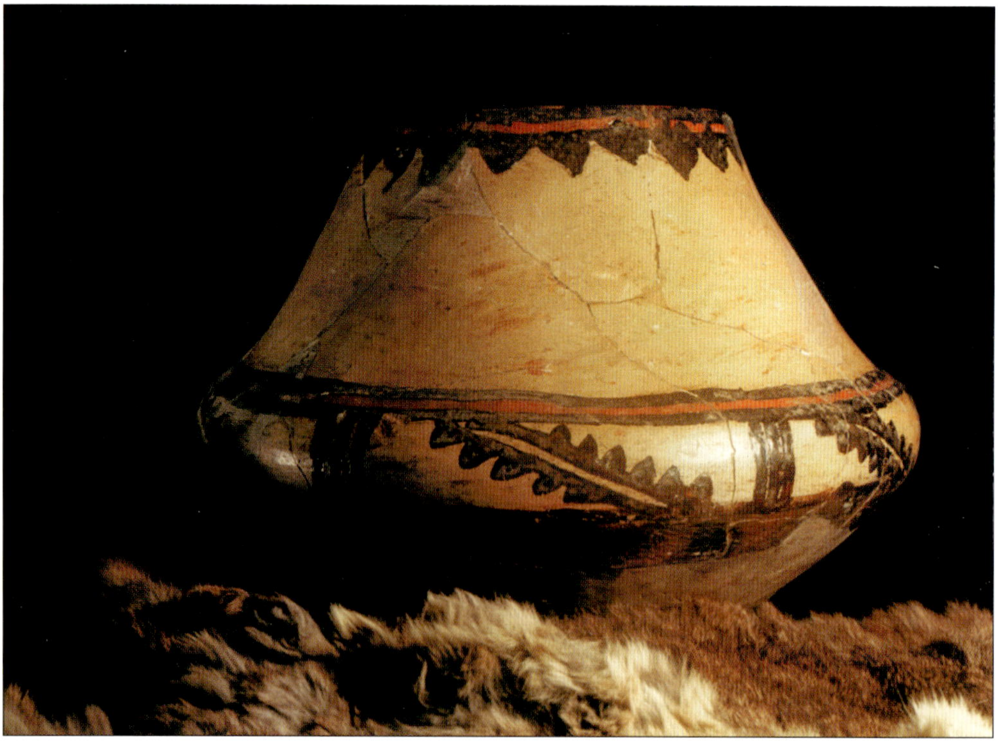

This exquisite Anasazi polychrome bowl, made about AD 1200, was discovered in the ruins of Cicúye Pueblo, east of Santa Fe. The pre-Columbian Anasazi inhabited what is now the American Southwest from about 500 BCE to AD 1400 and were the ancestors of most Pueblo Indians in New Mexico. Cicúye Pueblo lies within Pecos National Historical Park.

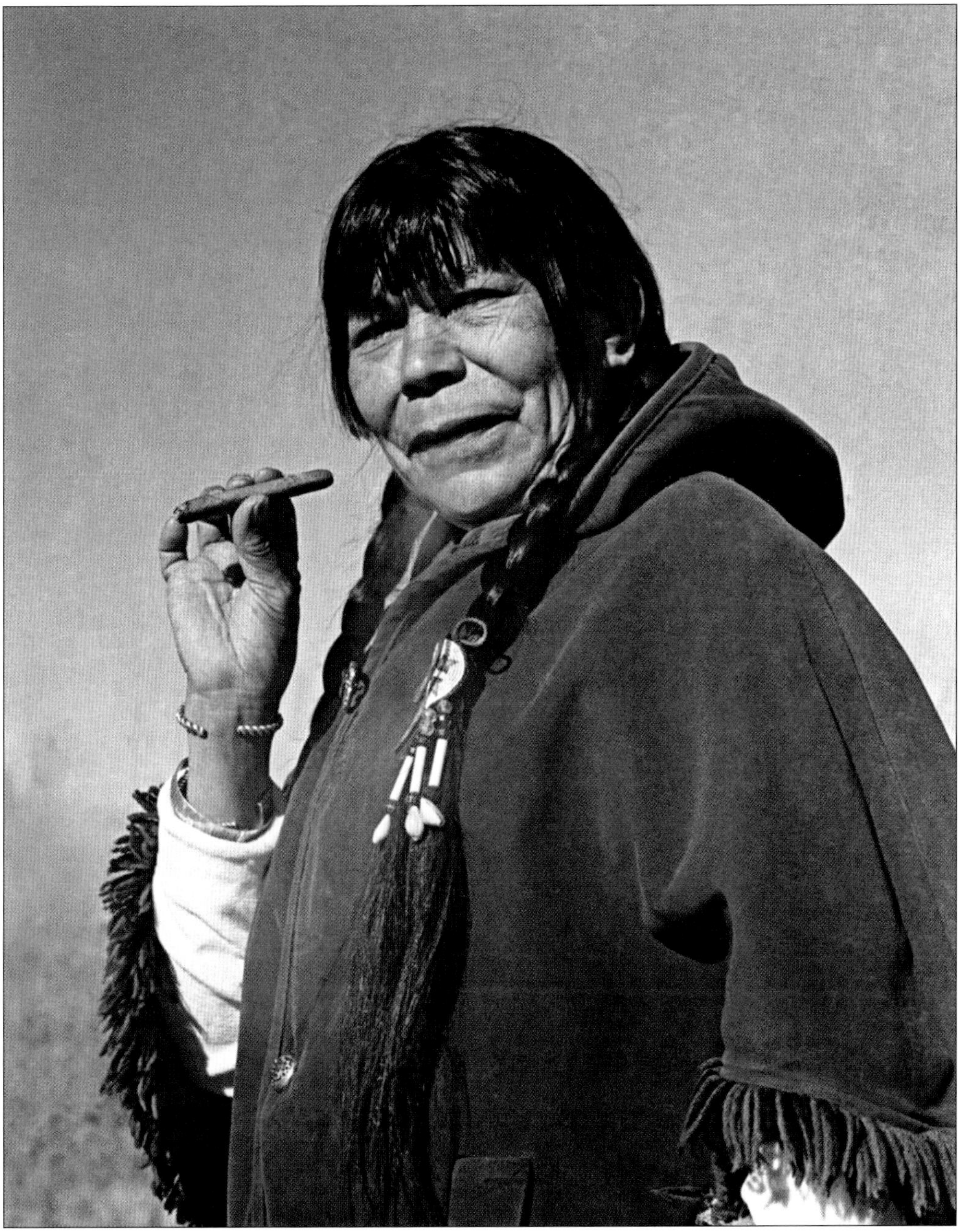

Elementary school teacher Geraldine DeCoteau Harvey (1916–2006), who was part Chippewa/Algonquin and part Oneida/Iroquois Indian, was originally from Wisconsin. She was one of the first American Indian women to graduate from college, obtaining a bachelor of arts degree from Sioux Falls College in South Dakota and, later, a master's degree from the University of Wisconsin. For many years, Harvey was head teacher at Tesuque Pueblo Elementary School, just north of Santa Fe, where she taught first and second grade Indian children. Harvey did not smoke in front of her students, but she loved a good cigar and was not bashful about puffing in public when decorum allowed. When she passed away at age 89 in 2006, a local newspaper noted that she would be "one tough act to follow." This photograph was taken at Tesuque Pueblo in 1973.

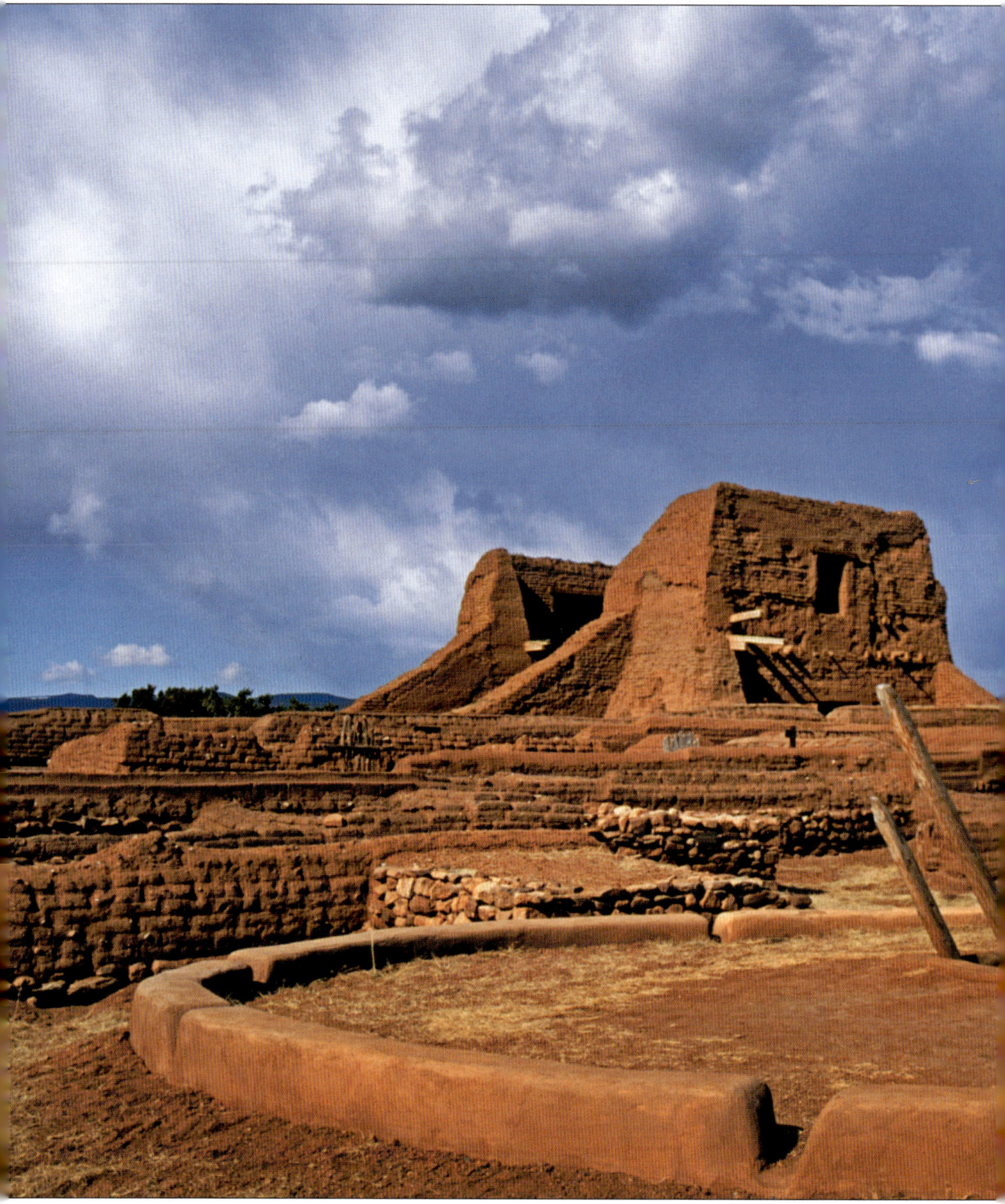

Located in the southernmost foothills of the Sangre de Cristo Mountains and distributed over several acres of rolling high-desert landscape, the ancient ruins at Pecos National Historical Park are breathtakingly beautiful. The remains of Cicúye (Pecos Pueblo), once the Southwest's largest and most powerful Anasazi pueblo, and a crumbling Spanish mission built sometime after 1693, straddle a low grass-covered ridge dotted with piñon, juniper, and native grasses. Unexcavated

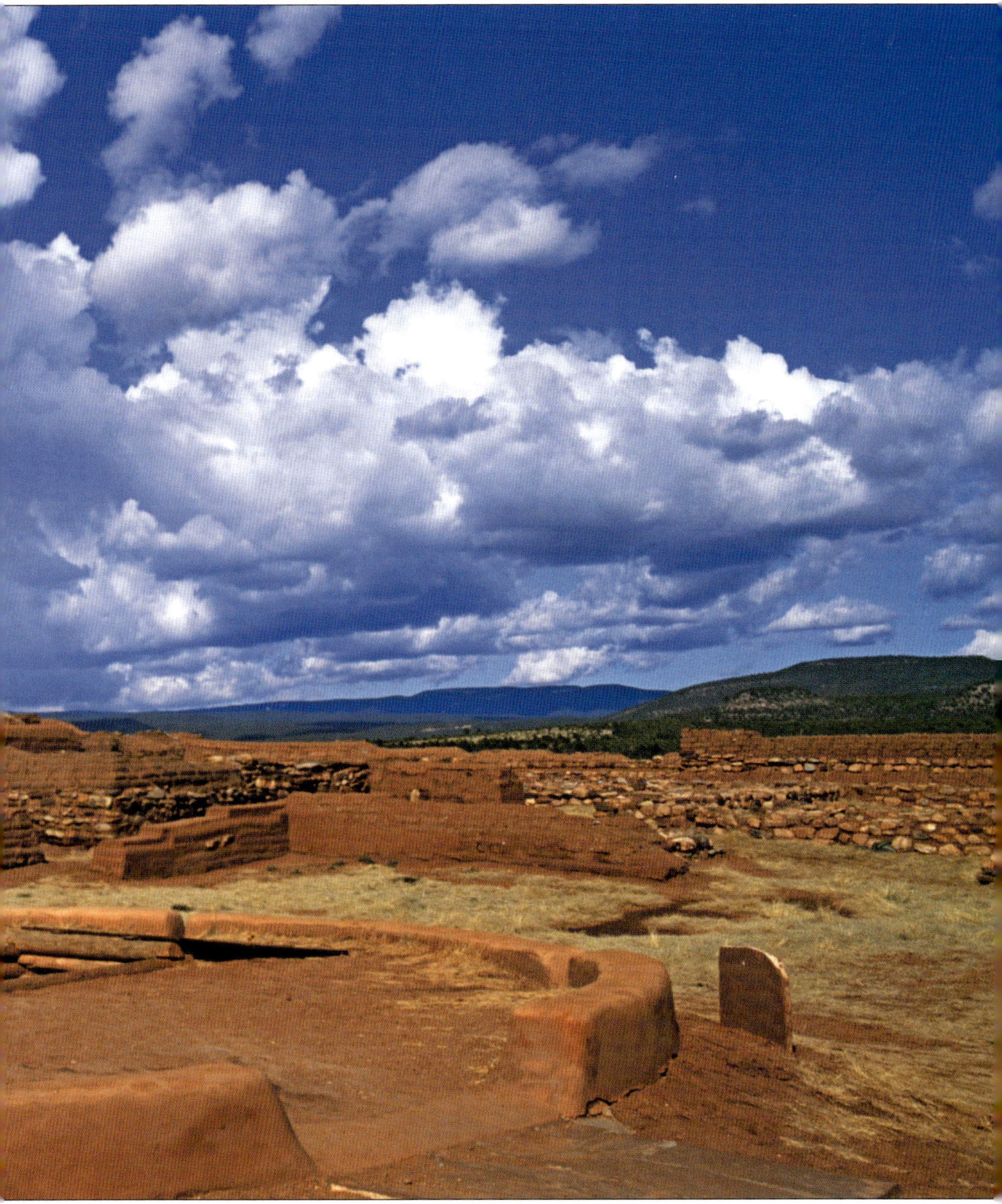

mounds of rubble at the park's north end are the remnants of a five-story "great house" that once sheltered 2,500 people. When Diego de Vargas led his small army to Santa Fe in 1693 to retake the city following the Pueblo Revolt, a contingent of 140 Cicúye warriors went with him to help in the upcoming battle.

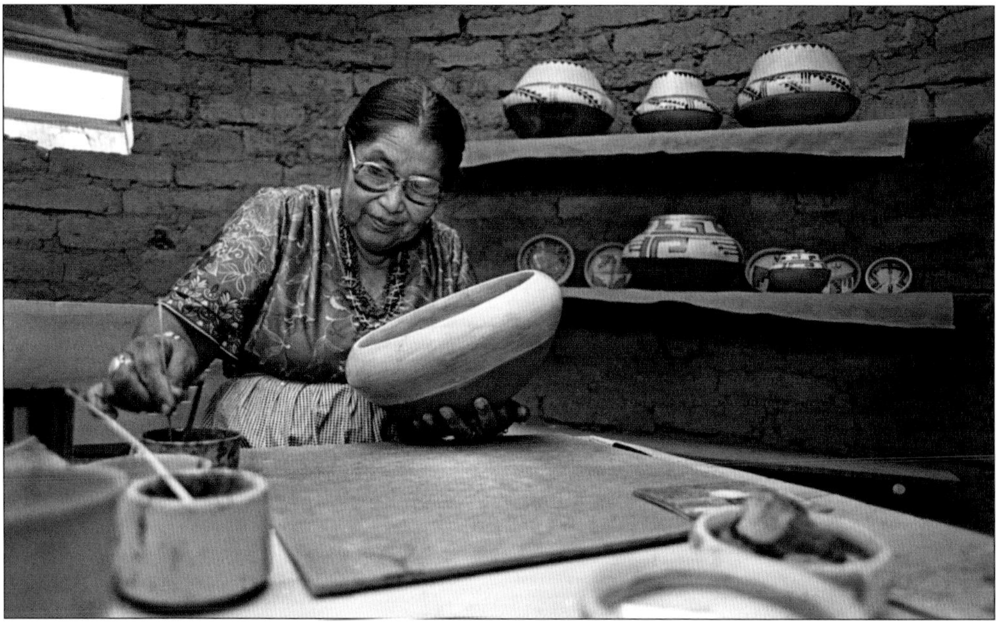

In 1838, after decades of drought, famine, and sickness had decimated the population of Cicúye Pueblo, the few surviving inhabitants abandoned their homes and were adopted by the people of Jemez Pueblo, 80 miles to the southwest. Photographed in 1977, this elderly Jemez potter is giving a pottery-making demonstration at Pecos National Historical Park. She claimed to have descended from one of those Cicúye survivors.

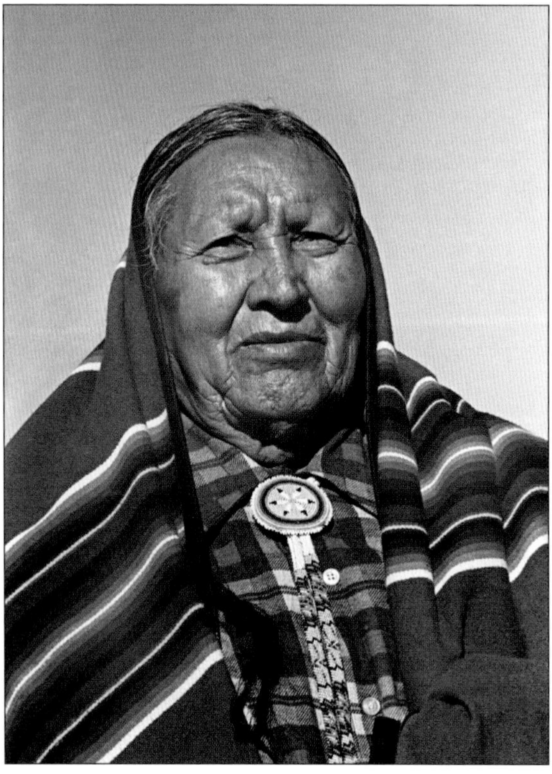

A tribal leader from San Ildefonso Pueblo oversees his community's Feast Day celebration in 1971. Spanish in origin, feast days honor the patron saints of the pueblos and provide an opportunity for non-Indians to participate in dances and other tribal activities. Some Indian families invite visitors into their homes on Feast Day, serving them traditional meals such as posole, green chile stew, and fresh *horno*-baked (oven-baked) bread.

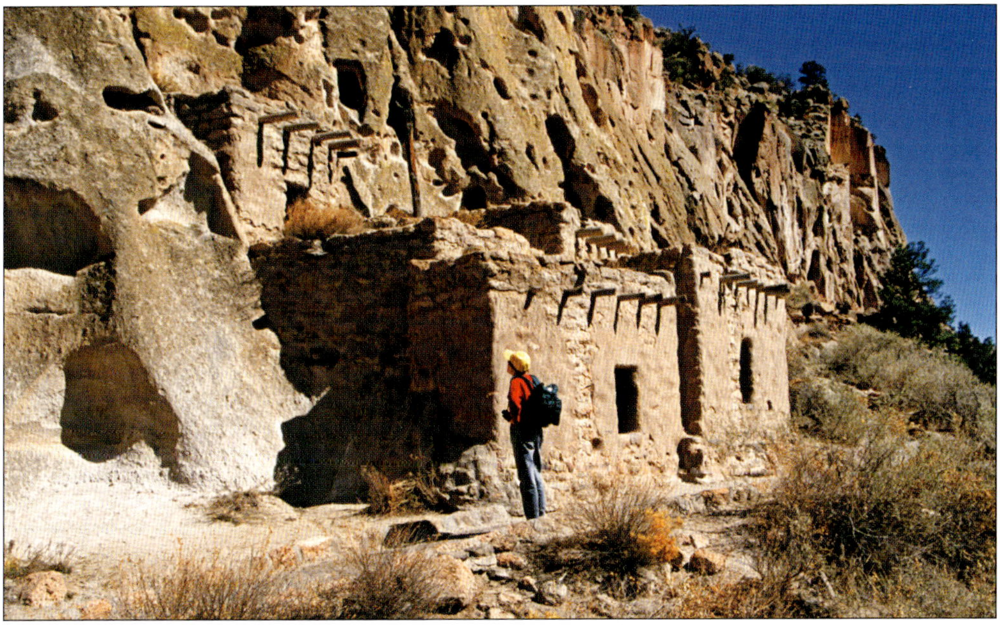

Located in the Jemez Mountains west of Santa Fe, Long House Ruins is a multistory Anasazi town that was constructed around 1350 in what is now Bandelier National Monument. Known as a talus village, it was built from hand-carved blocks of volcanic tuff and mortared together with mud. Anasazi migrants from Long House and other nearby villages probably started Cochiti Pueblo to the southeast after those settlements were abandoned around 1500.

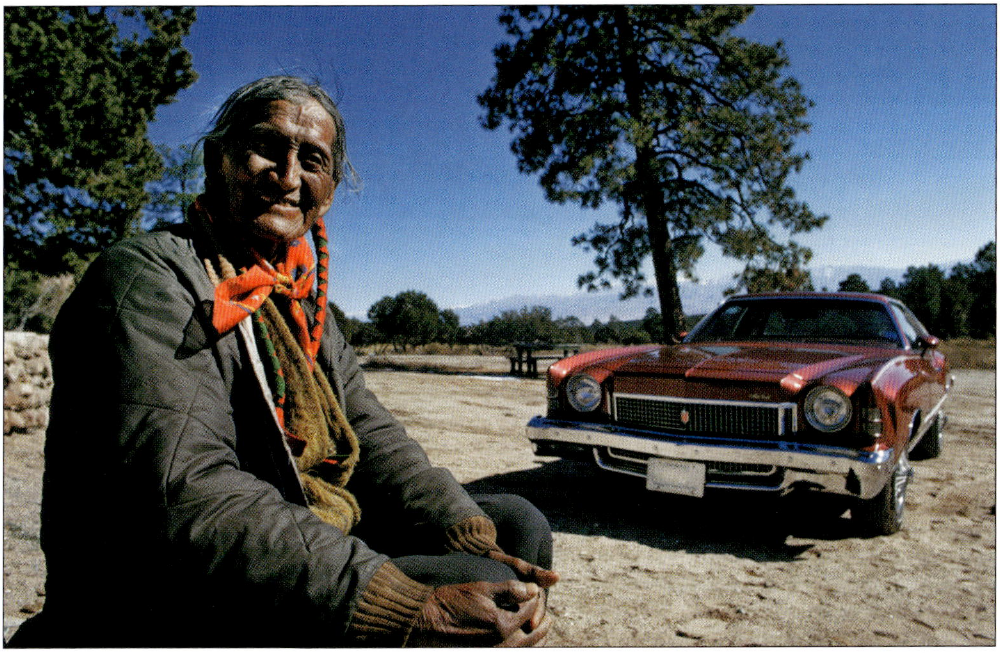

For many years, Santa Clara tribal member "Flint" Tafoya was the caretaker of Puye Cliffs—a long-abandoned Anasazi community in the Jemez Mountains, a few miles west of the Rio Grande. The Puebloans who once resided at Puye Cliffs abandoned the mountains around 1550 because of severe drought, migrating eastward to where they would build what is now Santa Clara Pueblo.

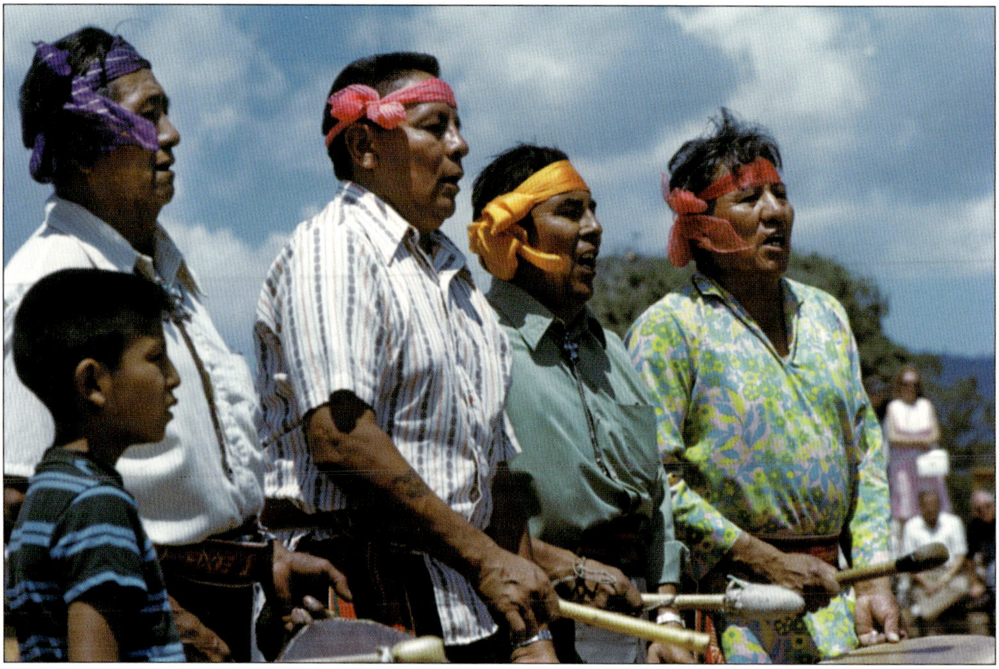

The group of Indian drummers and singers above accompanied pueblo dancers during a 1972 harvest ceremony at Santa Clara Pueblo. The Eagle Dance below was traditionally performed when divine intervention was needed in an Indian community. According to pueblo beliefs, eagles have the power to transport prayers to the gods. If the earth needed rain during the growing season or drier weather during harvest season so crops would not flood, dancers would ask eagles to convey their prayers to the spirits. The costumes and instruments used in these ceremonies are handmade and often handed down from generation to generation.

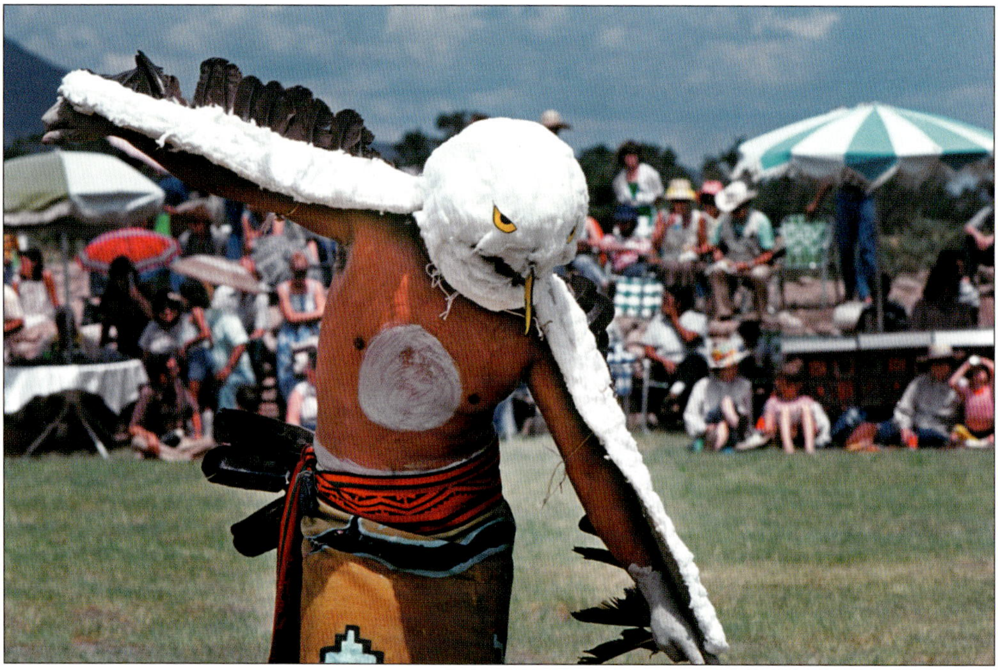

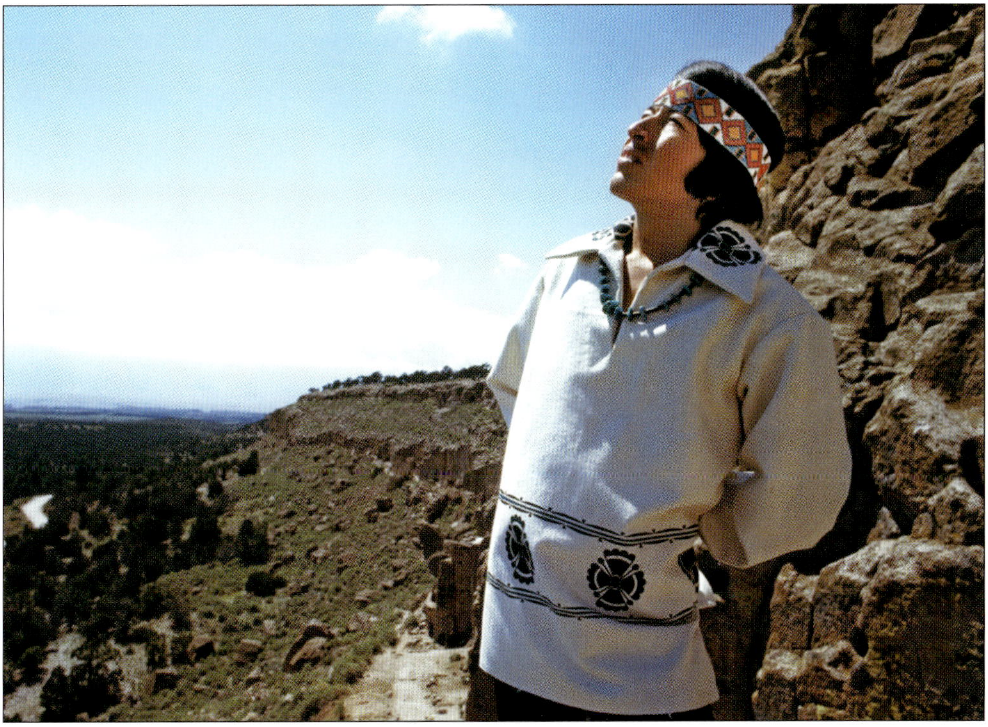

These two teenage models from Tesuque Pueblo are showing off a selection of Indian-made clothing, beadwork, and jewelry for a multipage fashion spread featured in an upscale Florida magazine in 1977. The craftsmen who designed and created the attire were not professionals; they were young Indian students attending a fine arts teaching program funded and overseen by Tesuque and several other northern New Mexico Indian pueblos. Both models wore jewelry and clothing that was probably similar to what their Anasazi ancestors had worn 1,000 years earlier. Archaeologists suggest that the prehistoric cultures in New Mexico commonly used cotton cloth for clothing, but no one knows whether the cotton was grown along the Rio Grande or bartered from tribes farther south.

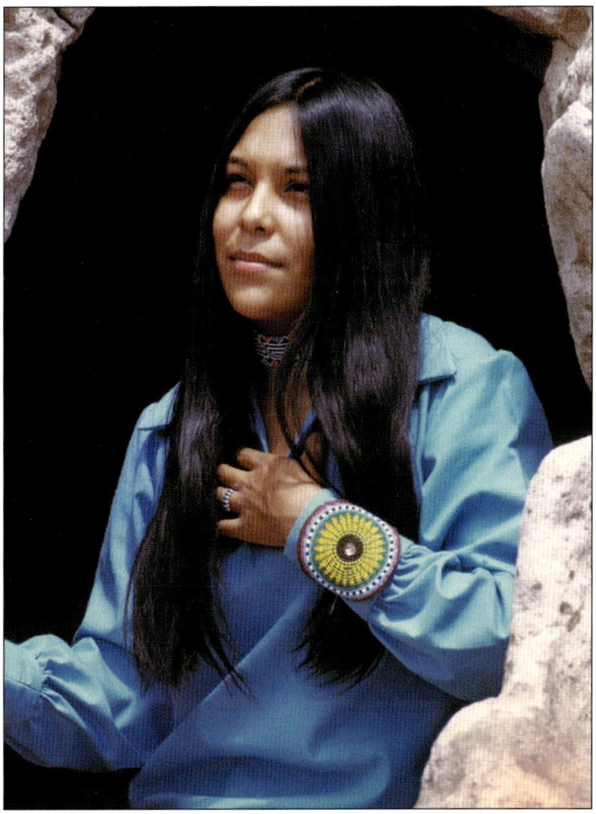

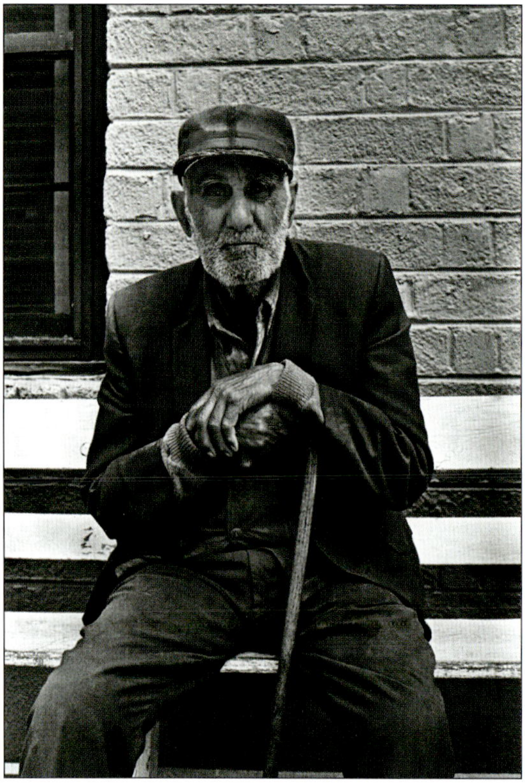

Spanish and Mexican government land grants were awarded to Santa Fe colonists in the 18th and 19th centuries to encourage the establishment of settlements outside the capital. Many of the remote mountain villages north and east of Santa Fe were founded as a direct result of these land grants. Often, the Hispanic mountain people who live in these isolated communities, such as those seen at left and below, are direct descendants of the original Spanish or Mexican settlers. Progress has always been late in coming to these areas. Even in the 1970s, roads leading to many of the towns were still unpaved, and some residents did not have electricity in their homes.

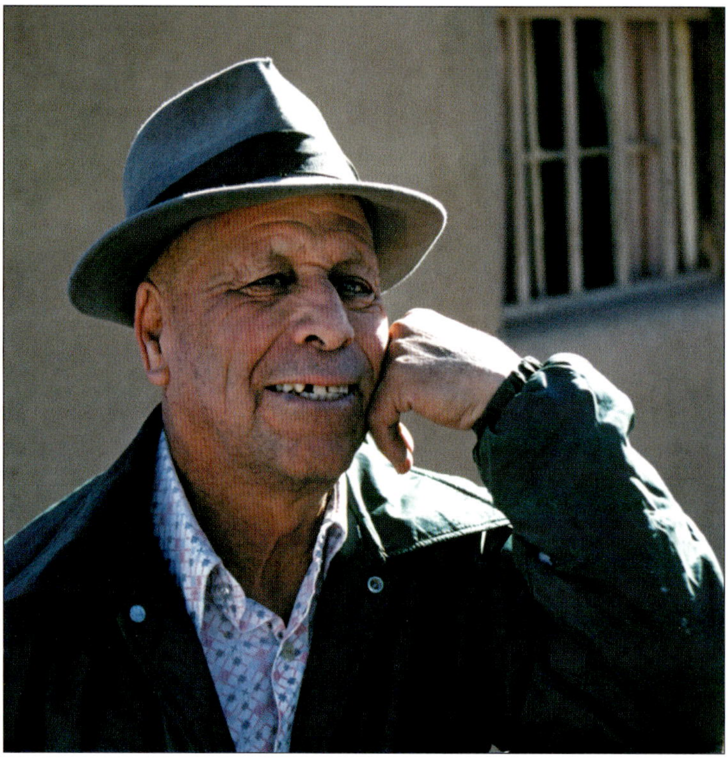

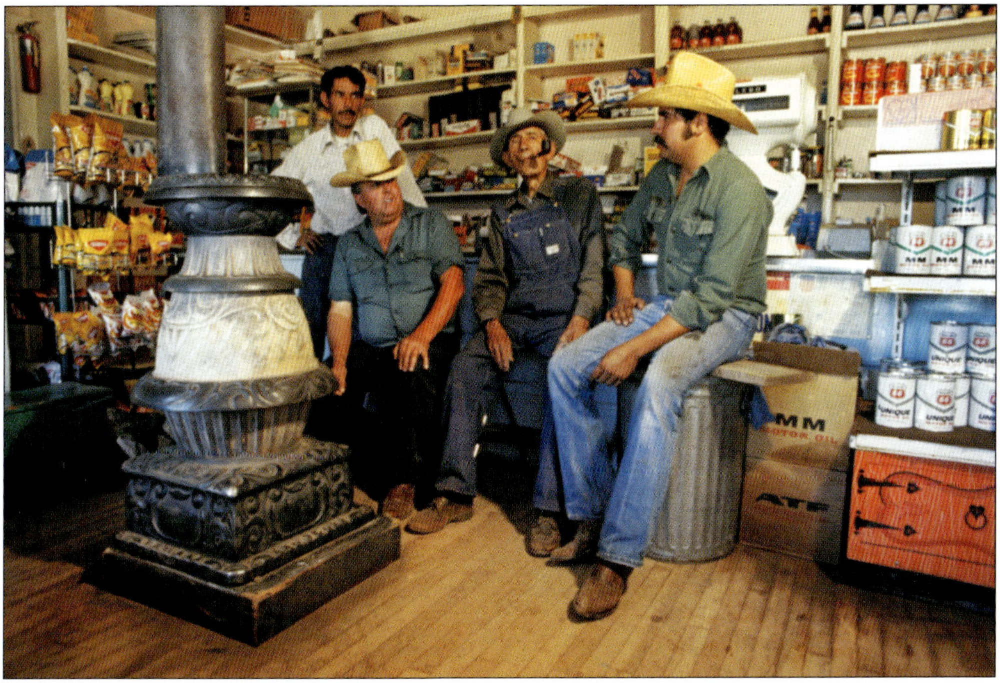

Above, local men from the colonial village of San Jose gather in the local mercantile on a Saturday morning for coffee and a gab session. The village was established around 1800 on the banks of the Pecos River as part of the San Miguel del Vado Land Grant. Later, San Jose was a primary river crossing for Santa Fe–bound travelers, many of whom were navigating the historic Santa Fe Trail in wagons. In the neighboring village of Ribera, the owner of the town's only gasoline station poses by his sole pump below. Electricity and indoor plumbing came late to both villages, and even in the late 1970s, when these photographs were taken, many homes still used outdoor privies.

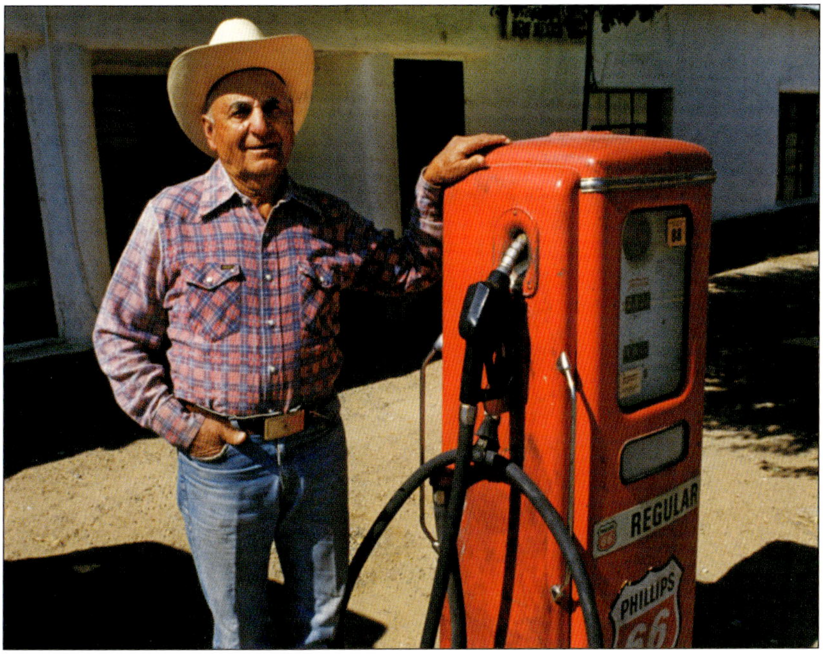

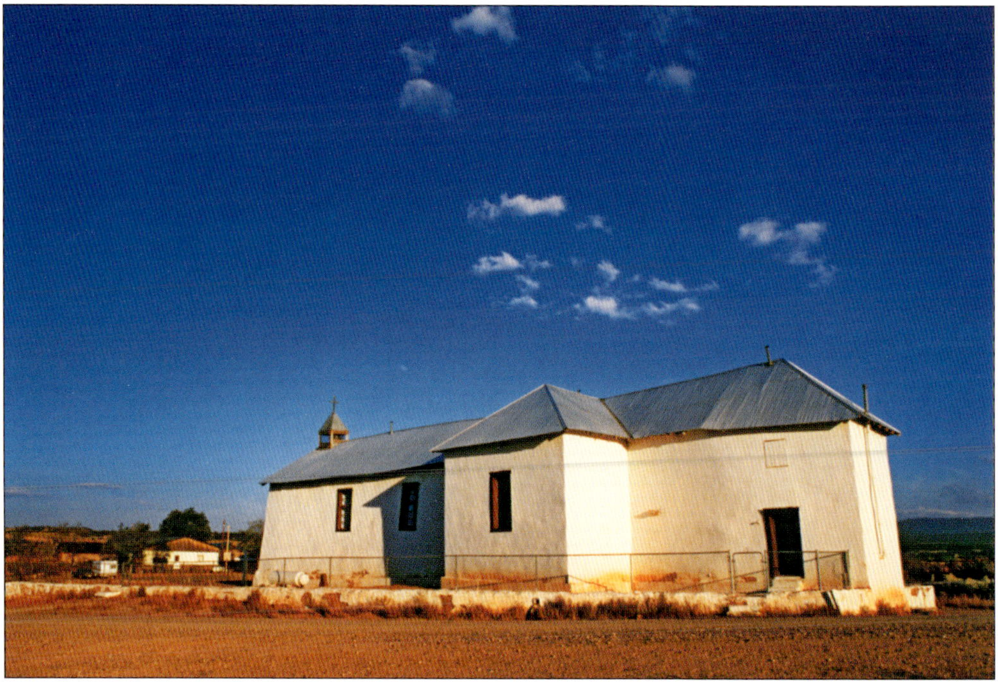

The Roman Catholic Church in the village of San Jose has served the religious needs of this community for several centuries. Sections of the adobe walls of the old structure are more than five feet thick, and although the exact age of the building is unknown, it was probably constructed shortly after the village was established in 1800. During the 1970s, the priest came only once a month to offer mass. In between priestly visits, the young caretaker below spent a few hours each day in the church, dusting the pews and trapping mice that chewed on the hymnals.

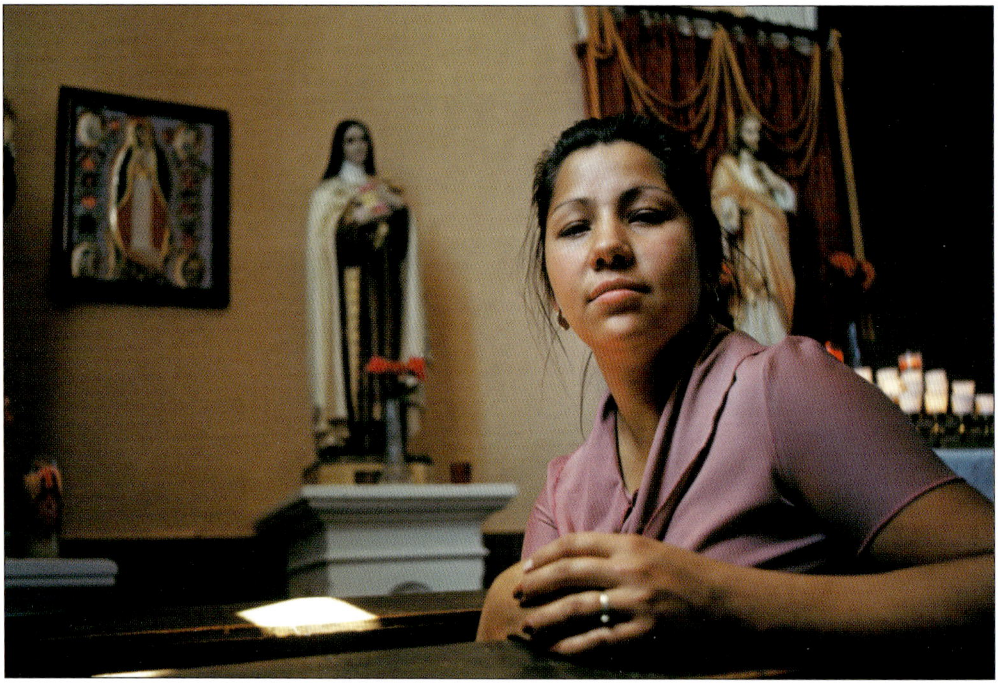

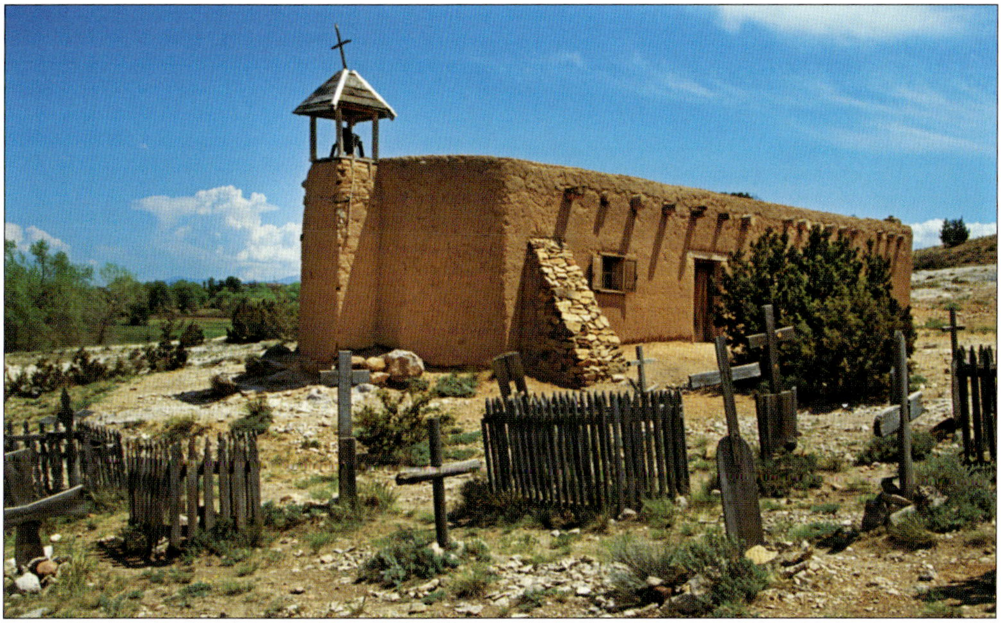

Los Hermanos Penitentes is a centuries-old Catholic sect whose members practice self-flagellation, as well as lifelike reenactments of the crucifixion of Christ on Good Friday. Adorned with only a simple cross, moradas (Penitente meetinghouses) like this one can still be found in many of the mountain villages around Santa Fe. The Penitentes are strongly frowned upon by the Catholic Church, but they continue to be active in secret, even in the 21st century.

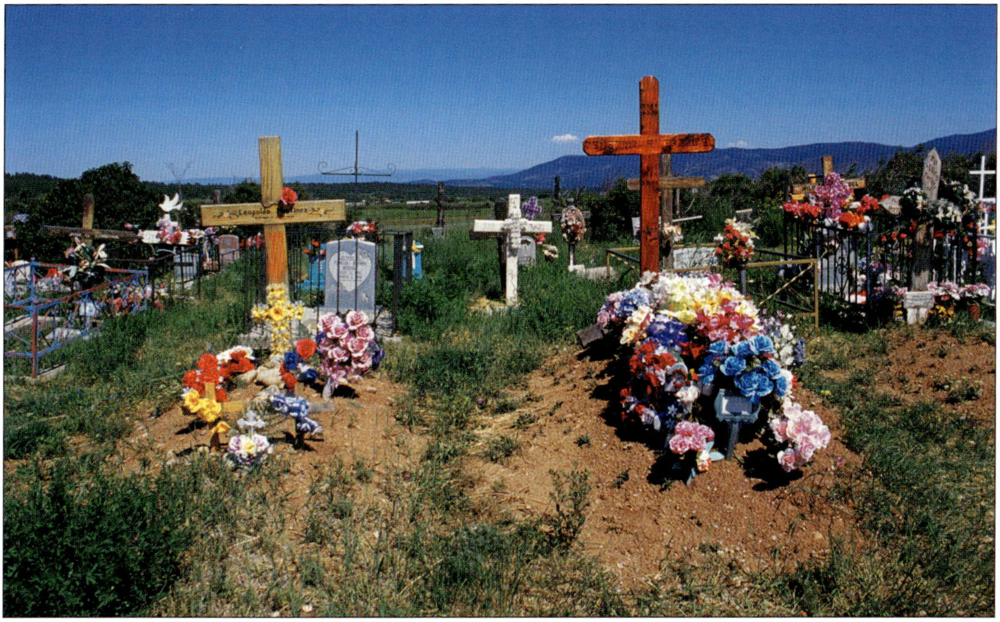

Plastic flowers and handmade wooden crosses adorn the graves of villagers in an ancient mountain cemetery near the Rio Santa Barbara northeast of Santa Fe. Not all the graves are old, of course, but some probably date back to the 18th century. The flowers might have been placed on the graves during Día de Muertos (Day of the Dead), when people of Mexican or Spanish heritage pay homage to ancestors and friends who have died.

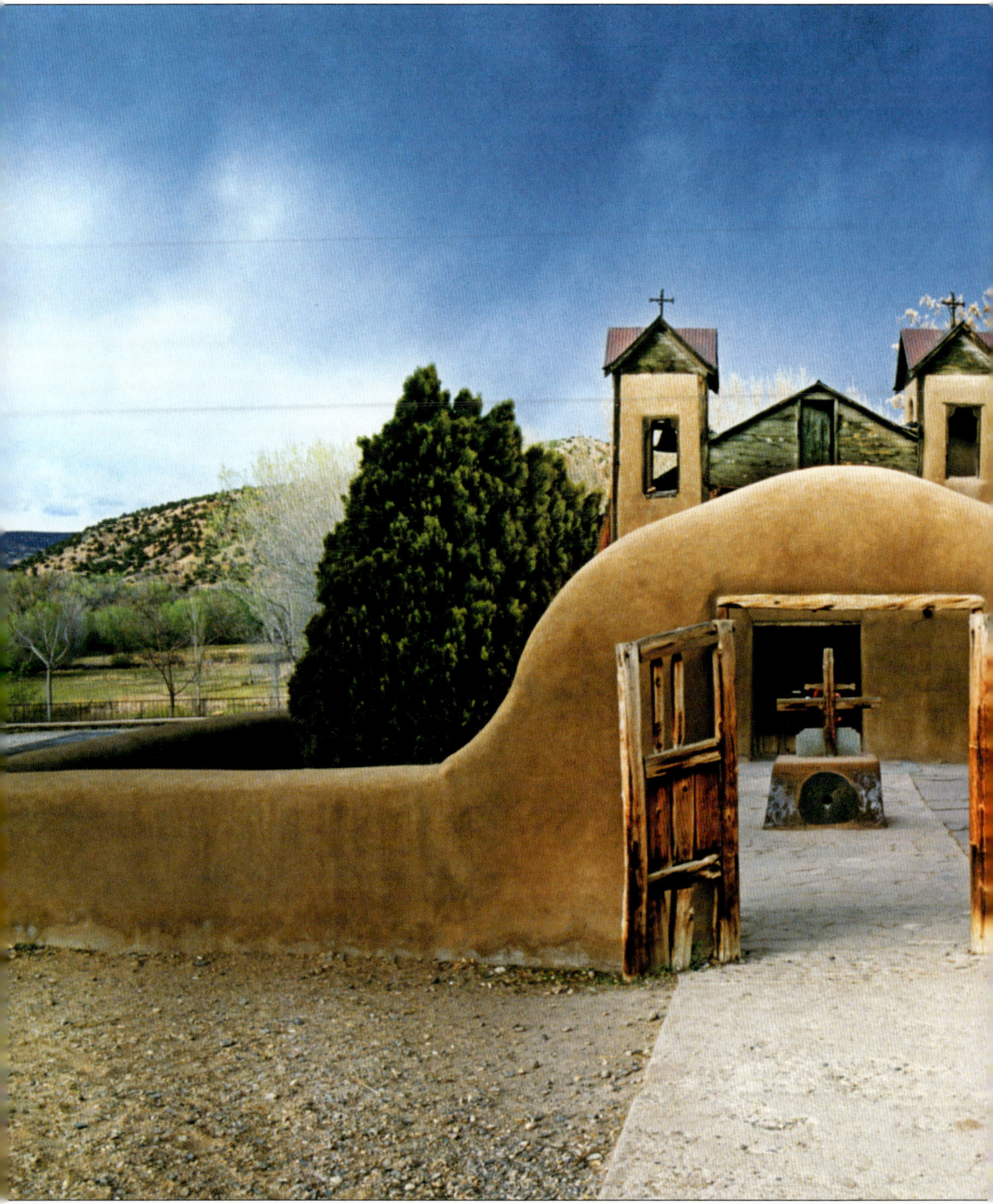

Called "the Lourdes of America" because of its alleged magical recuperative powers, El Santuario de Chimayo (The Sanctuary at Chimayo) is a tranquil place nestled into a cottonwood-filled valley on the western slope of the Sangre de Cristo Mountains, 28 miles from Santa Fe. The simple adobe architecture, built in 1814, is especially beautiful in the late afternoon when the tourists have left and the setting sun makes the mud-colored adobe walls of the chapel glow. For

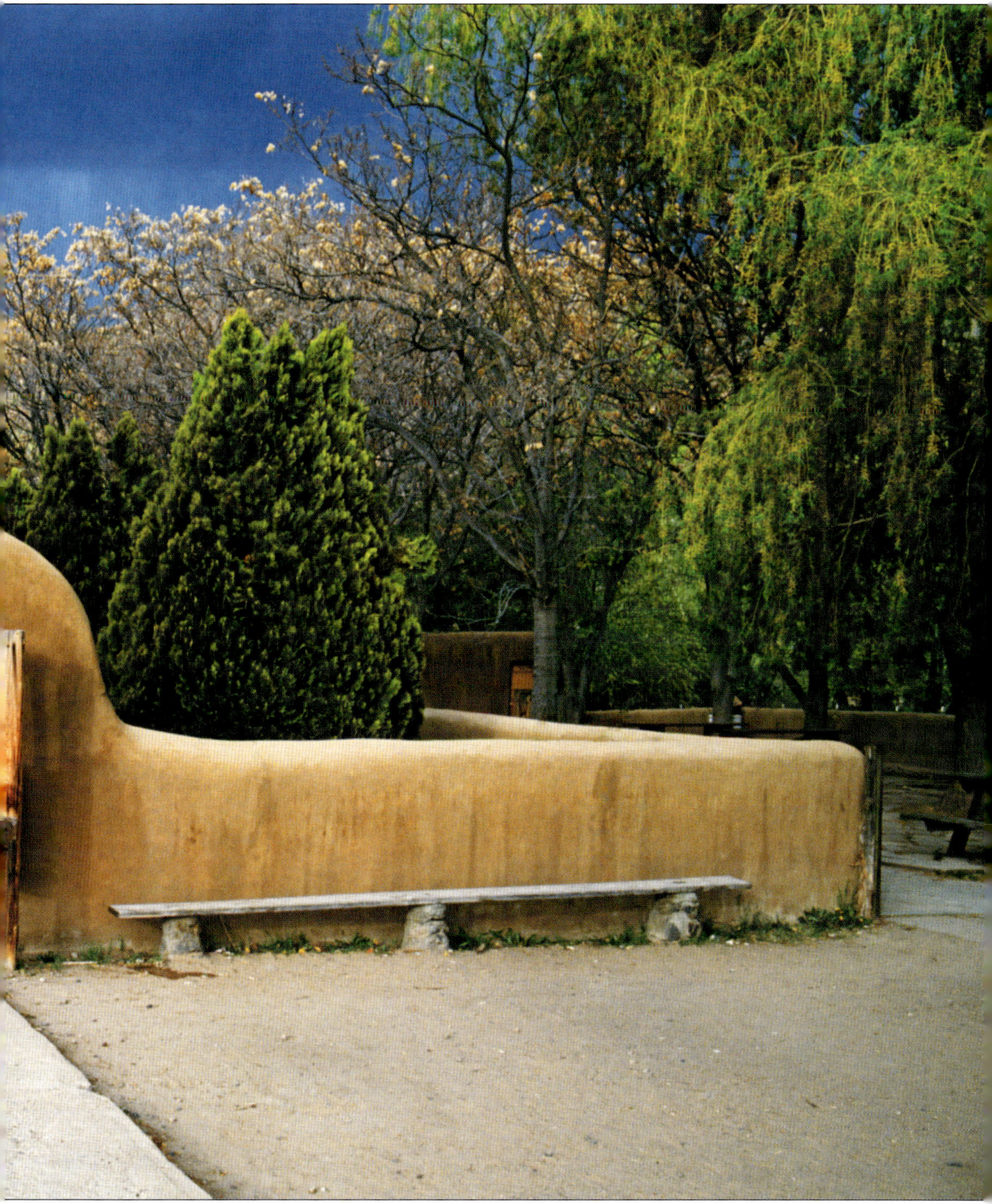

decades, pilgrims have flocked to the santuario during the week of Easter, with some walking or crawling all the way from Albuquerque. Visitors often carry away "holy dirt" from a hole inside the church in hopes of a miraculous cure for themselves or someone who could not make the trip. The chapel was declared a National Historic Landmark in 1970.

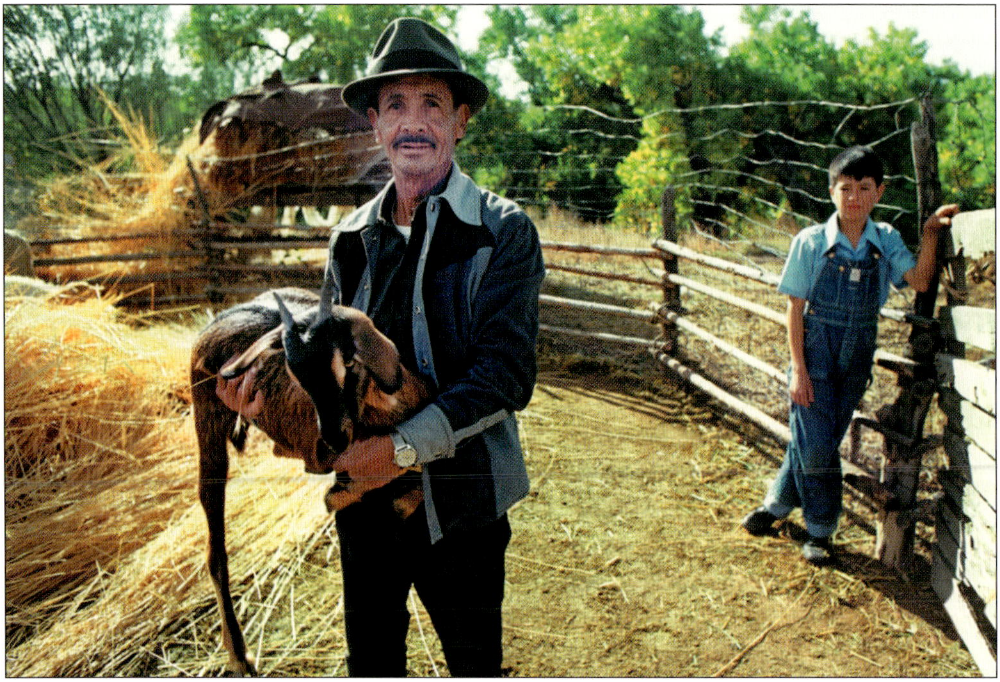

During the 17th and 18th centuries, El Rancho de las Golindrinas was an official encampment on El Camino Real de Tierra Adentro, the long and dangerous trail from Mexico City to Santa Fe. Known as a *paraje*—a place where weary travelers could find a good meal and perhaps even a bath before attending to whatever business had brought them to New Mexico—the ranch was the last stop before reaching the city, just a day's horseback ride away. In the early 1970s, after decades of neglect, Las Golindrinas was restored and opened to the public as a living historical museum. When these photographs were taken in 1973, many volunteer staff members were the descendants of Spanish and Mexican families who had actually traveled El Camino Real during the Spanish Colonial period.

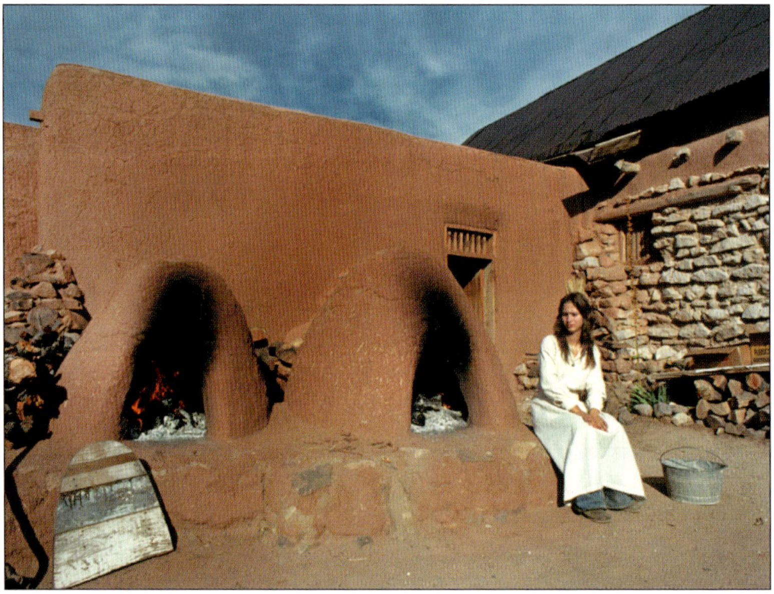

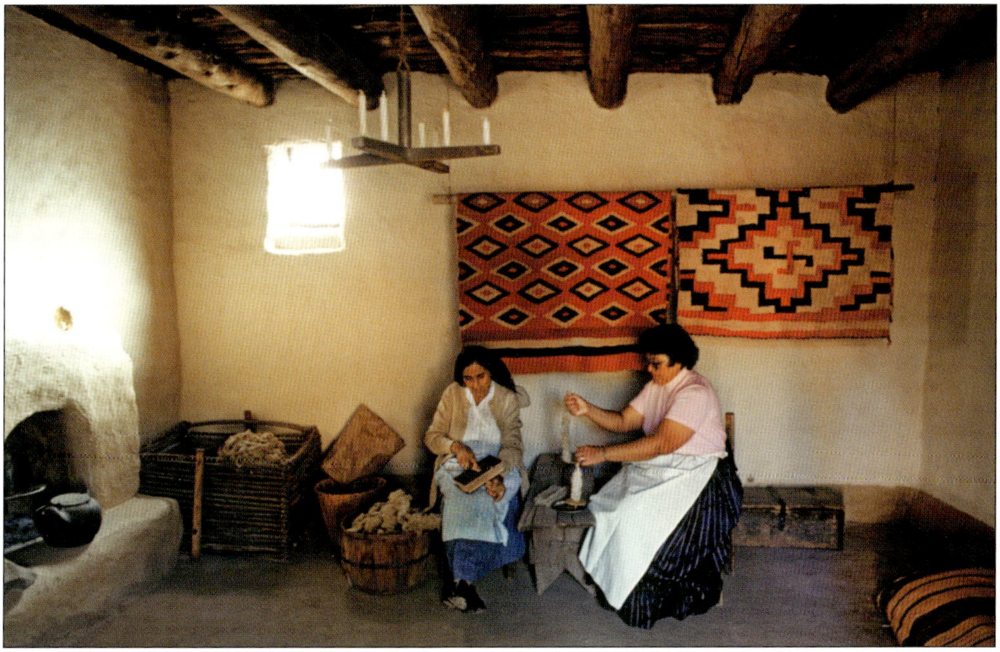

Museum volunteers at El Rancho de las Golindrinas have re-created many of the everyday household and farm activities that were part of life in the area's 17th- and 18th-century land grant villages. Some of those activities, such as goatherding (opposite page, above) and baking fresh bread in adobe hornos (opposite page, below), are still daily rituals for many rural Hispanic families. In Chimayo and other villages known for their traditional weavings, artisans often hand-card their wool (above). Cooperative hog butchering (below), or *la matanza* (the slaughter), is less common but is still practiced every autumn in communities such as Truchas and Penasco.

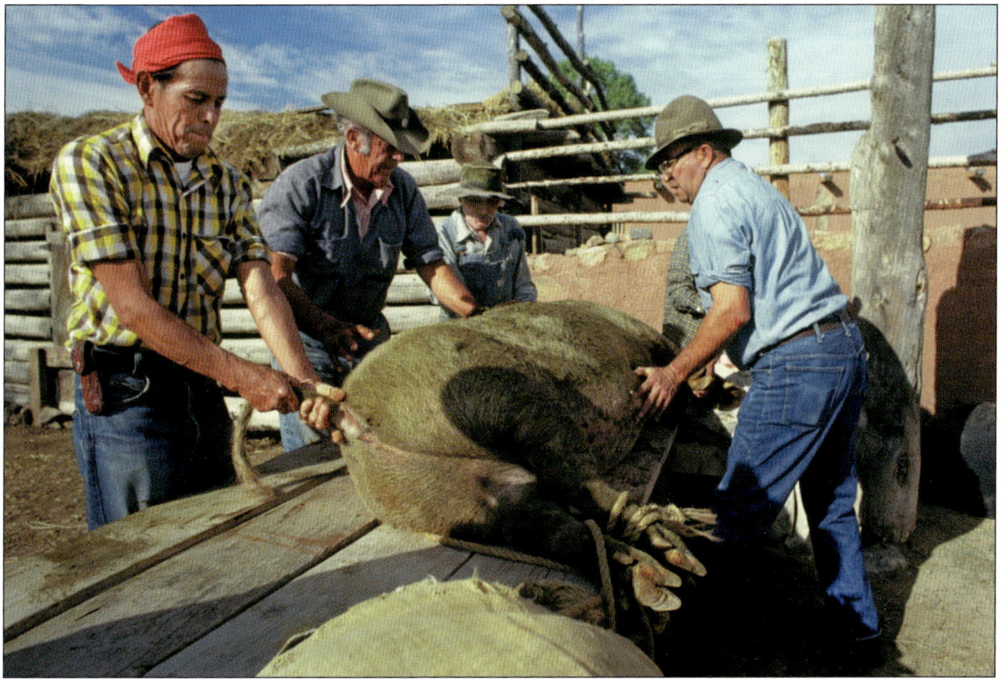

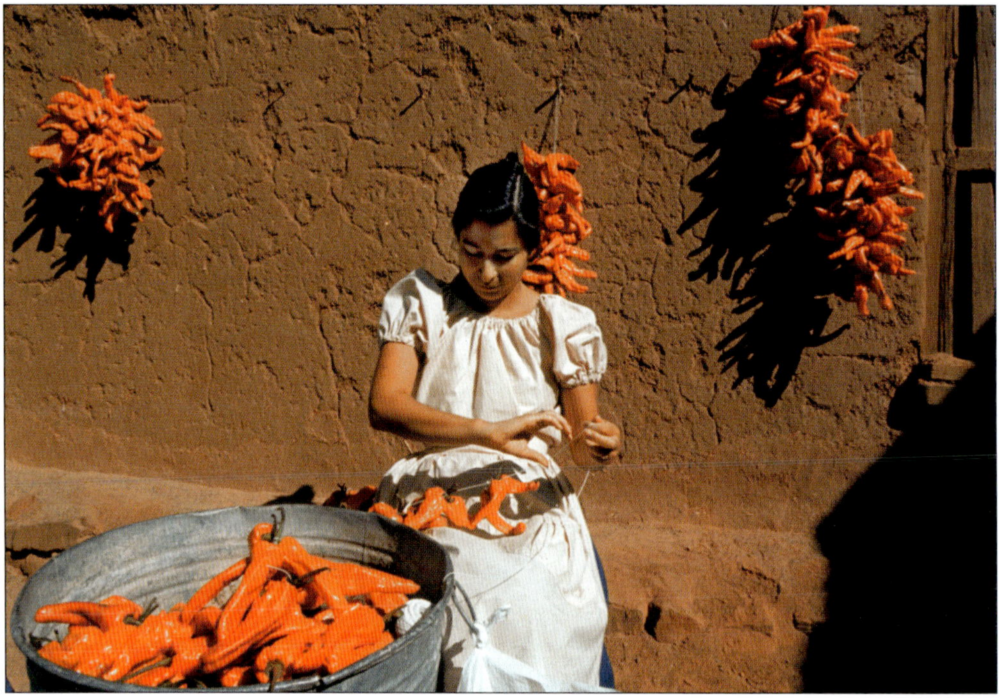

Strings of dried red chiles are often used as home decor, but at one time, most Santa Feans ate chile at every meal. Used mainly as a digestive, the spicy vegetable helped usher a heavily starched diet of pinto beans and corn tortillas through the digestive tract. The young woman above illustrates how early Spanish settlers strung pods of dried red chile into ristras to store them for consumption long after the harvest. Below, red and green chile pods, pumpkins, and dried corn embellish a classic pickup truck parked at a roadside fruit stand in the Rio Grande Valley north of Santa Fe. All three vegetables were developed and domesticated by Indians in North America several thousand years ago.

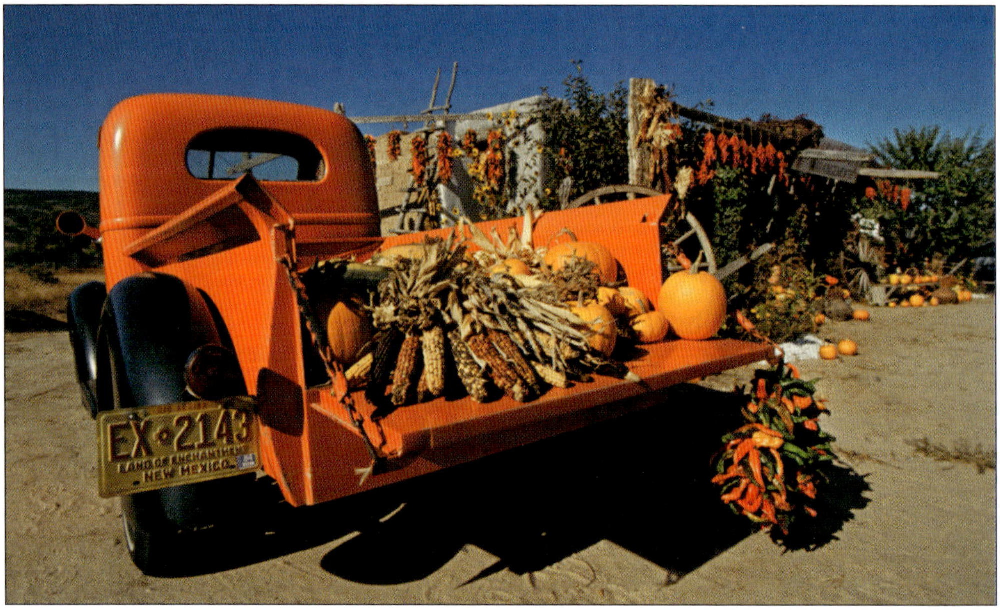

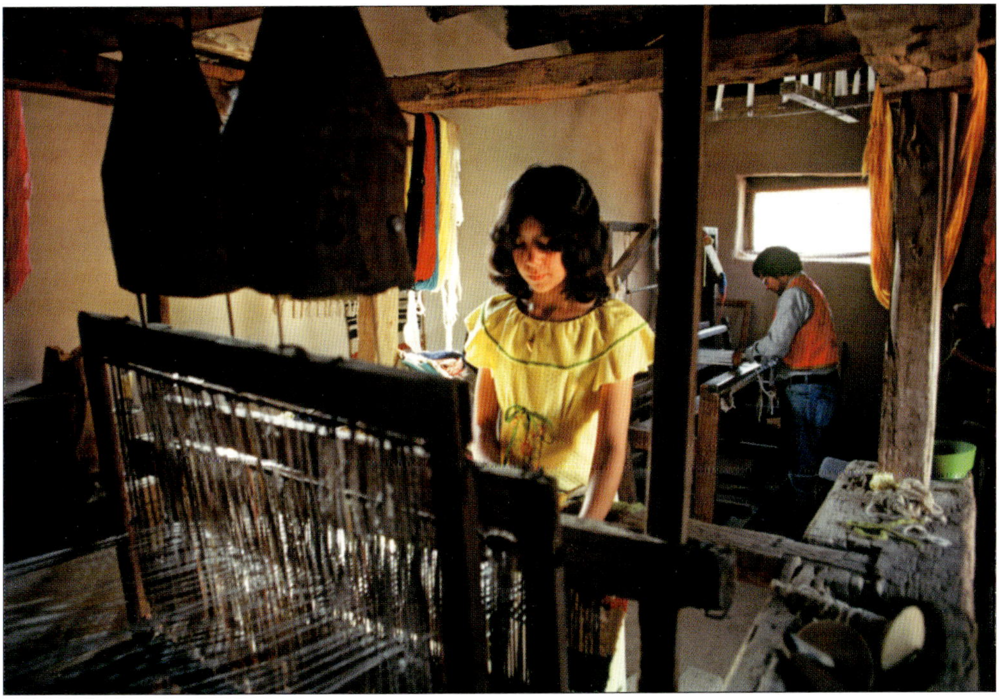

In the rolling foothills northeast of Santa Fe, the village of Chimayo is famous for the Santuario de Chimayo chapel (see pages 74 and 75), but it is also known for its talented weavers (above). Since the early 1700s, the Ortega and Trujillo families in Chimayo have been weaving naturally dyed wool rugs and blankets in what has become known as the Rio Grande–Chimayo style. Five miles up the road, in the tiny mountain village of Cordova, generations of Santeros—wood-carvers who whittle effigies of Catholic saints from slabs of pine, quaking aspen, or cottonwood—have been practicing this traditional form of folk art since about 1750 (below).

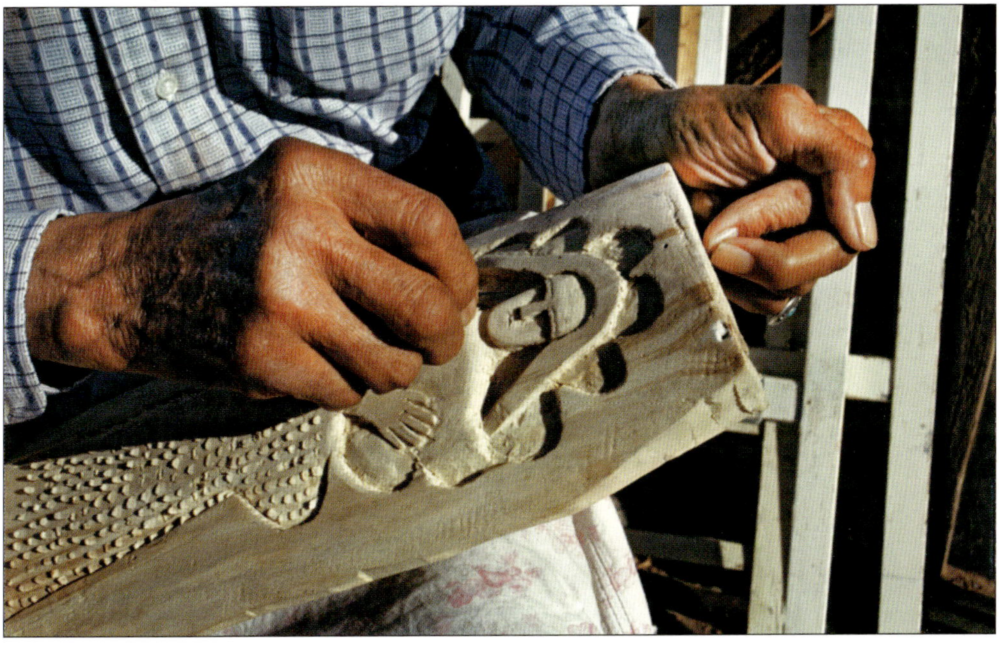

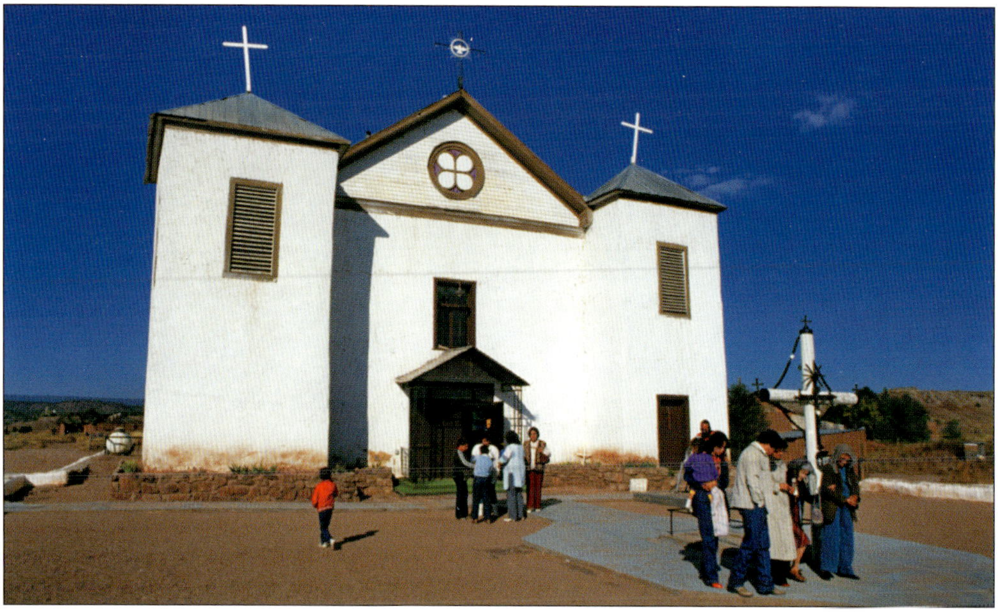

Daily life for Spanish colonists living in the small isolated villages surrounding Santa Fe during the 18th and early 19th centuries was not easy; most communities were held together by their sheer stubbornness and a strong belief in God and the Catholic Church. Government officials in the capital had little time or concern for these outlying villages or their problems, but the Church did. Often lacking a priest but filled with hand-carved bultos, santos, and retables (statues and icons of God, Jesus, and the saints), village churches became the foundations around which all other community life revolved. The beautiful *iglesia* (church) above, located in the village of San Miguel Del Vado, was constructed in 1805. Work on San Jose de Gracia Church, seen below in the village of Las Trampas, began in 1760 and finished in 1776.

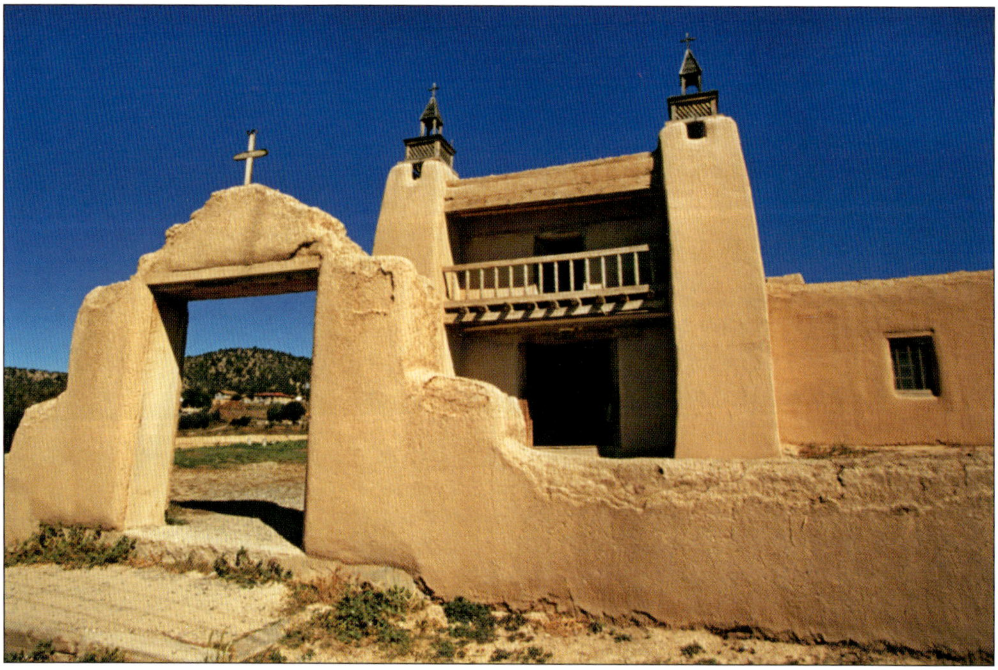

Five

The Great Santa Fe Outdoors

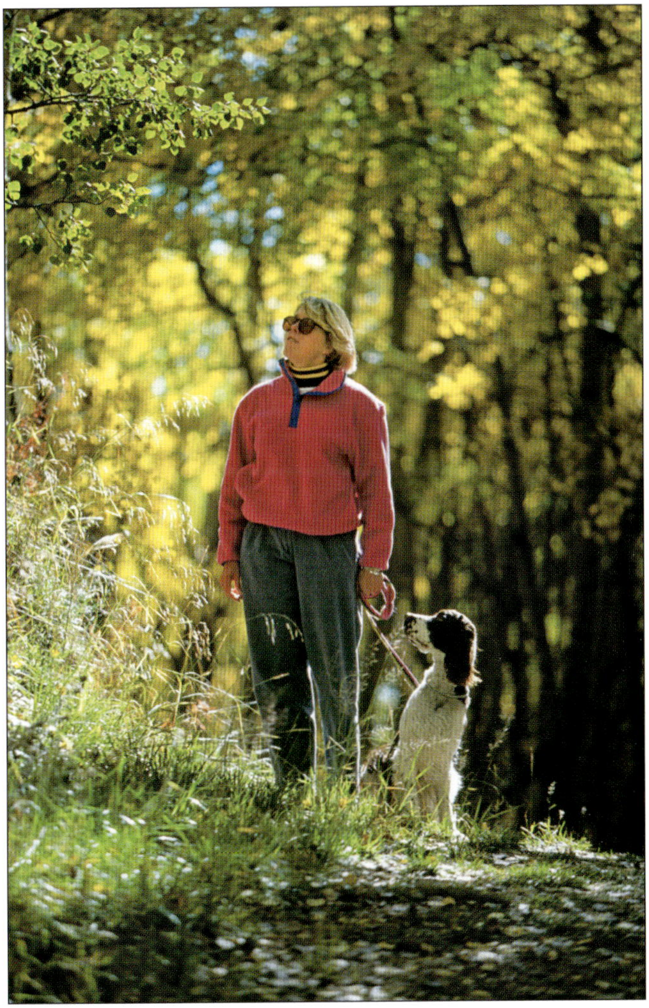

On the Aspen Vista Trail, high in the Sangre de Cristo Mountains above Santa Fe, a day hiker and her English springer spaniel enjoy an explosion of color as the aspen leaves change from green to gold in mid-October. The forest here is considered to have one of the best quaking aspen color changes in the western states.

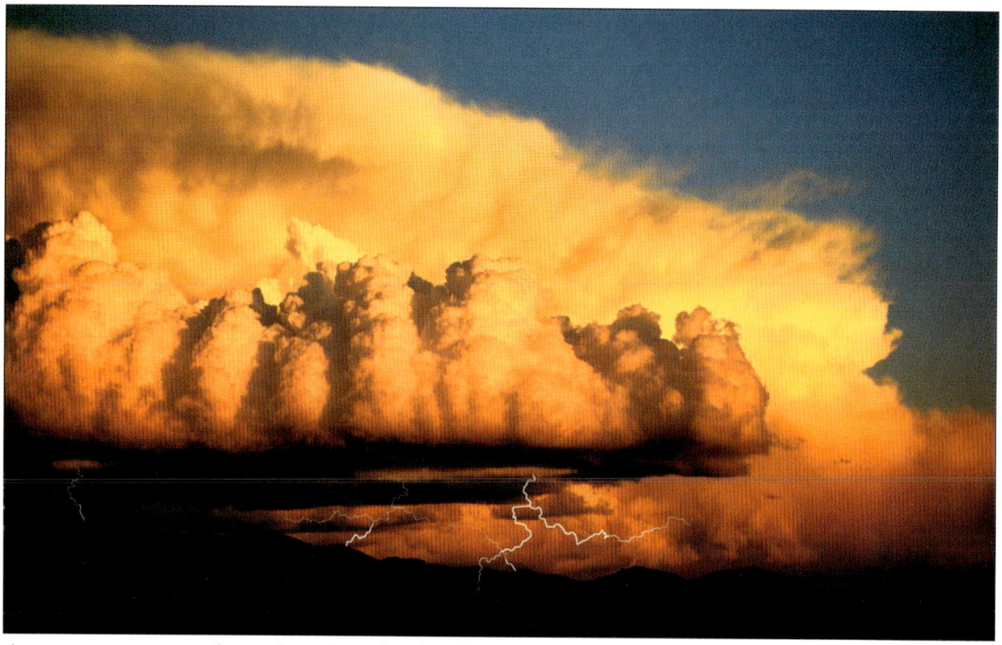

An enormous cumulonimbus thundercloud, flickering with lightning and bloated with rain, straddles the Sangre de Cristo Mountains above Santa Fe on a stormy August evening. Flotillas of these "super clouds" often build up over the mountains during late summer afternoons. The ensuing rainstorms can drop millions of gallons of water on the earth in a matter of minutes.

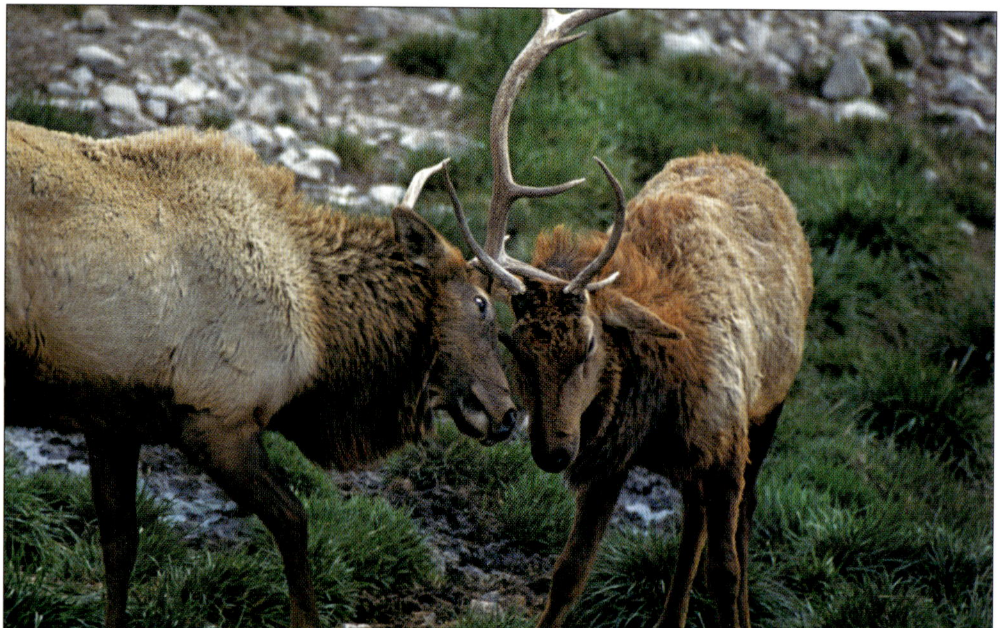

Two young Rocky Mountain bull elk spar for superiority in an alpine meadow as they prepare for the upcoming rut (breeding season), which usually occurs in September and October. The animals are part of a large and healthy elk herd that inhabits the 223,000-acre Pecos Wilderness, 20 miles northeast of Santa Fe.

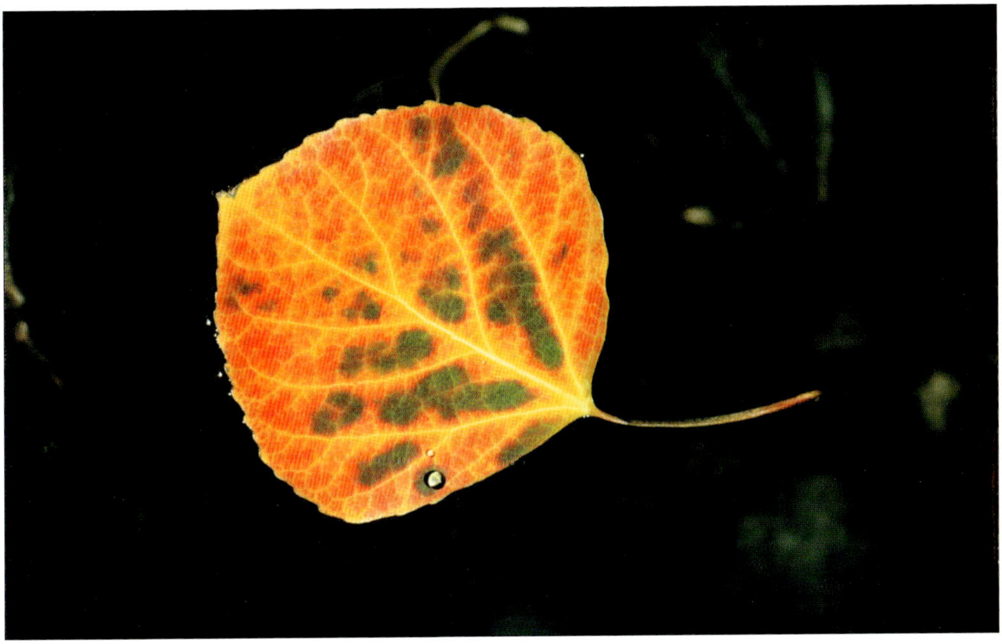

In mid-October, as the weather cools and nighttime temperatures drop below freezing in the mountains, a spectacular color change overtakes the miles and miles of quaking aspen groves found in the Santa Fe National Forest. An inch-long aspen leaf seems almost sculpted from gold as it floats in a pool of water on the upper Pecos River near the summer community of Cowels.

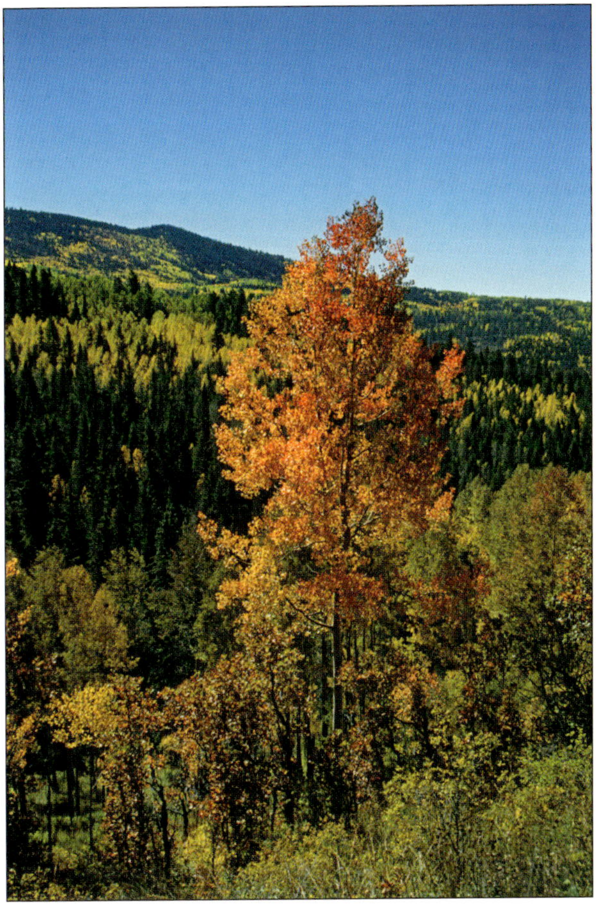

On nearby Hamilton Mesa, the autumn color bathes the mountains in brilliant yellows, reds, and golds when it reaches its peak. For more than a century, leaf lovers have traveled to the Santa Fe National forest every October to observe the annual color change.

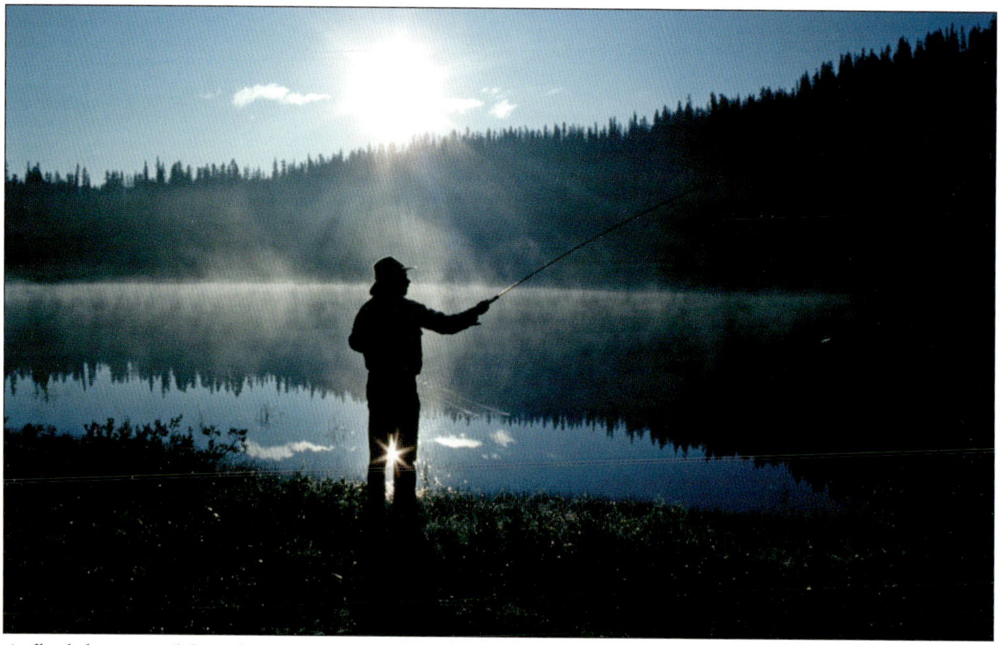

A fly fisherman (above) casts to rising brook trout and native cutthroats (below) just after dawn in an alpine lake, high in the backcountry of the Pecos Wilderness. Most of these lakes can only be reached on foot and are so remote that they are stocked with trout by New Mexico Department of Game & Fish helicopters. In the early 1970s, when these photographs were taken, only a few thousand people entered the wilderness each year, most of them backpackers in the summer or elk hunters in the fall. That number is considerably higher now, but the Pecos is still among the least used wilderness areas in the United States.

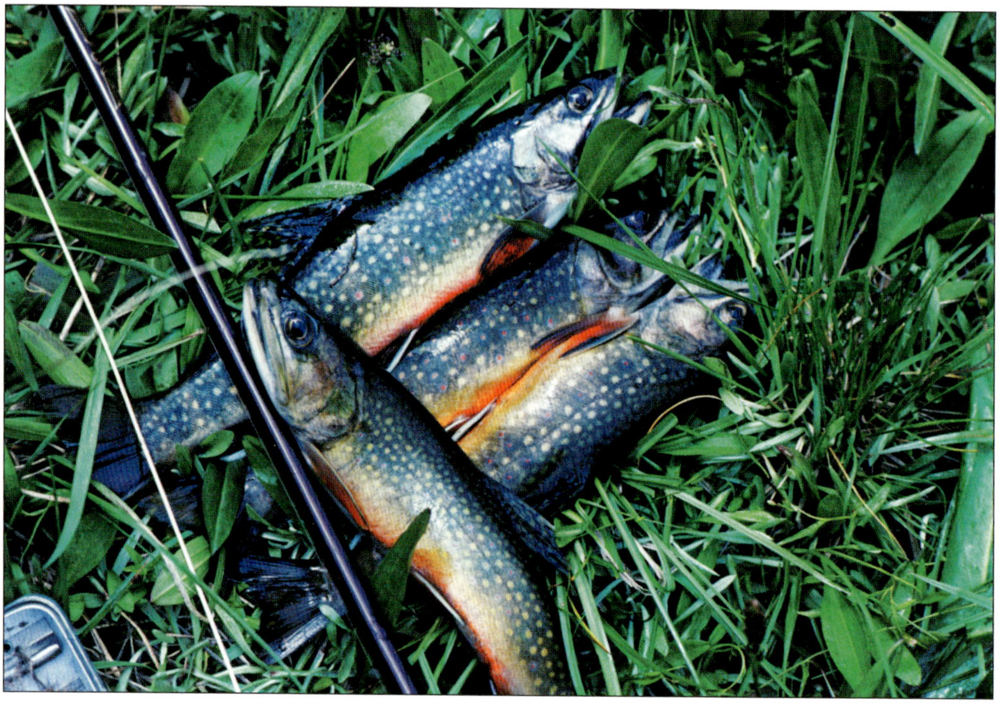

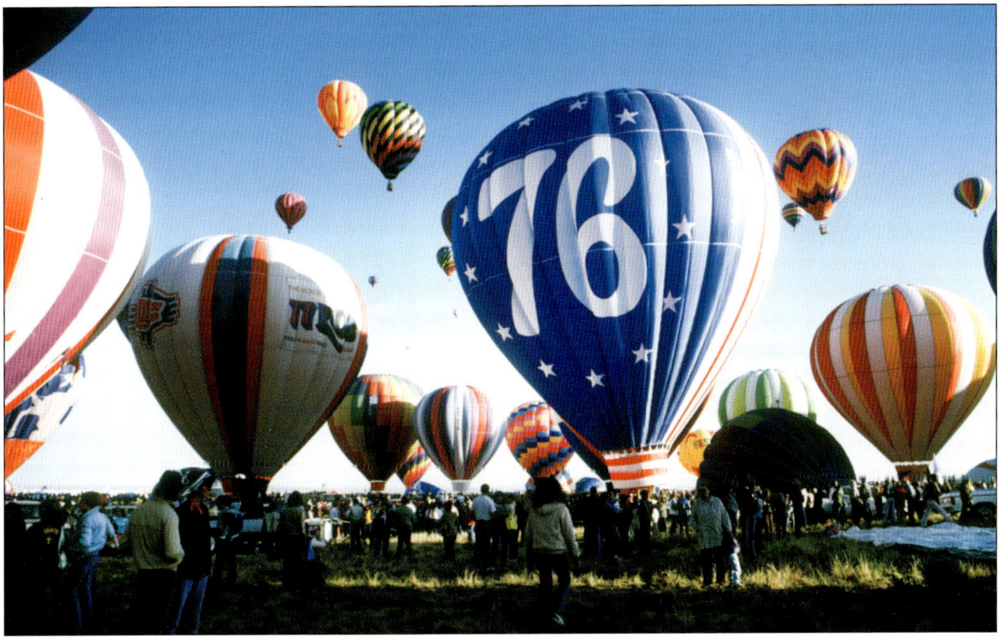

Albuquerque has been heralded as the hot air balloon capital of the world since the first International Balloon Fiesta took place there in 1972. Originally organized as a publicity stunt for a local radio station, the fiesta quickly evolved into the world's premier hot air balloon event, attracting as many as 750 lighter-than-air craft each October. Hot air balloons have been flying in Santa Fe for many years as well. Photographed in 1976, the small fleet of balloons below is preparing to lift off from a sports field on the city's south side. At least one commercial company in Santa Fe offers daily balloon flights to visitors during the summer.

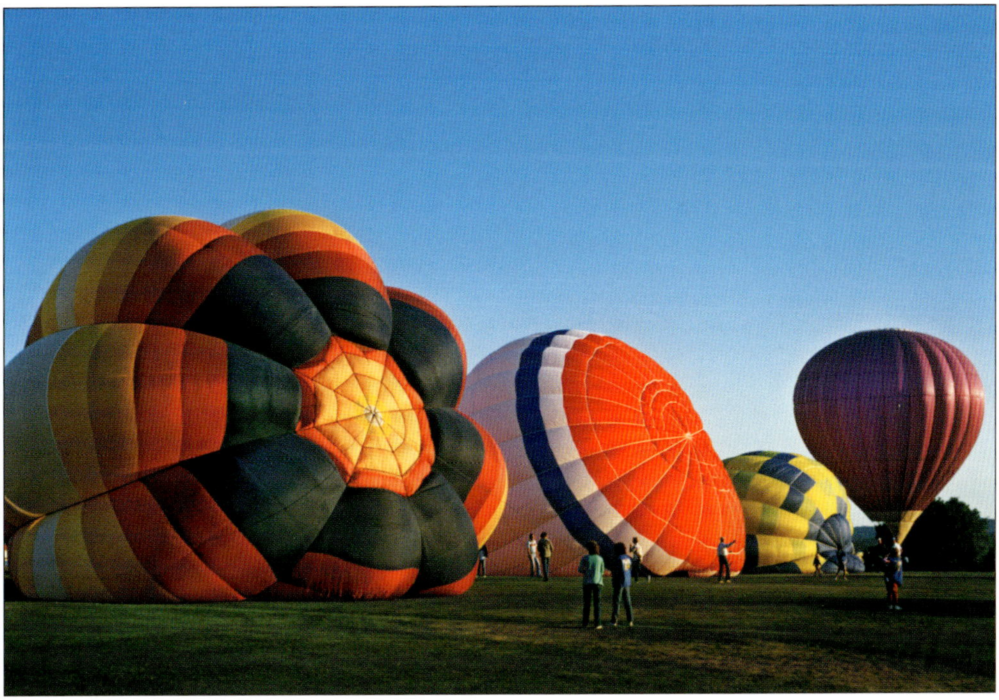

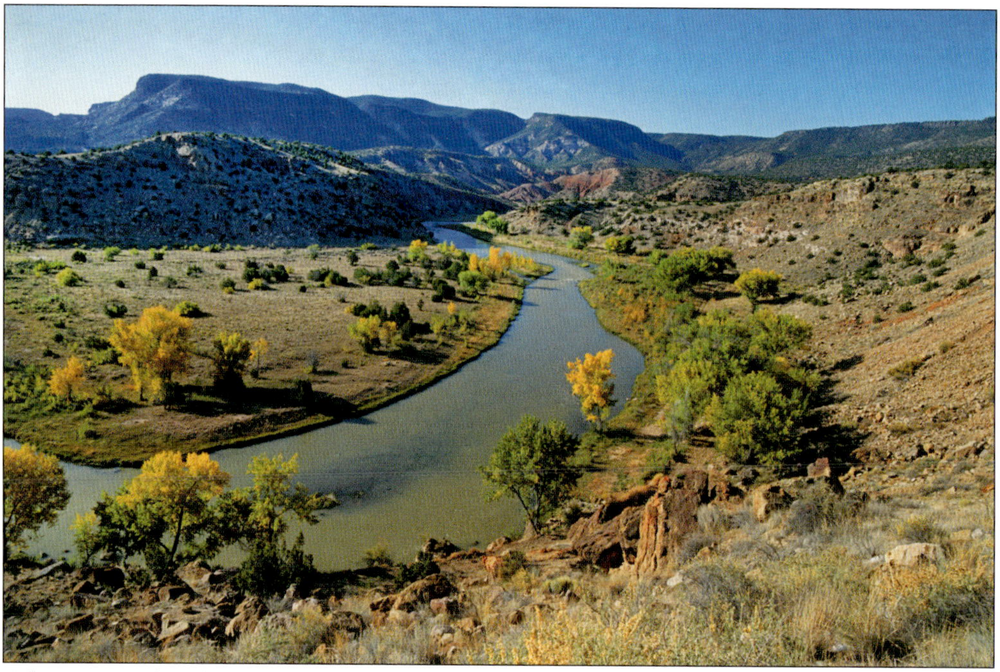

Adventure-seekers have been navigating northern New Mexico's rivers since durable rubber rafts were introduced to the general public in the 1950s. The Chama River (above), shown here near the village of Abiquiu, is a major tributary of the Rio Grande that is popular with families using smaller rafts, canoes, and kayaks. Its not-so-difficult Class III rapids and the beautiful high-desert canyon country through which it runs contribute to its appeal. A 25-mile-long segment of the river (below), from just south of El Vado Lake to just north of Abiquiu Reservoir, was officially designated as a protected Wild & Scenic area by the federal government in 1978.

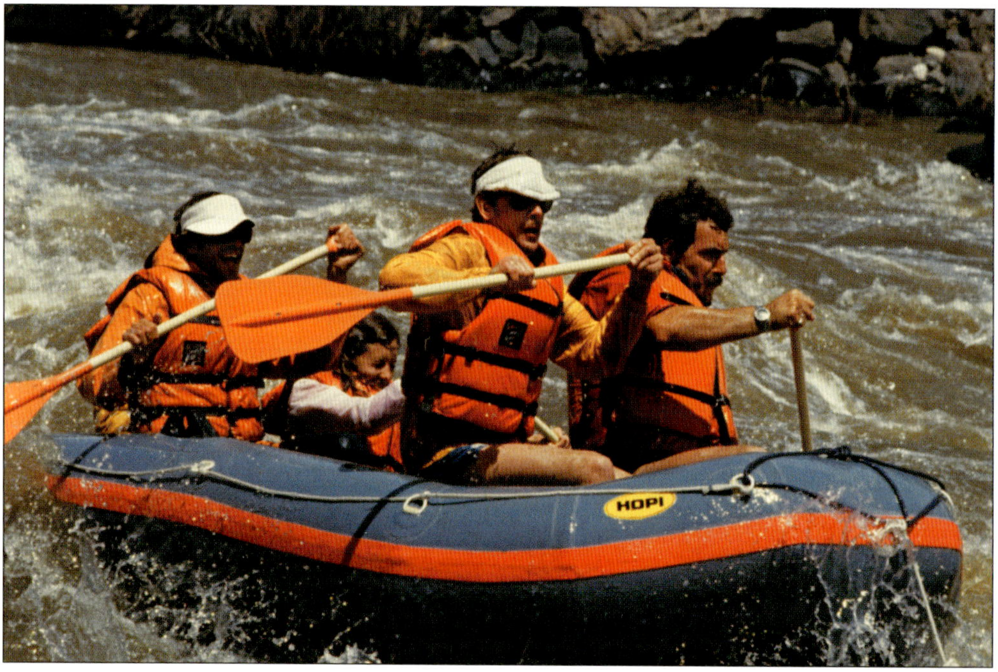

The king of white-water rafting rivers in northern New Mexico is the upper Rio Grande. Particularly stunning is the 74-mile-long, federally protected Wild & Scenic section of the river (right), encased by the 800-foot-deep Rio Grande Gorge. One of the first eight rivers in the United States to receive the National Wild & Scenic River designation in 1968, the upper Rio Grande is still among the least disturbed wilderness streams in the country. The most popular white-water rafting stretch is the 18-mile-long segment of boulder-studded water downstream from Taos Junction Bridge (below). Known as the Lower Gorge, it is paralleled by State Highway 68 and is ideal for day trips. The Upper Gorge (right), known locally as the Taos Box, cannot be reached by road and is far more difficult to access.

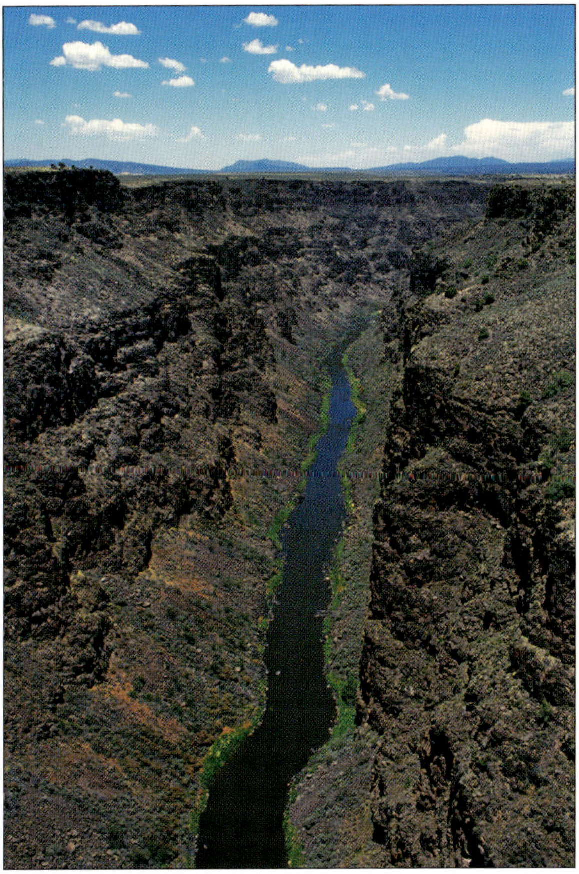

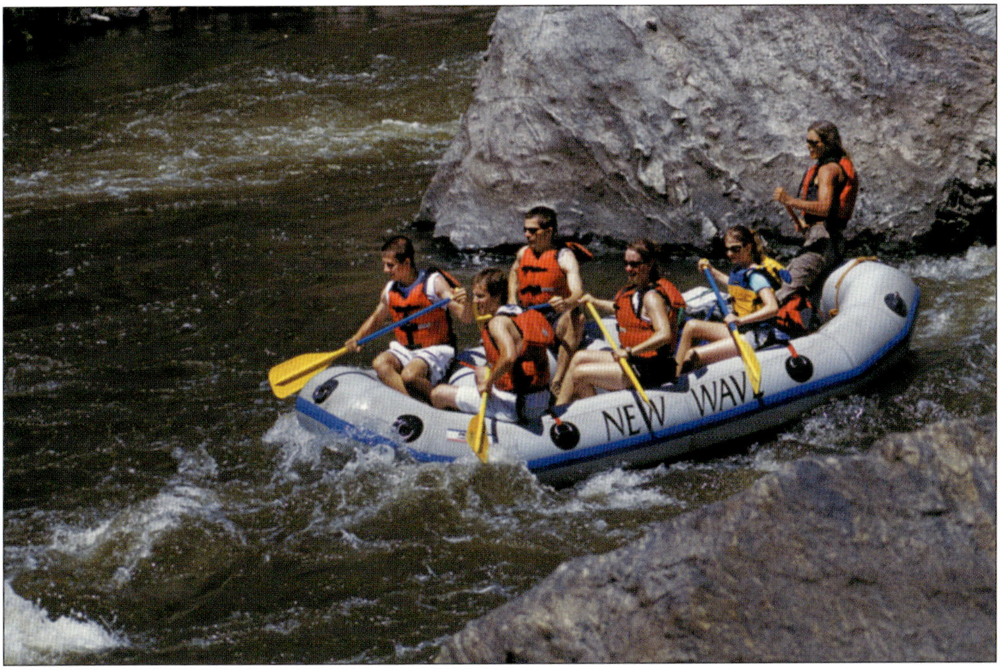

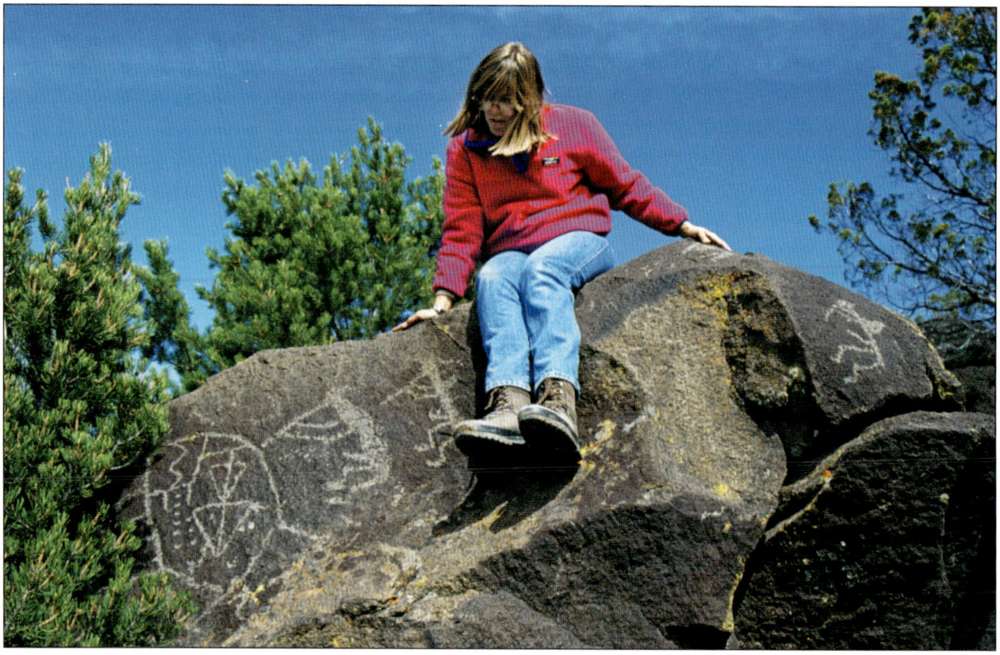

More than 700 years ago, an Anasazi artist painstakingly chipped these prehistoric rock carvings (known as petroglyphs) into the lava boulder above, just a few miles west of Santa Fe. The small figure on the right and the two larger figures in the middle are depictions of Kokopelli, a prehistoric fertility god who is also known as the humpbacked flute player. In the past 50 years, vandals have destroyed hundreds of Anasazi rock art sites in northern New Mexico. Even in federally protected Bandelier National Monument, vandals have stolen thousands of artifacts and disfigured many archaeological sites since the 1960s. Luckily, the restored 700-year-old Anasazi *kiva* (religious chamber) into which the hiker is climbing below has escaped defacement.

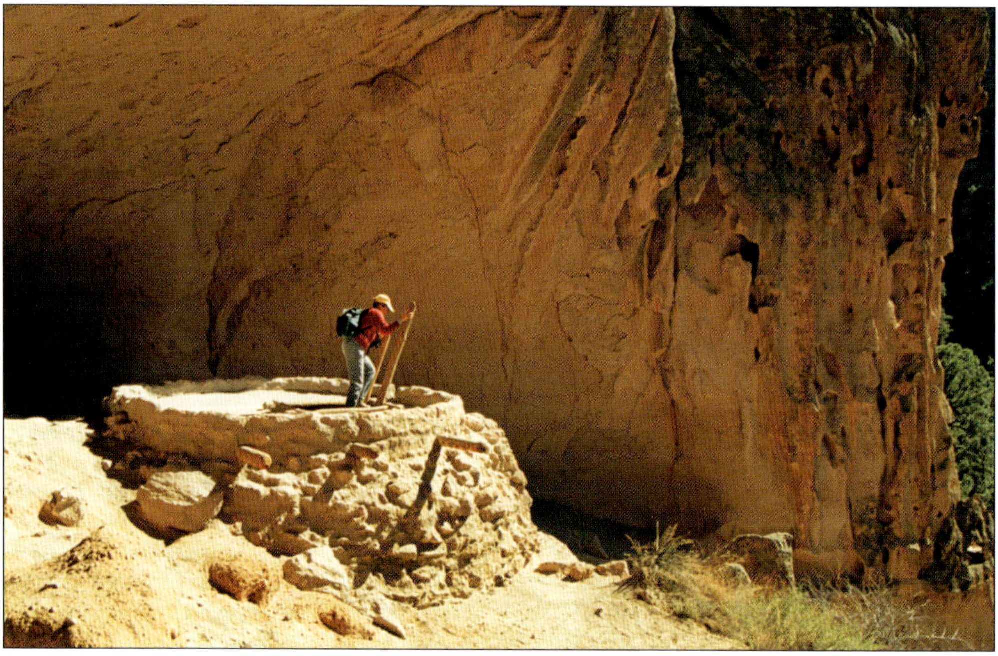

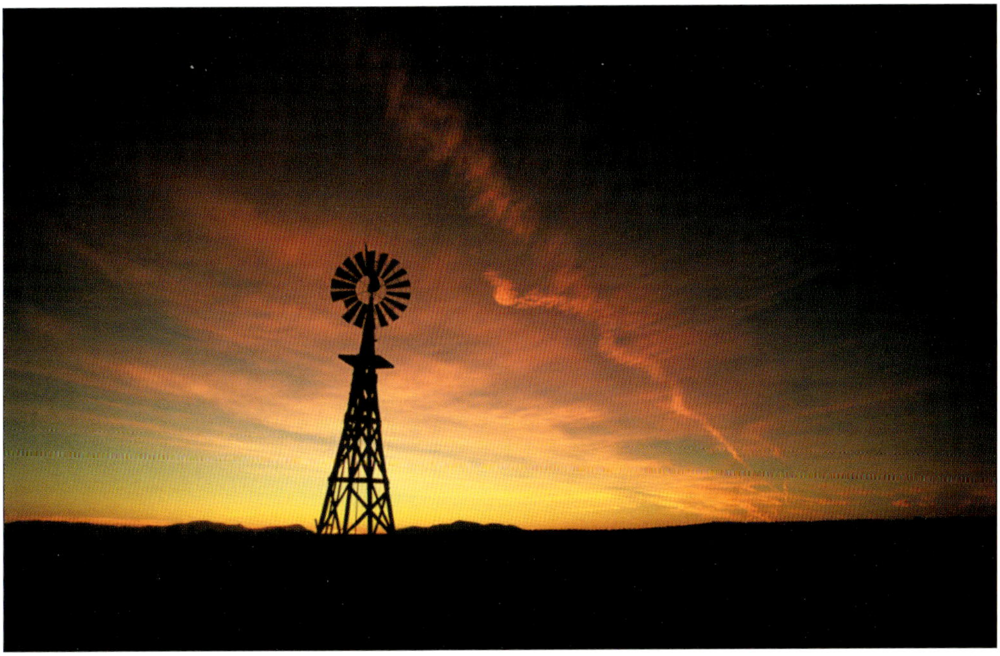

A creaky wooden windmill from about 1940 stands watch over the lonely juniper- and cholla-covered wilderness of the 460,000-acre Galisteo Basin, which begins a few miles south of Santa Fe. In the late 1800s, the basin was dotted with huge sheep and cattle operations, but overgrazing and bad land management caused most of them to disappear by the mid-1930s.

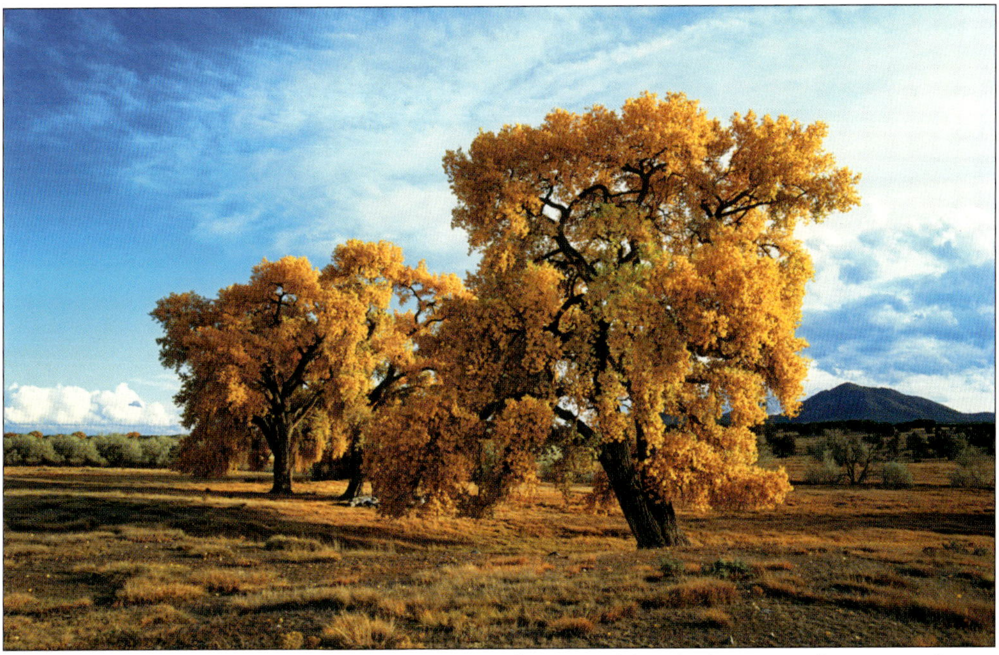

As the summer heat abates and early autumn nights get colder, the leaves on this grove of giant cottonwood trees turn bright yellow. Growing near a small seasonal creek on the west side of the Galisteo Basin, the trees are very large but probably not very old; cottonwood trees seldom live longer than a hundred years, even when they have a permanent source of water.

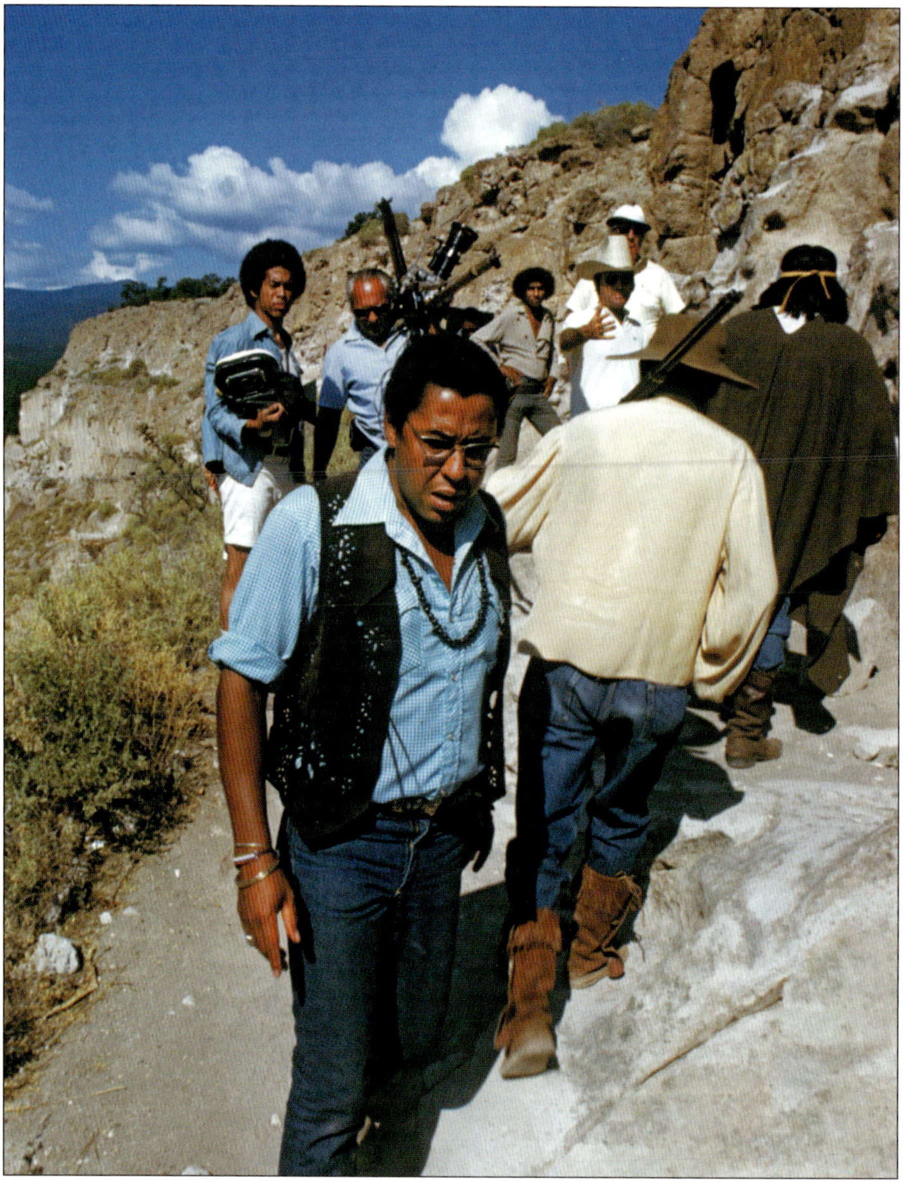

The motion picture industry discovered the extraordinary landscape around Santa Fe in the early 20th century, and by the 1970s, northern New Mexico had become one of Hollywood's favorite movie locations. Aggressively courted by the New Mexico film commission, dozens of highly respected directors and their film crews made their way to the state, bringing with them a multitude of top-name Hollywood stars. Talented director Gordon Parks Jr. (1934–1979) had already scored big in Hollywood with his action movie *Superfly* when he brought his crew and equipment to the ruggedly beautiful canyon country of the Santa Clara Indian Reservation in 1973. The movie he was filming, *Thomasina & Bushrod*, was meant to be a black counterpart to *Bonnie and Clyde*. A so-called blaxploitation film, made specifically for young, black, urban audiences, the movie was released in 1974 to mediocre reviews. Gordon Parks Jr. only made two other films after *Thomasina & Bushrod*. He was killed in 1979, along with three others, when their small airplane aborted takeoff and crashed near Nairobi, Kenya.

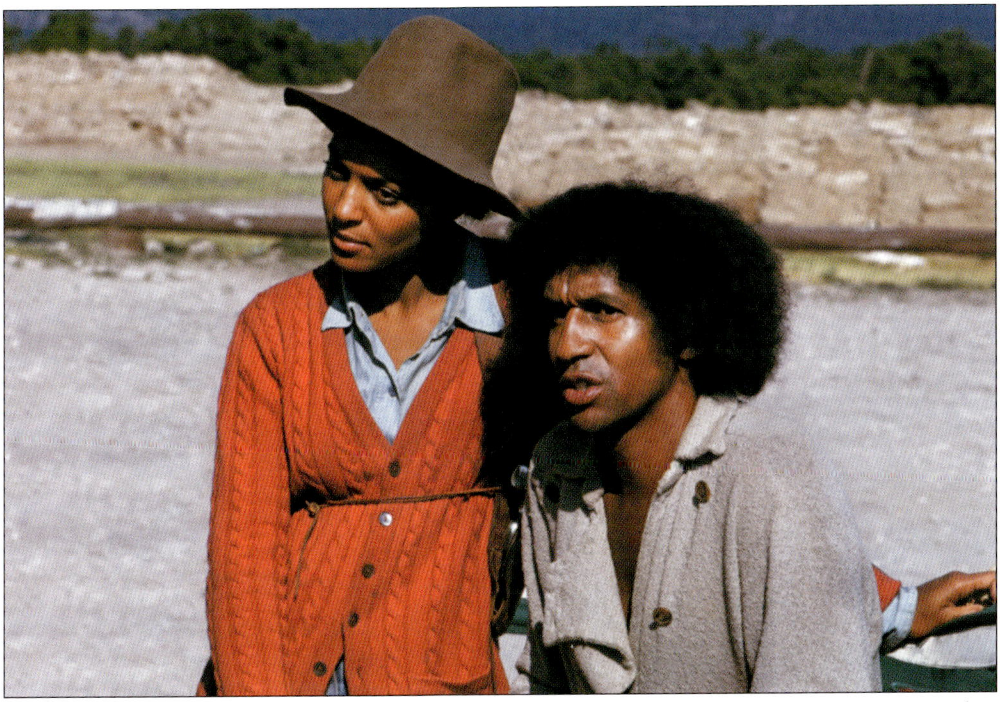

Above, actors Vonetta McGee (1945–2010) and Max Julien listen intently as director Gordon Parks Jr. describes a difficult sequence they are about to shoot during the filming of *Thomasina & Bushrod* in which actress McGee had to navigate a dangerous narrow rocky trail across the face of a steep cliff at a run. The beautiful backdrop of the Jemez Mountains below could be a landscape from one of John Ford's Western movies, but these cowboys are simply taking a break from fixing fences and checking free-roaming range cattle on a large northern New Mexico ranch.

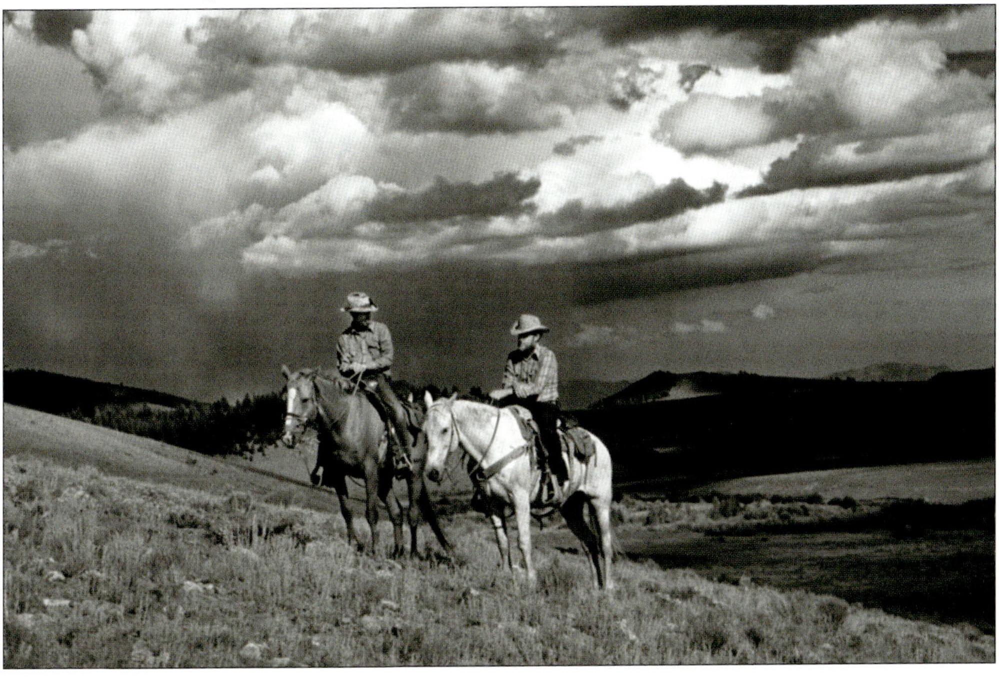

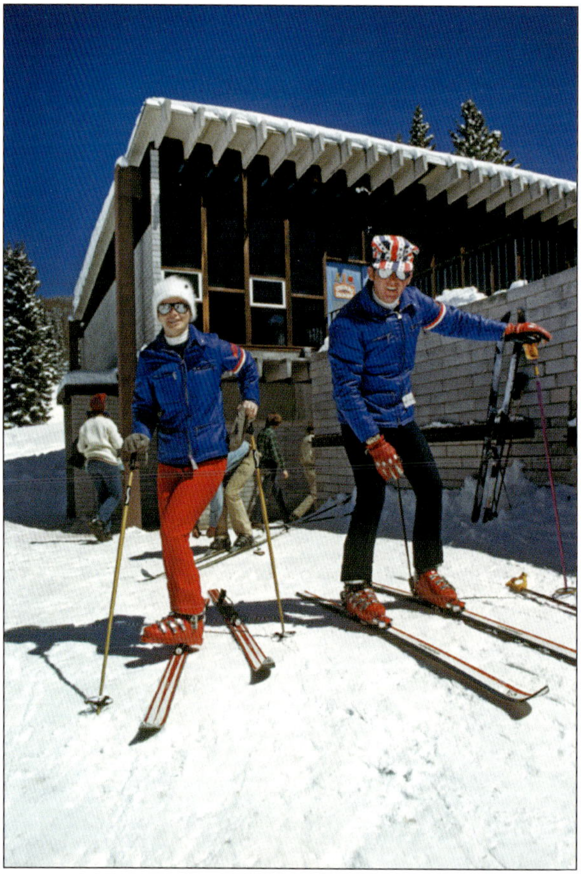

With an elevation of 10,350 feet, the Santa Fe Ski Basin, in operation since the early 1950s, is one of the highest ski areas in the United States. Located 16 miles from downtown Santa Fe at the end of State Highway 475, the basin offers skiers 77 different trails and a vertical drop of more than 1,700 feet. This photograph was taken in the early 1970s.

While navigating a powdery ski slope in the morning and getting a suntan in the afternoon is not always possible, neither is it an unusual occurrence in the Santa Fe area. In late spring and fall, temperatures may be in the 70s in town, even while snow is falling on the mountains above.

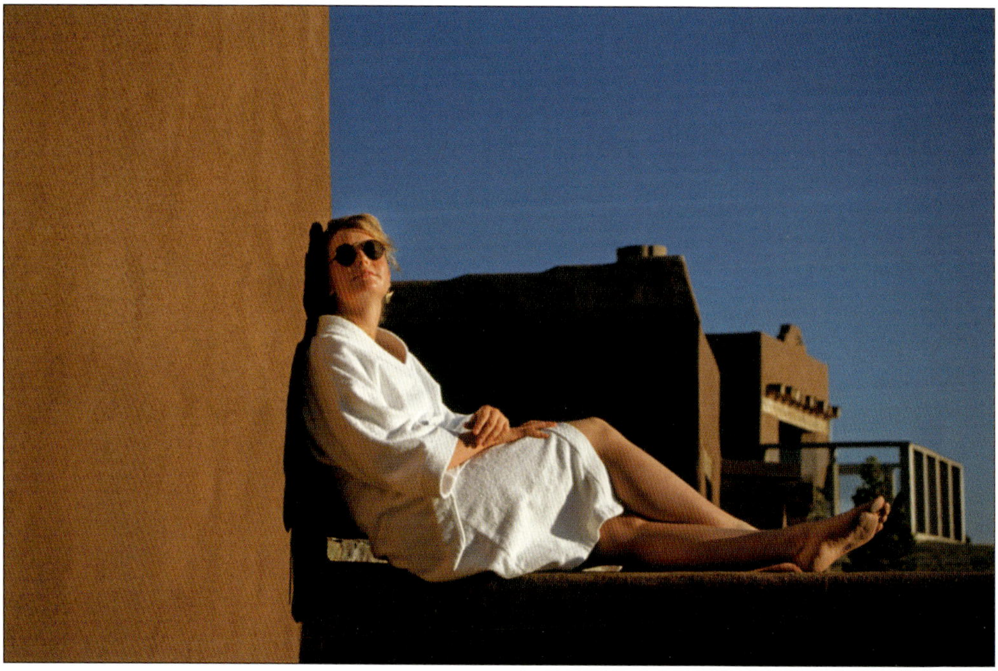

Although cross-country skiing is a popular sport today, it was almost unknown in the Santa Fe area until about 1970. There were no trails designed or designated specifically for skinny skis, so enthusiasts often made their own tracks alongside lightly used backcountry roads. The skis themselves were made of wood and were extremely heavy. Ski outfits usually consisted of jeans and a sweater, while ski boots resembled lightweight leather tennis shoes and offered no protection whatsoever from the elements. These photographs from 1973 show a young woman admiring the view from Upper Hyde Park Road (Ski Basin Road), and a couple enjoying a beautiful winter sunset from a snowy ridgeline near the Santa Fe Ski Basin.

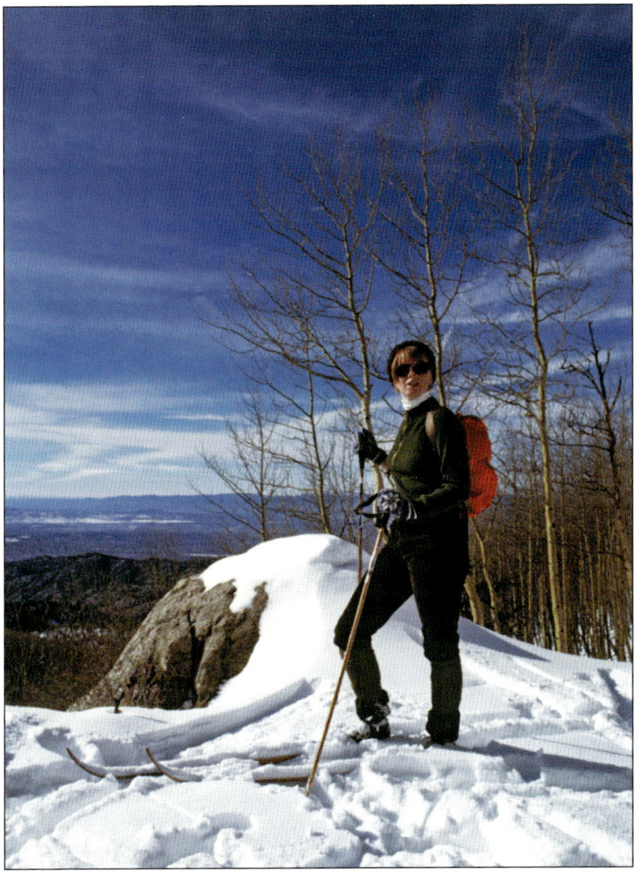

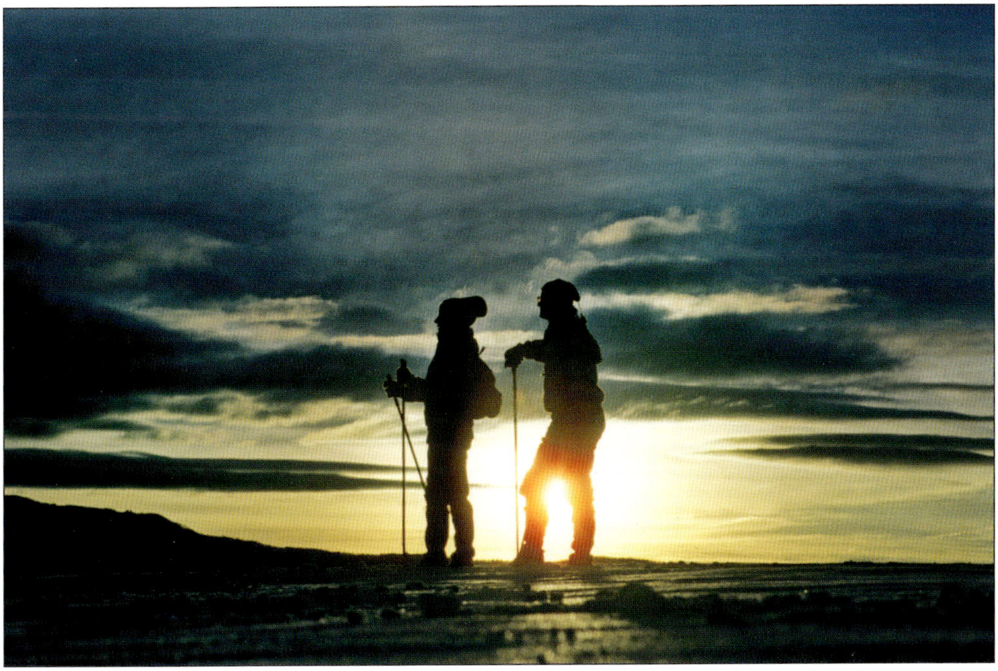

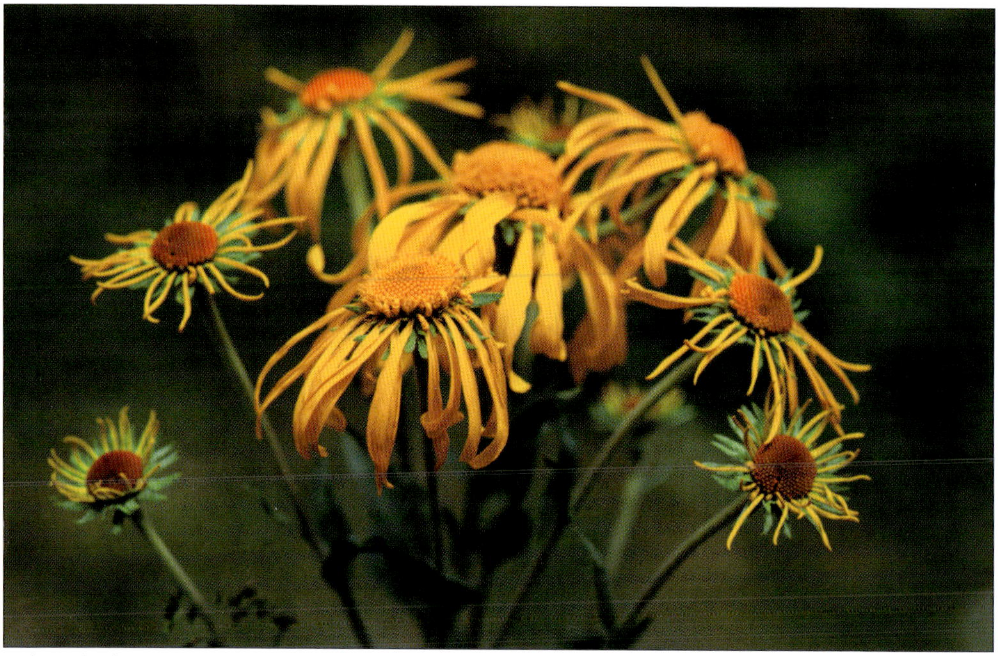

When the last mountain snows melt away and warm spring weather arrives, it ushers in an annual wildflower bloom in the moist alpine meadows of the Sangre de Cristo Mountains. A yellow bouquet of alpine sunflowers (above) brightens a Pecos Wilderness mountainside near Katherine Lake. Colorful black-eyed Susans (below), also known as cut-leaved cone flowers, bloom from July through September across most of New Mexico's northern mountains. These were growing near the Santa Fe Ski Basin. Spanish folk tales from colonial times claim that herbal tea made from the roots of a black-eyed Susan will kill worms and reduce the swelling caused by a snakebite.

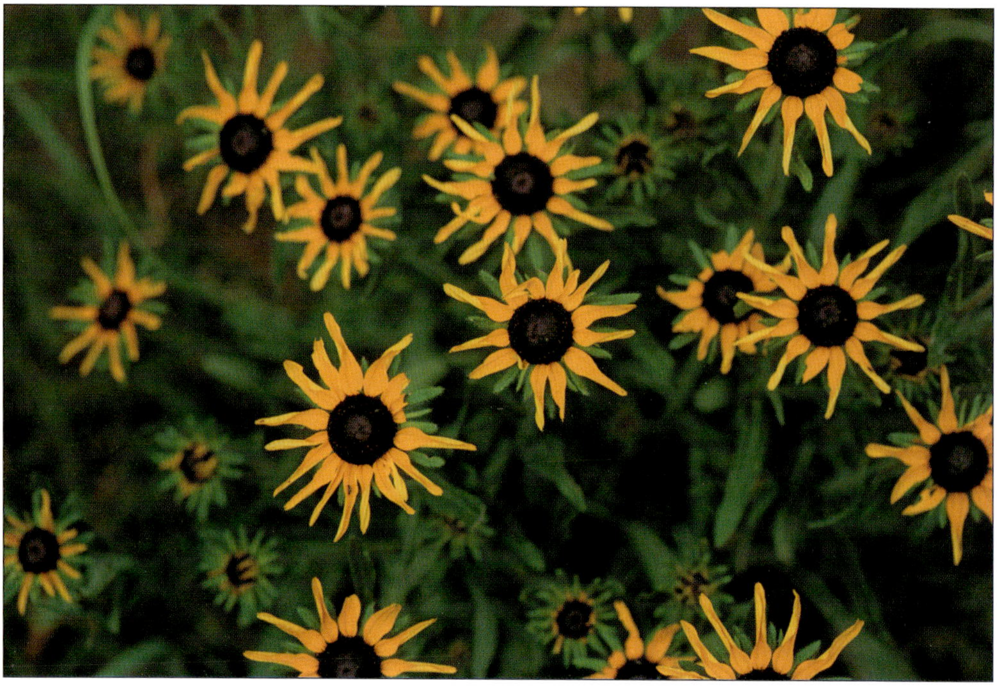